Key Stage 3
Classbook

Letts
EDUCATIONAL

Geography

NEW for September 2000

Adam
Arnell

First published 2000
Reprinted 2000

Letts Educational
9–15 Aldine Street
London W12 8AW
Tel 020 8740 2266
Fax 020 8743 8451

Design and page layout: Ken Vail Graphic Design, Cambridge

Illustrations: Vicky Squires, Graeme Morris (Ken Vail Graphic Design), SGA (Mike Lacey)

Colour reproduction by PDQ Digital Media Solutions, Bungay, Suffolk

Picture research by Brooks Krikler Research

British Library Cataloguing-in-Publication Data

A CIP record for this book is available from the British Library

ISBN 1 84085 420 0

Printed and Bound in Spain

Letts Educational Limited, a division of Granada Learning Limited. Part of the Granada Media Group.

Acknowledgements

The author would like to thank the students at King Alfred's Community and Sports College, Wantage, for their comments on early drafts of the book.

Maps in figures 107.1, 110.2, 110.3 and on pages 230–233 reproduced from Ordnance Survey mapping with permission of Her Majesty's Stationery Office, © Crown Copyright.

Maps in figures 106.1 and 109.1 from *Philip's Modern School Atlas*, reproduced by kind permission of the publishers.

Statistics on pages 234–5 (except HDI data) from *Philips Geographical Digest,* with permission.

HDI data on pages 234–5 from the *Human Development Report 1999* by United Nations Development Programme. Used by permission of Oxford University Press, Inc.

The author and publishers are grateful to the following for permission to reproduce photographs:
Adam Arnell: unit 1.2; AEATech: 83.3; Corbis: 7.1, 21.2, 21.4, 32.4, 41.2, 59.4, 76.3, 80.4, 82.3, 90.2, 92.2, 94.3, 98.3, 100.4, 101.3, 103.1, 103.2; Eye Ubiquitous: 13.4, 19.4, 24.1, 25.2, 28.3, 28.4, 31.3, 40.3, 65.2, 65.3, 66.2, 67.1, 67.2, 69.2, 70.2, 78.1, 84.2, 85.2, 88.2, 89.2, 89.4, 93.2, 98.1, 101.2, 114.3; Frank Spooner Pictures: 5.2, 6.4, 7.3, 8.4, 9.2, 12.1, 12.4, 14.1, 26.3, 35.4, 37.3, 37.4, 40.5 42.3, 44.2, 44.4, 45.3, 46.3, 47.2, 51.3, 51.4, 52.4, 53.2, 53.3, 54.2, 54.3, 55.3, 57.1, 57.2, 63.3, 63.4, 73.3, 90.1, 96.4, 104.3; James Davies Travel Photography: 18.3, 29.3, 30.1, 34.3, 34.5, 36.4, 48.2, 96.3, 102.3, 104.2; John Walmsley Photography: 1.3, 50.3, 105.1; Merry Hill Shopping Centre: 64.2; Milton Park: 62.3; Oxford Scientific Films: 11.1, 11.3, 13.1, 15.3, 16.4, 58.2, 60.2, 79.2; Skyscan: 19.2; Rex Features: 3.3; Wildgoose Publications: 49.2

Contents

Contents

Contents

Introduction

This Letts Geography Classbook has been designed and written to help you learn and understand the topics that you will cover during your Key Stage 3 Geography course. This book is intended to stimulate your curiosity about the natural and human worlds, about places from your local area to distant countries, and about our precious and fragile environment. While working through this book, you will be asked to think about how the way you live has an impact on the planet. You will be asked to consider other people's experiences, and how they might think about things differently. You will also learn about how governments, organisations and businesses influence the world.

The book is divided into 12 chapters, which together contain 114 units. Each unit begins with a list of key questions for you to investigate. The information that follows is written clearly so that you can read the unit yourself. Any new or technical words are highlighted in bold and explained in the key words section of each unit. There are also many maps, graphs, statistics, diagrams and photos for you to look at. These are as important as the writing, so study them carefully.

Each unit contains some questions that are intended to encourage you to think about the topic you are investigating. There is also a summary activity at the end of every unit. The summary activity will help you develop some of the ideas further. Many of the activities need geographical skills. Remember to look at the units on skills if you need extra help. Some summary activities may be completed using ICT. The symbol indicates where ICT is particularly appropriate. At the end of every unit is a summary to ensure you have understood the key points.

Throughout the book you are expected to use the enquiry approach to investigate topics. This means finding answers to a series of questions in a logical order. Although this book contains a wealth of information, it is hoped you will also use other sources. Most units contain links to excellent Internet websites, which can be used to carry out further work on a topic, and a separate section at the end contains a series of exciting Internet activities.

Many units contain case studies of real people and places. Remember to use an atlas to find where the places are. You will also find that many of the case studies have also been featured in recent educational television programmes. Viewed alongside this book, they will help bring geography to life.

We hope that you will find this book interesting to read and full of useful information. As well as helping you to be successful in your studies, we hope that you will be encouraged to think more deeply about the geography of the wonderful world in which we live.

1 Geographical enquiry

In this section of the book you will investigate the following things:
- What is geographical enquiry?
- What sources of evidence can be used in an enquiry?

Enquiry

Geography is about understanding the world we live in. It allows us to investigate the natural and human worlds, different places and the environment. Geography helps to explain why things are like they are now, and how they might change in the future.

An enquiry is about finding answers to geographical questions. Sometimes the questions are asked in a book, or are set by a teacher. At other times, students should be able to identify and then answer their own questions. An enquiry can take place over a single lesson, or last for several weeks.

Evaluating information

It is important to evaluate your information sources.

Check for the following:

- **Bias** – who has supplied the information?
- **Attitudes** – how do people's values and attitudes affect the information?
- **Accuracy** – is the information reliable and up-to-date?

▲ *Fig 1 Be critical about your information sources.*

Q1 What is an enquiry?

Identifying questions

Here are a selection of questions which can be adapted for a geographical enquiry.

- What is it?
- Where is it?
- When did it happen?
- How did it happen?
- Why did it happen?
- What were the effects?
- What might happen in the future?
- What do I think about it?
- What can I do about it?

A geographical enquiry does not have to contain all of these questions. Only use questions which fit the topic being investigated. Of course, it is very important that the questions are asked in a sensible order.

▲ *Fig 2 Using the internet. The internet offers a huge amount of information which can be used in a geographical enquiry. Be sure to evaluate the information.*

Sources of information

An enquiry should use information from several different sources (Fig 1). This geography classbook can be your starting point. **Evidence** should then be collected from some of the sources listed below.

- Internet– the largest possible source of information. Follow the links suggested in this book, or use a 'search-engine' to find useful web sites (Fig 2).
- TV and video programmes – videos can provide good visual and factual information.
- Information books – library books written about the topic. Try your school library, or join your local library; it's free!
- Newspapers – newspapers often have geographical stories and photos, especially after a natural disaster such as an earthquake.
- Fieldwork – the collection of 'first-hand' data outside the classroom is an important geographical enquiry skill (Fig 3) (see unit 105).

- Questionnaires – surveys of friends, family or the public can also provide useful 'first-hand' data.
- CD ROMs – general CD ROMs such as encyclopaedias are good sources of information. You may also be able to use geography CD ROMs. Never just print out information.
- Organisations and companies – many organisations and companies will send you free information if you write to them and ask.

> **Q2** Suggest a source of information that may be **biased**.
>
> **Q3** Suggest a source of information that may be out-of-date.

Presentation

An enquiry can be presented in many different forms. It can be presented as a report, a letter, a newspaper or magazine article, a leaflet, a talk or even a web page.

▲ **Fig 3** Collecting information first-hand through fieldwork can be part of a geographical enquiry.

Key words

biased – gives a one-sided view of an issue

evidence – information used to make a point

SUMMARY

- An enquiry is a geographical investigation.
- Enquiry involves asking and answering a sequence of questions.
- Several different sources of information should be used to provide evidence.
- Evidence should be evaluated carefully.
- Enquiries may be presented in many different ways.

SUMMARY activity

Write a sequence of geographical enquiry questions on a topic of your choice.

2 The Earth

In this section of the book you will investigate the following things:
- What is the Earth?
- How was the Earth formed?
- What is the Earth made of?
- How has the Earth changed?

Structure of the Earth

The Earth is one of nine planets orbiting the Sun. The Earth was formed around 4600 million years ago. Dust and gas produced in the **'Big Bang'** came together to form planets. One of these planets is the Earth. In the beginning the Earth was not solid, but over time the outside has cooled to form a hard rock **crust**.

The Earth's crust varies in thickness. Under the oceans it is only between 5 km and 10 km thick. On the land it is between 25 km and 90 km thick. Beneath the crust there are a number of layers of rock (Fig 1). The thickest layer is the **mantle**. The mantle is hot enough to melt but is kept solid by huge pressure. Although the mantle is solid, it is able to flow very slowly like plasticine.

At the centre of the Earth is the **core**. The core is very dense and probably made of nickel and iron. The inner core is thought to be solid, whereas the outer core is liquid and able to flow. The core reaches about 5500 °C.

Seismic waves

How do we know what is beneath the Earth's crust? Although we cannot see inside the Earth, earthquakes give us a big clue. Earthquakes cause two types of **seismic wave**: push waves and shear waves. Push waves can travel through solids and liquids. This means they can travel all the way through the Earth to the other side. However, shear waves cannot travel through liquids. As shear waves only reach half way round the world this suggests that there is liquid rock at the Earth's core (Fig 2).

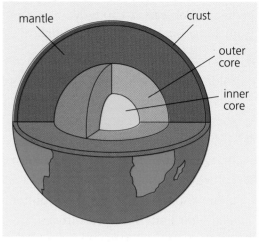

▲ **Fig 1** The structure of the Earth.

Q1 When was the Earth formed?

Q2 How was the Earth formed?

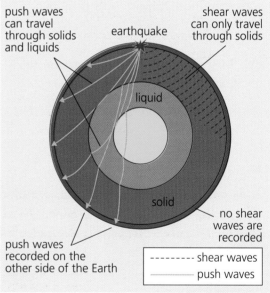

▲ **Fig 2** Seismic waves.

Q3 What is the difference between push waves and shear waves?

 USGS home page http://www.usgs.gov/

Moving continents

Look carefully at a world map. You can see how the continents look as if they would fit together, like a jigsaw puzzle. South America would slot in very neatly next to Africa. There is also other evidence that in the past all the continents were joined together. For example, identical fossils have been found in different continents thousands of kilometres apart, a mountain chain in the USA matches mountains in Europe, and some rocks in Britain were formed in a desert! For these thing to be possible the continents must have moved. Fig 3 shows how the continents have very slowly spread apart.

The Earth 200 million years ago

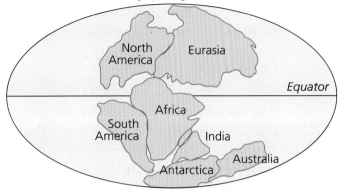

The continents are joined together forming a supercontinent

The Earth today

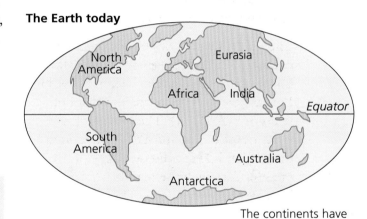

The continents have broken apart and spread out

Q4 List three pieces of evidence which show that the continents used to be joined together.

▲ **Fig 3** The Earth 200 million years ago and today.

Key words

Big Bang – the formation of the universe
core – the centre of the Earth
crust – the solid skin of rock around the Earth's surface
mantle – the semi-solid mass of rock beneath the crust
seismic wave – shock wave produced by earthquakes

SUMMARY

■ The Earth was formed from hot dust and gas in the 'Big Bang'. The inside of the Earth is still cooling down.
■ The Earth is divided into different layers of rock: crust, mantle, outer core and inner core.
■ Seismic waves from earthquakes help us 'see' into the centre of the Earth.
■ The continents used to be joined together. 200 million years ago they broke apart and have very slowly spread out.

SUMMARY activity

Draw a diagram to show the different layers of the Earth. Add labels to describe each layer. Underneath the diagram, explain how we know what is inside the Earth.

 USGS – plate tectonics http://wrgis.wr.usgs.gov/docs/parks/pltec/pltec1.html

3 Plate tectonics

In this section of the book you will investigate the following things:
- How is the Earth's crust divided into plates?
- How do tectonic plates move?
- Where do earthquakes and volcanoes occur?

Tectonic plates

The Earth's crust is not one solid piece. It is broken into huge slabs of rock called **tectonic plates**. There are seven major plates and twelve smaller ones (Fig 1). Tectonic plates are lighter than the rock in the mantle. This means that the plates are able to 'float' on top of the mantle. The major tectonic plates are larger than continents.

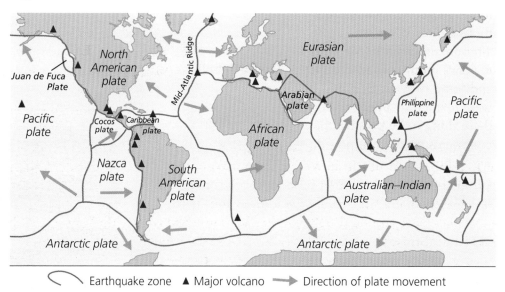

Earthquake zone   ▲ Major volcano   ➡ Direction of plate movement

▲ **Fig 1** The Earth's major tectonic plates.

There are two different types of tectonic plate. The lightest and thickest plates are called continental crust. Continental crust forms the land but can also extend under the sea. Because continental crust is light it cannot sink into the mantle and be destroyed. This means that continental crust can be very old.

The second type of tectonic plate is called oceanic crust. Oceanic crust is thinner but made from heavier rock. Because it is heavy, oceanic crust can be pushed down into the mantle. Oceanic crust is then melted and destroyed in the mantle. Oceanic crust is continually being destroyed in one place, and renewed in another.

Q1 What is a tectonic plate?

Q2 What is the difference between continental and oceanic crust?

 NASA – plate tectonics http://observe.ivv.nasa.gov/nasa/earth/tectonics/Tectonics1.html

Plate movement

The Earth's core is extremely hot. Heat escapes from the core and rises up into the mantle. This heat causes **convection currents** in the semi-solid rocks of the mantle. The convection currents cause the mantle rock to move very slowly in a circular motion. The movement of the rock in the mantle drags the tectonic plates along (Fig 2). In this way, the tectonic plates move by a few centimetres every year. In our lifetimes the plates will only move a few metres. But over millions of years, plates can move the whole way around the Earth! This process is called **plate tectonics**. It explains how the continents, which used to be joined together, have spread apart.

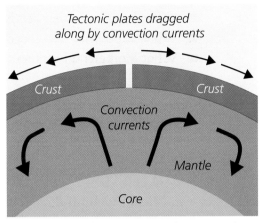

Tectonic plates dragged along by convection currents

▲ **Fig 2** Movement of tectonic plates.

Q3 What causes convection currents?

Earthquakes and volcanoes

Fig 1 shows the location of the world's major volcanoes and earthquake zones. It shows that earthquakes and volcanoes are found together in long narrow bands. For example, there is a large band of volcanoes and earthquake sites around the Pacific Ocean. This band is known as the 'Ring of Fire'. Notice how close the bands of earthquakes and volcanoes are to where the tectonic plates meet. This map shows us that most earthquakes and volcanoes occur at **plate boundaries** (Fig 3). Earthquakes and volcanoes can be very useful for learning about the movements of the Earth's crust.

▶ **Fig 3** *San Andreas Fault – an example of a plate boundary.*

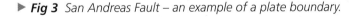

Key words

convection current – a transfer of energy as heat causing movement in a circular direction

plate boundary – the point where two tectonic plates meet

plate tectonics – theory explaining how the Earth's crust is able to move

tectonic plate – a large, rigid section of the Earth's crust

SUMMARY

- ■ The Earth's crust is broken into several large pieces called tectonic plates.
- ■ There are two types of crust: oceanic and continental crust.
- ■ Tectonic plates move because of convection currents in the mantle.
- ■ Earthquakes and volcanoes are located at tectonic plate boundaries.

SUMMARY activity

Describe the distribution of earthquakes and volcanoes around the world. Use an atlas to name some countries which have volcanoes, and which have experienced earthquakes.

4 Plate boundaries

In this section of the book you will investigate the following things:
- What happens when tectonic plates move apart?
- What happens when tectonic plates collide?
- What happens when tectonic plates slide past each other?

The Earth's tectonic plates are moving very slowly around the surface of the planet. In some places, plates are moving apart from each other. In other places they are pushing together. Some plates are sliding sideways past each other. The places where tectonic plates meet are called plate boundaries. There are four different types of plate boundary.

Constructive boundaries

A **constructive boundary** is where two plates are moving apart from each other. As the two plates pull apart, rock in the mantle melts. Molten rock in the mantle is called **magma**. Magma erupts at the surface as liquid rock called **lava**. As the lava escapes it builds up mountains called volcanoes. Volcanic eruptions at constructive boundaries are quite gentle, but may continue for many years (Fig 1).

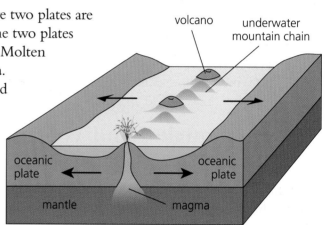

▲ **Fig 1** Constructive plate boundary.

Most constructive boundaries are under the sea. Millions of years of eruptions have formed underwater mountain chains. The most famous is the Mid-Atlantic Ridge. Sometimes a volcano grows so high that it can make an island, for example, Tristan da Cunha or Surtsey.

Q1 What is the difference between magma and lava?

Q2 How was Tristan da Cunha formed?

Destructive boundaries

A **destructive boundary** occurs where oceanic and continental plates collide. The heavier oceanic plate is forced underneath the continental plate. As the plate is pushed down into the mantle it melts. The melted crust forms magma. The magma slowly rises up towards the surface. If it reaches the surface it forms dangerous explosive volcanoes (Fig 2).

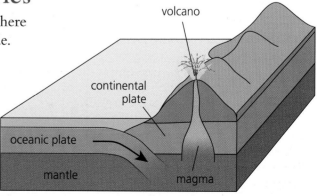

▲ **Fig 2** Destructive plate boundary.

 PBS mountain maker http://www.pbs.org/wgbh/aso/tryit/tectonics/

The force of one plate sliding over another is enormous. Often they become stuck and then move suddenly. This sudden movement causes earthquakes. The combination of earthquakes and volcanoes make destructive plate boundaries dangerous places to live.

Q3 Why do volcanoes occur at destructive boundaries?

Collision boundaries

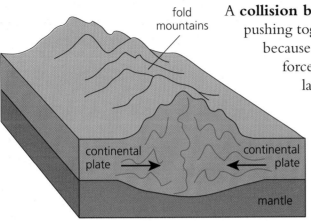

▲ *Fig 3* Collision plate boundary.

A **collision boundary** is where two continental plates are pushing together. Neither plate will sink into the mantle, because they are made from lighter rocks. As they are forced together, both plates buckle up forming large mountains. Mountains made in this way are called fold mountains. The Himalayas are a very large chain of fold mountains (Fig 3).

No volcanoes are produced at collision boundaries, but violent earthquakes can happen when the plates suddenly move.

Q4 How are fold mountains formed?

Conservative boundaries

In some places, tectonic plates are sliding past each other. This process is not smooth because the plates become locked together. Over many years, tension builds up at the plate boundary. Suddenly the rocks break and one plate shoots forward (Fig 4). This movement causes powerful earthquakes. The most famous **conservative boundary** is the San Andreas Fault in California.

▶ *Fig 4* Conservative plate boundary.

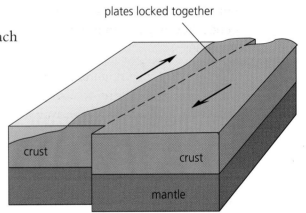

Key words

collision boundary – where continental plates collide

conservative boundary – where two plates slide past each other

constructive boundary – where two plates move apart from each other

destructive boundary – where an oceanic plate slides underneath a continental plate

lava – molten rock at the Earth's surface

magma – molten rock beneath the Earth's surface

SUMMARY

- There are four types of plate boundary.
- New crust is created at constructive boundaries.
- Old crust is destroyed at destructive boundaries.
- Fold mountains are formed at collision boundaries.
- No crust is created or destroyed at conservative boundaries.

SUMMARY *activity*

Draw a simple labelled diagram of each type of plate boundary. Underneath describe the hazards of living near each type. Which do you think is the most dangerous plate boundary?

5 Volcanoes

In this section of the book you will investigate the following things:

■ **What are volcanoes?**
■ **What causes volcanoes?**
■ **What different types of volcano are there?**

An erupting volcano is one of the most awesome sights on Earth. A volcano is formed where molten rock, called magma, forces its way to the Earth's surface. Magma is produced many kilometres below the crust, in the mantle. Because the magma is very hot it rises towards the Earth's surface. If it reaches the surface, it may either flow out gently as liquid lava, or explode violently as **volcanic bombs** and ash. The lava or ash builds up to form cone-shaped mountains. It is these cone-shaped mountains we call volcanoes.

Q1 What is a volcano?

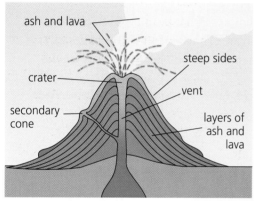

▲ **Fig 1** *Composite volcano.*

Types of volcanoes

There are over 1500 volcanoes around the world, but not all of them are active. A volcano which is active has erupted recently and is expected to erupt again. There are over 800 active volcanoes in the world today. A volcano which has not erupted in recorded history is described as dormant, or sleeping. A dormant volcano might erupt one day again in the future. A volcano which is never expected to erupt again is said to be extinct. An extinct volcano has not erupted for many thousands of years.

Composite volcanoes

Q2 Why are dormant volcanoes dangerous?

There are several different types of volcano. One of the most common is called a composite volcano (Fig 1). Composite volcanoes occur at destructive plate boundaries. The type of lava produced at destructive plate boundaries is thick and sticky. This means that when a composite volcano erupts it can be very violent. Ash and lava can be ejected several kilometres into the air. After this violent explosion, thick slow-moving lava can erupt and build up a layer on top of the ash. Each time the volcano erupts it adds further layers of ash and lava.

Composite volcanoes are extremely dangerous when they erupt. The biggest danger is called a **pyroclastic flow**. A pyroclastic flow is a cloud of red hot gas and ash which rushes down the side of the volcano at over 200 km/hour. A pyroclastic flow flattens and burns anything in its path. When Mount St Helens (USA) erupted in 1980, a pyroclastic flow flattened trees up to 25 km away (Fig 2).

▲ **Fig 2** *Mt St Helens erupting.*

 Volcano world http://volcano.und.nodak.edu/vw.html

During an eruption, mudflows may also occur. Melted ice or rainfall mixes with volcanic ash to form deadly rivers of mud. Mudflows can travel for many kilometres, washing away roads and bridges. Later, thick layers of volcanic ash settle over the surrounding land. Houses and farmland are buried, leaving the whole area uninhabitable.

Occasionally, shock waves from an underwater volcanic eruption cause very large sea waves called **tsunami**. Tsunami travel at up to 500 km per hour and when they reach land they can be over 30 metres high. Tsunami can cause devastation many miles away from the site of the volcanic eruption.

Q3 What are the four main hazards when a composite volcano erupts?

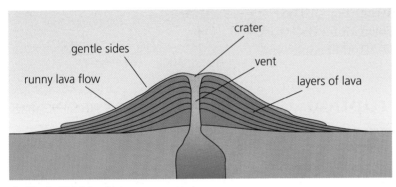

▲ **Fig 3** Shield volcano.

Shield volcanoes

Shield volcanoes occur at constructive plate boundaries (Fig 3). Lava produced at constructive plate boundaries is thin and runny. Thin, runny lava can travel a long way before it cools and turns solid. As a result, shield volcanoes are wide with gently sloping sides. Volcanic eruptions from shield volcanoes are frequent but not explosive. This means they are less likely to result in loss of life.

Q4 Why do shield volcanoes and composite volcanoes have different shapes?

Date	Volcano	Deaths	Major cause of death
1783	Laki, Iceland	9 350	Starvation
1815	Tambora, Indonesia	92 000	Starvation
1883	Krakatau	36 417	Tsunami
1902	Mt Pelee, Martinique	29 025	Pyroclastic flow
1980	Mt St Helens, USA	61	Pyroclastic flow
1982	El Chichon, Mexico	2 000	Pyroclastic flow
1985	Ruiz, Colombia	25 000	Mudflows
1991	Pinatubo, Philppines	800	Building collapse and disease
1997	Soufrière Hills, Montserrat	19	Pyroclastic flow

◄ **Fig 4** Volcanic eruptions.

Key words

pyroclastic flow – a cloud of gas and ash ejected from a volcano

tsunami – a sea wave up to 30 metres high caused by earthquakes and volcanic eruptions

volcanic bomb – lava exploded into the air which turns solid as it falls

SUMMARY

■ A volcano is an opening in the Earth's crust from which lava and ash erupts.

■ Volcanoes may be classified as active, dormant or extinct.

■ Composite volcanoes are made from layers of ash and thick lava.

■ Shield volcanoes are made from runny lava.

SUMMARY activity

Draw a timeline of volcanic eruptions, using the data in Fig 4. For each eruption, show the number and cause of deaths. Suggest why starvation no longer occurs.

Cascades Volcano Observatory http://vulcan.wr.usgs.gov/home.html

6 Montserrat

In this section of the book you will investigate the following things:
- What caused the volcanic eruption on Montserrat?
- What type of eruption occurred?
- What were the effects of the eruption on people, the economy and the enviroment?
- How have people responded to the eruption?

In 1995, a volcano began to erupt on the Caribbean island of Montserrat (Fig 1). The volcano, which had been dormant for 350 years, has shattered the lives of the 12000 people who lived on the island.

▲ **Fig 1** The location of Montserrat.

Cause of the eruption

Montserrat is close to a destructive plate boundary. The North and South American plates are sinking underneath the Caribbean plate. As the American plates sink into the mantle they are melted and destroyed (Fig 2). The melted plates become magma, which rises to the surface to form a chain of volcanic islands. The volcano which erupted on Montserrat is a composite volcano. Composite volcanoes are made from ash and thick lava, and erupt extremely violently.

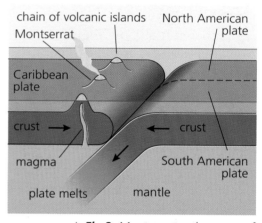
▲ **Fig 2** Montserrat – the cause of the eruptions.

The eruption

In July 1995 a volcano called Soufrière Hills began to give off clouds of ash and steam. Scientists predicted that the volcano would soon erupt. People living in the danger zone, the south of the island, were evacuated to the north. In 1996 the volcano erupted. Fiery volcanic bombs were hurled out at 200 km per hour. **Pyroclastic flows** flattened and burned buildings and trees. Ash was blasted high into the air. When the ash settled it covered over two-thirds of the island, burying buildings and farmland. The volcano has continued to erupt regularly, and the southern part of the island is still off limits (Fig 3).

Q1 Why was the eruption on Montserrat so violent?

Q2 Use Fig 3 to calculate how far ash erupted from the volcano has travelled.

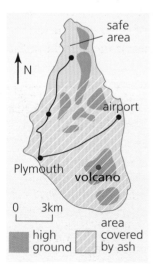

safe area

airport

Plymouth

volcano

0   3km

high ground

area covered by ash

▲ **Fig 3** Montserrat after the eruptions.

Volcano World – Soufrière Hills, Montserrat
http://volcano.und.nodak.edu/vwdocs/current_volcs/montserrat/montserrat.html

Effects

Many people have left Montserrat as **refugees**. The original population of 12 000 is now less than 4000. Most refugees have either moved to Antigua or Britain. The people who have stayed on Montserrat have a difficult life. Over 60% of the housing was destroyed. Today, people have to live in crowded conditions in the north of the island. There is a lack of clean water and sewage facilities. There is no proper hospital, and few schools are open (Fig 4).

▲ *Fig 4* Effects of the eruptions on Montserrat.

Q3 Draw a sketch map of Montserrat. Label it to show how the people, the economy and the environment have been affected by the eruption.

Q4 Why do you think some people have chosen to stay on Montserrat?

Before the eruption most people worked either as farmers or in the tourist industry. There is little left of either industry. Most fields are buried under several metres of ash, and any goods that are grown are difficult to export because the main port is closed. The island is now considered too dangerous for tourists and the airport has closed. The loss of income has further reduced people's quality of life.

Montserrat used to have many trees and plants. Many of these are now dead. They have been burned by pyroclastic flows, buried by ash, or poisoned by acid rain. Much of the wildlife has also disappeared. Off the coast, coral reefs and sea creatures are dying. They have been buried by ash washed into the sea by rain.

Aid

Aid has been sent to the people of Montserrat from different areas. Other Caribbean countries sent food, shelters and medical help. **Non-government organisations**, such as the Red Cross, have also provided medicines and doctors. The British government offered £2600 to every adult in compensation. They also promised £42 million to rebuild houses, the hospital and the airport. The people of Montserrat did not think this was enough, and they rioted in protest.

Key words

aid – help given in the form of food, medical supplies, skilled people or financial loans

non-government organisation – an organisation which provides aid, but is not tied to any government

pyroclastic flow – a cloud of gas and ash ejected from a volcano

refugee – a person forced to leave their home by war or natural disaster

SUMMARY

■ The eruption on Montserrat happened because it is on a destructive plate boundary.

■ The volcano erupted volcanic bombs, pyroclastic flows and ash.

■ The economy, based on farming and tourism, has been very badly affected.

■ Over half the population have left Montserrat. Many people are angry that there was not more help from Britain.

SUMMARY activity

Write a letter from a person in Montserrat to the British Prime Minister. In the letter say what you need, and why the British government should help you.

7 Living with volcanoes

In this section of the book you will investigate the following thing:
- **What are the benefits of living close to volcanoes?**

Volcanoes are one of the most powerful and destructive forces on Earth. In a single eruption they are able to destroy everything for miles around. Yet 360 million people around the world live and work next to volcanoes. Despite the dangers, volcanoes offer people many benefits.

Fertile soils

Mt Etna is an active volcano on the Italian island of Sicily. On average, Mt Etna erupts every ten years. Each time it erupts, it threatens the homes and farmland of the one million people who live on its slopes (Fig 1). People choose to live close to the volcano because of the high quality farmland. Ash erupted from the volcano weathers quickly to form very fertile soil. The rich soil is excellent for growing vines and fruit trees. Farmers can produce very high yields of crops. The money earned from selling the crops is thought to be worth the risks of a possible volcanic eruption.

▲ **Fig 1** *Mount Etna overlooking the town of Randazzo.*

Q1 Why are volcanic areas good for farming?

Geothermal energy

People living in volcanic areas can have access to cheap electricity and hot water. Underground water is heated by hot and molten rock deep in the crust. When the water is brought to the surface it turns to steam. The steam is used to drive turbines to produce electricity (Fig 2). Hot water brought to the surface can be used directly for central heating. Electricity and hot water produced in this way is called **geothermal energy**.

▲ **Fig 2** *Geothermal energy.*

 USGS – living with volcanoes http://vulcan.wr.usgs.gov/Living With/Framework.html

New Zealand has a large geothermal energy plant at Wairakei. Fifty boreholes bring steam to the surface. The steam drives nine turbines to produce 150 megawatts of electricity. Unfortunately, the Wairakei plant has caused environmental problems. Too much water has been taken out of the rocks. As a result **geysers** and **mudpools** have dried up.

Tourism

Volcanic landscapes can be spectacular. Tourists visit volcanic areas to see unusual features such as craters, lava flows, hot bubbling mud pools and geysers. A very popular volcanic tourist destination in New Zealand is Rotorua (Fig 3). Rotorua is a crater lake, formed when a volcano exploded thousands of years ago. Close to Rotorua is an area with brightly coloured mud pools and geysers. One geyser gushes up to 18 metres into the air!

Hotels, restaurants and shops have been built in the area to cater for tourists. Many local people are employed in the tourist industry. This means the people of Rotorua benefit economically from living in a volcanic area.

Q2 Draw a flow diagram to show how geothermal energy is produced.

Q3 How might geothermal energy benefit, and harm, the environment?

▲ **Fig 3** Rotorua, New Zealand.

Q4 What makes volcanic areas attractive to tourists?

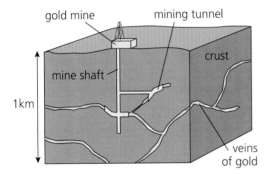

▲ **Fig 4** Mining for gold in South Africa.

Minerals

Several valuable minerals are found in volcanic areas. Hot liquids and gases move through cracks in the crustal rocks. The gases and liquids deposit minerals, such as copper, lead and gold in long 'veins' (Fig 4). Precious gem stones such as diamonds and sapphires are also found in volcanic areas. South Africa is a country with gold and diamond mines. Thousands of people are employed in mining them.

Key words

geothermal energy – heat and electricity produced from hot underground water

geyser – a jet of hot water and steam which erupts from a hole in the ground

mudpool – a pool of hot mud which bubbles with volcanic gases

SUMMARY

- Millions of people around the world live near to volcanoes.
- Volcanic ash and lava weather to make fertile soil.
- Geothermal energy can be produced in volcanic areas.
- Tourism in volcanic areas brings economic benefits.
- Valuable minerals, such as gold and copper, are mined in volcanic areas.

SUMMARY activity

Imagine you are an estate agent selling a house in Rotorua. Design an advert to persuade people that it is a good idea to live in a volcanic area.

8 Earthquakes

In this section of the book you will investigate the following things:

■ What causes earthquakes?

■ How are earthquakes measured?

■ What are the effects of earthquakes?

Every year, about 6000 earthquakes are recorded around the world. Most are too small to be felt by people. However, a small number are powerful enough to cause wide-scale devastation.

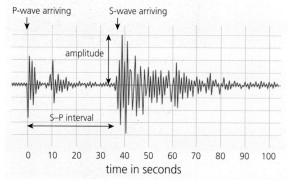

▲ **Fig 1** *Earthquake focus and epicentre.*

Cause

Earthquakes occur mainly on plate boundaries that are moving towards, or past, each other. As the plates move, friction locks them together. Over many years pressure builds up until eventually the rocks snap along a weak area called a **fault** line. The stored energy is released and it travels outwards as **seismic waves**. These seismic waves, or shock waves, cause the Earth's crust to shake up and down, and from side to side.

The place underground where the rock snaps is called the **focus**. The earthquake focus can be deep or shallow. A deep focus happens in the mantle, whereas a shallow focus happens in the crust. An earthquake with a shallow focus causes more damage at the surface. The place at the surface directly above the focus is called the **epicentre**. Rings of seismic waves spread out from the epicentre like ripples in a pond (Fig 1).

Q1 What causes earthquakes?

Q2 What are the focus and epicentre?

▲ **Fig 2** *Seismograph recordings.*

Q3 What is the difference between the Richter scale and Mercalli scale?

Q4 Which scale do you think is more useful?

Recording and measuring

Scientists record seismic waves from earthquakes on **seismometers**. Seismometers are so sensitive that they can pick up earthquake vibrations from the other side of the world. Earthquake vibrations are shown as a seismograph (Fig 2). The strength of an earthquake is described using two different scales. The Richter scale measures the total amount of energy released. The Richter scale is logarithmic. This means a level 5 earthquake is 10 times more powerful than a level 4 earthquake. The other scale used is called the Mercalli scale. The Mercalli scale measures the amount of damage caused by the earthquake. The scale ranges from 1 to 12 (Fig 3).

Effects

Primary effects are hazards which happen immediately an earthquake strikes:

Building collapse – buildings which have not been built to withstand earthquakes may collapse, trapping and killing the people inside (Fig 4). In some cases the land becomes liquefied and buildings actually sink.

Falling objects – objects, such as signs, may fall from buildings. Glass falling from broken windows is a major hazard. Glass falling from a ten-storey building is able to cut through a car roof.

Secondary effects are problems faced in the hours and days after an earthquake:

Fire – gas pipes ripped open in an earthquake may catch fire. If enough buildings are on fire, a firestorm can develop.

Tsunami – huge waves, up to 30 metres high and travelling at 500 km hour, can occur after an earthquake which happens out at sea.

Disease – cholera and typhoid may spread through the population of an area if the water supply has been cut off.

Communications – buckled roads and railways, and fallen telephone cables, make travelling and communicating difficult.

Economy – factories may have to close, and people lose their jobs. The country will have to spend millions of pounds on repairs.

No	Effects
1	Detected only by instruments
2	Slight vibrations, hardly noticed
3	Slight vibrations, noticed by people not moving
4	Moderate, felt by people moving about
5	Quite strong, loose objects fall over
6	Strong, slight damage to buildings
7	Very strong, walls crack
8	Destructive, chimneys fall
9	Ruinous, buildings collapse
10	Disastrous, many buildings destroyed
11	Very disastrous, few buildings left standing
12	Catastrophic, total destruction

▲ *Fig 3* *The Mercalli scale.*

▲ *Fig 4* *Earthquake in Turkey, 1999.*

Key words

epicentre – the point on the Earth's surface directly above the focus of an earthquake
fault – a line of weakness in rock
focus – the point underground where the energy of an earthquake is released
seismic wave – shock waves or vibrations caused by an earthquake
seismometer – sensitive instrument used to measure earthquakes

SUMMARY

- Earthquakes are caused by sudden movements of the Earth's crust.
- Earthquakes are measured using either the Richter or Mercalli scales.
- The effects of earthquakes can be divided into primary and secondary effects.

SUMMARY activity

Describe how the effects of an earthquake might vary under the following conditions:
- *in a richer country or a poorer country*
- *in a rural area or an urban area*
- *during the daytime or at night*
- *in an inland area or coastal area.*

 USGS earthquake information centre http://www.neic.cr.usgs.gov/

9 Kobe earthquake

In this section of the book you will investigate the following things:
- What caused the Kobe earthquake?
- What were the effects of the earthquake?
- How did people respond to the disaster?

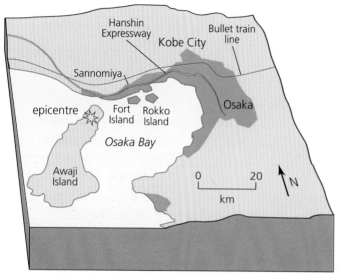

▲ **Fig 1** Kobe and Osaka.

Each year Japan has around 2000 earthquakes. Luckily, most of these are not powerful enough to do much damage. The Japanese have spent a lot of time and money studying earthquakes. They are trying to predict where the next 'big one' might strike. However, nobody was expecting the earthquake which struck Kobe in 1995. Kobe is a coastal city on the main island of Honshu (Fig 1). At 5.46 a.m. on 17 January 1995, an earthquake measuring 7.2 on the Richter scale struck the city. The earthquake lasted only 20 seconds, but caused terrible human suffering and damage estimated at £80 billion (Fig 2).

Cause of the earthquake

Japan lies in the middle of four **tectonic plates**. The huge Pacific plate is moving west at 10 cm every year. As it moves, it is forced underneath the North American and Philippine plate. The Philippine plate is also sliding underneath the Eurasian plate (Fig 3). The immense pressure of these movements has created **faults** (cracks) in the crust in Japan. There is a fault running through the Kobe area, but it had not moved for 50 years. Because it had not moved for such a long time, an enormous amount of pressure had built up. When the fault suddenly did move, shock waves spread out causing the earthquake. The **epicentre** of the earthquake was on Awaji Island in the Akashi Straits.

Q1 Where is Kobe?

Q2 Draw a labelled diagram to explain the cause of the earthquake.

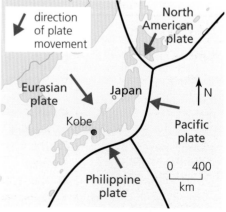

▲ **Fig 2** Collapsed building in Kobe.

▲ **Fig 3** Plate boundaries around Japan.

 EQE Kobe disaster report http://www.eqe.com/publications/kobe/kobe.htm

Effects of the earthquake

The primary effect of the earthquake was damage to buildings. Many older buildings collapsed completely. Wooden buildings in the poorer area of Kobe, Nagata, were flattened. Although wood is more flexible than concrete, the walls could not support the heavy tile roofs. A number of tall concrete buildings 'pancaked'. This means the walls gave way and each floor piled up on top of the one below. In the bay area, the soil liquefied during the earthquake. Buildings sank down into the ground and settled at dangerous angles (Fig 2).

The most devastating secondary effect was fire. Paraffin heaters and gas cookers set fire to buildings. The fire was made worse by gas escaping from broken gas pipes. The fire services could do little to help. Water mains had burst in the earthquake and the roads were blocked. In total 190 000 buildings were either destroyed or damaged and 300 000 people lost their homes and had to live in temporary shelters (Fig 4).

Q3 Draw a table to show the primary and secondary effects of the earthquake.

Human response

A few days after the earthquake, people became angry with the government. They said that the government had not done enough to help them. They claimed that:

- the emergency services took too long to arrive;
- the emergency services gave up looking for survivors after only 24 hours;
- there was a lack of rescue equipment, such as thermal image cameras;
- the government turned down assistance from other countries;
- the poorer part of the city received less help.

Q4 Why did the emergency services take a long time to reach earthquake victims?

Deaths	4 569
Injuries	14 679
Fires	175
Aftershocks	1 320
Schools	85% damaged
Industry	12% destroyed
Ports	90% destroyed
Bullet train	130 km of track closed

▲ **Fig 4** Data on the Kobe earthquake.

Key words

epicentre – the point on the Earth's surface directly above the focus of an earthquake

fault – a line of weakness in rock

tectonic plate – a large, rigid section of the Earth's crust

SUMMARY

- The earthquake was caused by the movement of tectonic plates.
- The major primary effect of the earthquake was building collapse.
- The major secondary effect of the earthquake was fire.
- The Japanese government was accused of not doing enough to help.

SUMMARY activity

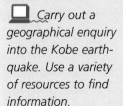

Carry out a geographical enquiry into the Kobe earthquake. Use a variety of resources to find information.

 Kobe City homepage http://www.city.kobe.jp/index-e.html

10 Prediction and preparation

In this chapter you will investigate the following things:
■ How can earthquakes and volcanic eruptions be predicted?
■ How can people prepare for earthquakes and volcanic eruptions?

The world's population is increasing. This means more and more people are living in areas at risk from earthquakes and volcanoes. Scientists try to predict when an earthquake will strike or a volcano will erupt. Meanwhile, governments do their best to prepare their citizens.

Earthquake prediction

Earthquake **prediction** is extremely difficult. Scientists have some idea of where earthquakes are likely to happen, but not when. Only one earthquake has been successfully predicted: in China, in 1975.

One method of predicting where the next earthquake will strike is to map previous earthquakes. Areas which have not had an earthquake for a long time are more at risk. Sometimes warning signs are given before an earthquake. A series of small tremors, called **foreshocks**, may signal a large earthquake in the near future. A change in water levels in wells or small movements of the ground, may also be warnings. Many people believe that animals are able to sense earthquakes before they happen. Catfish, rats and pigs have been seen behaving strangely before an earthquake.

Earthquake preparation

Much can be done to prepare for earthquakes. Buildings can be built to withstand severe shaking. In richer countries, high-rise buildings can be built with deep **foundations**, often made of rubber. The rubber absorbs the shock waves and protects the building. Concrete is reinforced with steel, allowing buildings to twist and sway. In case of fire, sprinkler systems are built in (Fig 1). In poorer countries, people cannot afford buildings like these. However, it is still possible to build safer buildings. For example, wood should be used, rather than bricks, because wood is more flexible. Other measures governments can take are to have emergency guidelines and practice drills. In Japan and California, all school children are trained what to do in case of an earthquake.

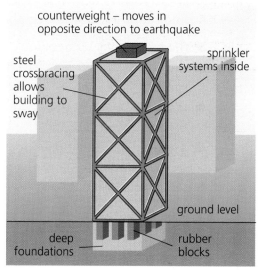

▲ *Fig 1* Earthquake-proof building.

Q1 Why are the numbers of deaths caused by earthquakes increasing?

Q2 Why are areas which have not had an earthquake for a long time more at risk?

Q3 Why are buildings made from wood and steel more likely to survive an earthquake?

 USGS – Earthquake Information: Reducing Hazards http://quake.wr.usgs.gov/

Volcanic eruption prediction

Improvements in technology are making it easier to predict volcanic eruptions. **Satellites** are used to monitor the temperature and shape of active volcanoes. If either of these change, it may show that the volcano is filling up with magma. On the ground, scientists monitor the volcano with very sensitive instruments. Gas readings of sulphur dioxide and carbon dioxide are taken. An increase in either of these gases may signal an eruption. Also, seismometers are used to record any earthquakes. Earthquakes are caused when the magma pushes upwards and fills the volcano before it erupts (Fig 2).

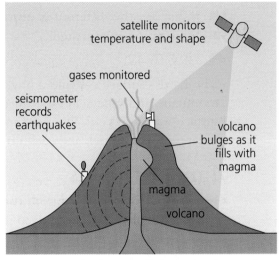

▲ **Fig 2** *Predicting volcanic eruptions.*

Q4 How does a change in the shape of a volcano warn that it might erupt?

Volcanic eruption preparation

Being able to predict volcanic eruptions means it is easier to prepare for them. Hazard maps are produced, showing the areas most at risk from an eruption. People can then be evacuated from these areas (Fig 3). Although it is not possible to stop a volcano from erupting, people have had some success at diverting lava flows. In Italy, lava flows from Mt Etna were bombed to divert them away from a village. In Iceland, sea water was sprayed on to lava flows to turn them solid. This action saved the main port.

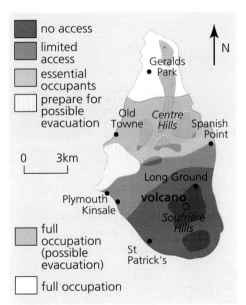

◀ **Fig 3** *A volcano hazard map for Montserrat (before 1997 eruption).*

Key words

foreshock – a small earthquake before a large one

foundations – part of a building that is below the ground

prediction – warning of an event before it happens

satellite – a computerised device orbiting the Earth

SUMMARY

■ It is possible to predict where earthquakes might happen, but not when.

■ Buildings can be made to withstand earthquakes.

■ Volcanic eruptions can usually be predicted.

■ Evacuation is the most effective response to a volcanic eruption.

SUMMARY *activity*

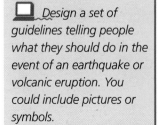

Design a set of guidelines telling people what they should do in the event of an earthquake or volcanic eruption. You could include pictures or symbols.

 USGS – Earthquake Monitoring http://vulcan.wr.usgs.gov/Monitoring/Framework.html

11 Rocks

In this section of the book you will investigate the following things:
- What are the different groups of rocks?
- How are rocks formed?
- How do rocks influence landforms?

The Earth's surface contains a huge variety of landforms. In some places there are mountains and valleys, in other places, gentle hills or flat plains. Why does the Earth's surface vary so much? The most important reason is the type of rock. There are three different types of rock and each one creates different landforms.

Igneous rocks

Igneous rocks are formed from **magma**. Magma is molten rock from deep inside the Earth. Because magma is hot it rises through the Earth's crust. If it reaches the surface, it forms a volcano. Volcanoes erupt liquid rock called lava. Lava cools quickly to form new rock called basalt. Because it cools so quickly, basalt has very small crystals. Often magma does not reach the Earth's surface. Instead it cools inside the crust. When magma cools inside the crust it forms rock called granite. Because granite takes a long time to cool, it develops large interlocked crystals. Granite is a very hard rock and takes a long time to wear away. Granite forms upland areas such as mountains and moors (Fig 1).

▲ *Fig 1* Hay Tor, Dartmoor.

Q1 How are igneous rocks formed?

Q2 How can you tell whether igneous rock cooled inside or outside the crust?

Sedimentary rocks

Sedimentary rocks are formed from other rocks, or the remains of living creatures. Rocks at the Earth's surface are worn down by the weather. The particles of worn down rock are carried by rivers to the sea. When they reach the sea they sink to the bottom and build up in layers. Over millions of years the particles are squashed together by the layers above. Eventually they become stuck together and form new

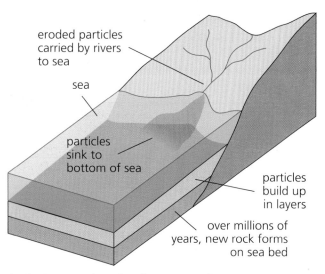

eroded particles carried by rivers to sea

sea

particles sink to bottom of sea

particles build up in layers

over millions of years, new rock forms on sea bed

▲ *Fig 2* Formation of sedimentary rock.

rock. Rocks formed in this way include sandstone and clay (Fig 2). Clay is a very soft rock and forms flat lowland areas.

Some sedimentary rocks are formed from the remains of dead sea creatures. When the creatures died their shells and skeletons sank to the sea floor. These built up in layers and were compressed to form chalk and limestone (Fig 3). Chalk is harder than clay and forms gentle hills. Limestone is quite a hard rock and can form spectacular mountains and gorges.

◀ **Fig 3** *Chalk cliffs: the layers of rock are visible.*

Q3 What are sedimentary rocks made from?

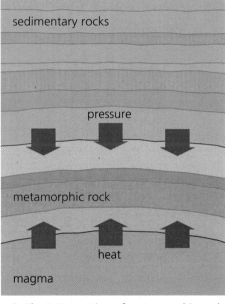

▲ **Fig 4** *Formation of metamorphic rock.*

Metamorphic rocks

Metamorphic rocks are formed from other rocks during volcanic activity, or earth movements. Rocks which come into contact with magma are heated and turned into another type of rock. Limestone heated by magma is turned into marble, and sandstone is turned into quartzite. Sometimes extreme pressure can also alter rocks. Clay can be changed into slate by great pressure (Fig 4). Metamorphic rock is usually quite hard and forms upland areas.

Q4 Explain how marble and slate are formed.

Key words

igneous – rock formed from magma

magma – hot molten rock

metamorphic – rock formed from other rocks under extreme heat and pressure

sedimentary – rock formed from particles of other rocks or dead sea creatures

SUMMARY

- Landforms are influenced by the type of rock.
- Igneous rock is formed from magma, either cooled at the surface, or underground.
- Sedimentary rock is formed on the sea bed from particles of rock or skeletons.
- Metamorphic rock is formed from igneous or sedimentary rock.
- Metamorphic rock is formed only in areas of volcanic activity or earth movement.

SUMMARY *activity*

Design a crossword puzzle on the topic of rocks. Exchange your crossword with your classmates.

 British Geological Survey http://www.bgs.ac.uk/

12 Weathering and erosion

In this section of the book you will investigate the following things:
- What is weathering?
- What is erosion?

How do weathering and erosion shape the land?

The Earth's surface is constantly changing. **Weathering** and **erosion** are wearing away the land and shaping mountains, hills, valleys and coastlines. Weathering slowly breaks down rocks at the Earth's surface. Weathering is caused by rain, changes in temperature, plants and animals. Erosion wears rock away, and removes the loose particles. Erosion is caused by glaciers, rivers, wind and the sea.

◀ **Fig 1** *The Taj Mahal in India is being weathered by acid rain caused by pollution.*

Chemical weathering

Rainwater is naturally a very weak acid, because of carbon dioxide in the air. Acidic rainwater is able to break down certain types of rock, such as chalk and limestone. Chalk and limestone are made from calcium carbonate, which reacts with weak acid. Acidic rainwater dissolves the rock, especially along cracks or joints. When rainwater seeps below the surface in limestone areas, it dissolves the rock to form huge caves. Chemical weathering also attacks buildings made from limestone. Chemical weathering of buildings is a growing problem in cities. Air pollution from cars and power stations is making rainwater more acidic (Fig 1).

Q1 What is the difference between weathering and erosion?

Q2 How are people increasing the amount of chemical weathering?

Q3 Why is an increase in chemical weathering a problem?

Freeze-thaw weathering

Weathering can happen very quickly when it is cold. Water seeps into cracks in the rock. When the temperature falls below 0 °C, the water turns to ice and expands. As it expands it causes great pressure. This pressure widens the crack. When the temperature warms up, the ice turns back to water.

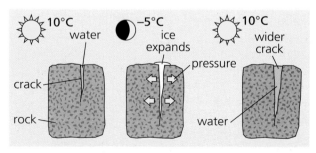

▲ **Fig 2** *Freeze-thaw weathering.*

USGS Weathering and erosion http://wrgis.wr.usgs.gov/docs/parks/misc/gweaero.html

The water seeps further into the crack, where it will later freeze again. Eventually the rock will break apart and large pieces will fall away (Fig 2). These pieces of broken rock pile up to form **scree**. Freeze-thaw weathering is common in mountain areas, such as the Lake District.

Q4 Why does freeze-thaw weathering not happen often in very cold areas?

Onion-skin weathering

Onion-skin weathering happens in areas with a large temperature range, such as deserts. During the day it can be very hot, up to 40 °C. Surface layers of rock are heated, causing them to expand. At night the temperature may fall to around freezing. The surface layers cool and contract. This causes the rock to weaken. The surface layers of rock may split away. Because the rock peels away in layers, it is called onion-skin weathering (Fig 3).

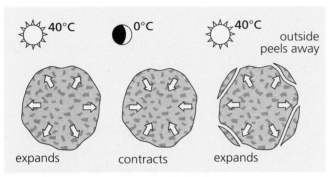

Q5 Why is weathering in deserts called 'onion-skin' weathering?

▲ **Fig 3** Onion-skin weathering.

Biological weathering

Plants and animals are also able to break up rocks. Plant roots can grow into cracks in the rock. The roots put pressure on the cracks and widen them. Eventually the rock may break apart (Fig 4). Burrowing creatures such as moles and worms also help to break up soft rocks, such as clay.

▲ **Fig 4** Biological weathering.

Key words

erosion – wearing away of the land

scree – piles of broken rock

weathering – the natural breakdown of rocks

SUMMARY

■ Weathering is the breakdown of rocks by weather and living things.

■ Erosion is the wearing away and removal of rock by wind, rivers, sea and ice.

■ Weathering and erosion shape rocks at the Earth's surface to create landforms such as mountains, valleys and coastlines.

SUMMARY activity

Design a series of labelled diagrams to show biological weathering.

 Weathering and erosion school study http://schoolsite.edex.net.uk/192/text/envhome.htm

13 Limestone landscapes

In this section of the book you will investigate the following things:
- How is limestone formed?
- What landforms occur in limestone areas?

Limestone

Limestone is a sedimentary rock. It was formed hundreds of millions of years ago, when warm tropical oceans were full of tiny sea creatures. As the creatures died, their shells and skeletons fell to the sea floor. Over many years they built up in thick layers and were stuck together to form new rock. Later, movements of the Earth's crust lifted the limestone high above sea level (unit 3). Today, we can still see the layers in limestone. These layers are called **bedding planes**. Limestone also has many cracks, caused when it was lifted out of the sea. The cracks are called **joints**. Water is able to flow through the bedding planes and joints in limestone. This means the rock is **permeable**.

Q1 Why does limestone contain fossils?

Q2 Why is limestone permeable?

Surface landforms

Limestone is a very hard rock, but it can be dissolved by rain water. Limestone is made of calcium carbonate, which is alkaline. Rainwater is acidic, so it reacts with the limestone and dissolves it. This is a very slow process. Only around 1 cm of limestone is dissolved every 100 years!

Rainwater attacks the limestone at its weakest points, the joints and bedding planes. This results in a unique landform at the surface. As the joints are worn away, blocks of stone are left behind. The enlarged joints are called **grykes**, and the blocks are called **clints**. This landscape is called a limestone pavement. There is a good example of a limestone pavement in the Yorkshire Dales (Fig 1).

Q3 What is a limestone pavement?

▲ **Fig 1** *Limestone pavement.*

Underground landforms

Very few rivers flow over the surface in limestone areas. Rivers disappear down holes called swallow holes. A swallow hole forms where a joint has been completely dissolved. Once underground, the river continues to dissolve the limestone. At first it

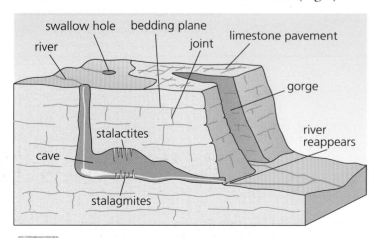

◀ **Fig 2** *Limestone features.*

 National Park Service – Mammoth Caves http://www.pbs.org/wgbh/aso/tryit/tectonics/

forms tunnels, then caves and then huge caverns (Fig 2). The largest limestone cave system in the world is the Mammoth Caves in the USA. The Mammoth Caves are 560km long.

Limestone caves contain beautiful features called stalactites and stalagmites (Fig 3). These form when water drips from the roofs of caves. Each drip deposits a tiny amount of dissolved calcium carbonate. Over hundreds and thousands of years the calcium carbonate builds up to form icicle-shaped columns. Columns hanging from the roof are called stalactites. Those rising from the floor are called stalagmites. If stalactites and stalagmites

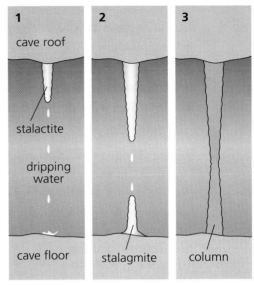

▲ Fig 3 *Formation of stalactites, stalagmites and pillars.*

meet, they will form a pillar. In some places, the roof of a large cavern collapses. This forms a spectacular steep-sided valley, often with a river flowing through it. A valley formed in this way is called a **gorge**. Gordale, in the Yorkshire Dales, is an example of a limestone gorge (Fig 4).

Q4 What is the difference between stalactites and stalagmites?

Q5 How is a gorge formed?

◄ Fig 4 *Gordale Gorge, Yorkshire Dales.*

Key words

bedding plane – a horizontal crack between layers of rock

clint – block of stone on a limestone pavement

gorge – a deep steep-sided valley

gryke – weathered joint on a limestone pavement

joint – a crack in the rock

permeable – allows water to flow through joints in the rock

SUMMARY

- Limestone is a sedimentary rock formed from the remains of ancient sea creatures.
- Limestone is weathered at the surface to form limestone pavements.
- Limestone is dissolved underground to form caves and caverns.

SUMMARY activity

Some people explore new limestone caves as a hobby. Imagine you have just discovered a new cave system. Draw a map of your caves and label the features you found.

 The stupid page of rocks http://www.geocities.com/RainForest/Canopy/1080/

14 River basins

In this section of the book you will investigate the following things:

- What is a river basin?
- What are the different parts of a river basin called?
- How do rivers erode, transport and deposit material?

Rivers play a very important part in shaping the landscape. As they flow from high land to low land, they erode soil and rock. The eroded pieces are transported downstream and later deposited. New landforms are created by these processes of **erosion** and **deposition** (Fig 1).

▲ **Fig 1** Rivers erode, transport and deposit.

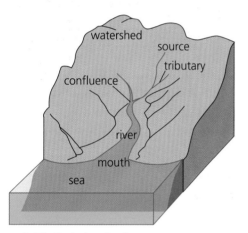

▲ **Fig 2** A river basin.

Q1 How can a river have several sources?

Q2 Why does a river become deeper towards its mouth?

River basins

Rivers begin in upland areas. The place where they begin is called the source. Rivers flow downhill from their source, until they reach the sea or a lake. The place where the river enters the sea or lake is called the mouth. During the journey from source to mouth the main river is joined by other rivers. This means a river can have several sources. The name given to a smaller river joining the main river is a tributary. The point where a tributary joins the river is called a confluence. When more water enters the river from a tributary, the river channel becomes wider and deeper. This means a river becomes larger as it flows from its source to its mouth.

The area of land containing the river and its tributaries is called a drainage basin, or **river basin** (Fig 2). This is because the rivers drain the land of all the rain that falls in the area. The area of high land which separates two drainage basins is called the watershed.

Erosion

The faster a river flows, the more energy it has to erode its bed and banks. A river erodes in four different ways (Fig 3).

- Hydraulic action – the force of the water wears away the bed and banks of the river channel.

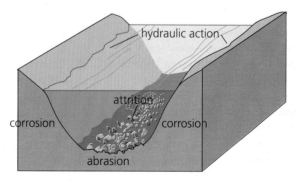

▲ **Fig 3** River erosion.

 Centre of Ecology and Hydrology http://www.nwl.ac.uk/ih/

28

- Abrasion – pebbles carried by the river rub the bed of the river channel and wear it away.
- Corrosion – the river water is able to dissolve some rocks, such as limestone.
- Attrition – stones carried by the river collide. When they collide they knock pieces off each other. The stones become smaller and rounder as they travel down the river.

Transportation

The stones and soil which have been eroded are called the river's load. A lot of energy is needed to transport the load downstream. The river **transports** the load in four different ways (Fig 4).

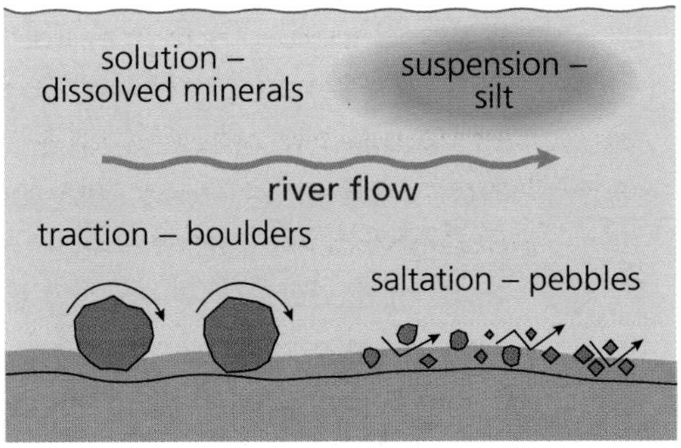

▲ ***Fig 4*** *River transportation.*

- Traction – the heaviest rocks and boulders are rolled along the river bed. Traction only happens when there is a lot of water in the river, such as during a flood.
- Saltation – the flow of the river water bounces stones and pebbles along the river bed.
- Suspension – the small pieces of eroded soil float in the river. When a river is transporting material like this, the water looks brown and cloudy.
- Solution – some minerals, such as calcium carbonate in limestone, are dissolved by water. The dissolved minerals are carried downstream in the river water.

Deposition

When a river slows down, it loses energy and has to deposit its load. Most of the load is deposited when the river enters the sea or lake. The heaviest material, rocks and boulders, are deposited first. The lightest material, silt, is deposited last. The minerals in solution become salt in the sea.

Q3 When does a river deposit its load?

Q4 Which material does it deposit first?

Key words

deposition – the dumping of the river's load when it slows down
erosion – the wearing away of the land
river basin – an area of land drained by a river and its tributaries
transportation – the movement of eroded material downstream

SUMMARY

- Rivers drain an area of land called a river basin.
- Rivers shape the land through erosion, transportation and deposition.
- There are four types of erosion.
- There are four types of transportation.
- Eroded material is deposited when a river slows down.

SUMMARY *activity*

Design a web page to explain to people how a river erodes, transports and deposits material. Use labelled diagrams to show the processes.

Global Rivers Environmental Education Network http://www.igc.apc.org/green/resources.html

15 Upper valley river landforms

In this section of the book you will investigate the following things:
- What shape are river valleys in upland areas?
- How do interlocking spurs form?
- Why do some rivers have waterfalls and gorges?

Most rivers begin in areas of high land with steep slopes. Along this upper part of a river's course, its energy is used to erode the land downwards. This results in landforms such as V-shaped valleys, interlocking spurs, waterfalls and gorges.

V-shaped valleys

River valleys in upland areas are steep-sided and narrow. They are called V-shaped valleys because they form the shape of the letter V. V-shaped valleys are formed as the river erodes downwards (vertically), leaving steep valley sides. The valley sides are slowly broken down by **weathering**. The loose weathered material is washed into the river by rainfall. The river transports this material downstream as part of its load (Fig 1). The river's load in upland areas has a lot of large rough rocks and boulders. This is because they have not yet been eroded by attrition. In upland areas the river can look rough and fast flowing. In fact, the rocks and boulders slow the river down.

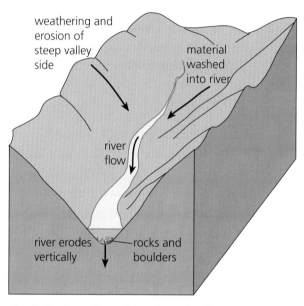

▲ **Fig 1** Formation of a V-shaped valley.

Q1 What shape are river valleys in upland areas?

Q2 Why do upland river valleys have steep sides?

Interlocking spurs

Rivers begin to twist and turn as they flow downhill. They flow from side to side, avoiding areas of harder rock which are more difficult to erode. A series of hills form on either side of the river valley. The name given to a hill on the inside of a river bend is a **spur**. Because the river is curving from side to side, these hills become interlocked (Fig 2). Therefore, a series of interlocking spurs are formed by river erosion.

Q3 Why do rivers begin to flow from side to side?

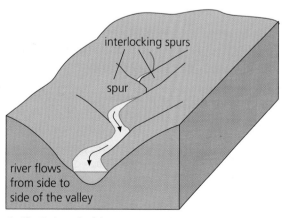

▲ **Fig 2** Interlocking spurs.

Waterfalls

The most spectacular sight along the course of a river is a waterfall (Fig 3). Waterfalls usually occur where there is a band of hard rock lying on top of softer rock. The river erodes the softer rock more quickly than the hard rock. This forms a 'step' in the river, where the water falls vertically. At the base of the waterfall, the falling water erodes the softer rock, and undercuts the hard rock. An **overhang** develops. Eventually the overhang will collapse under its own weight. The rock which breaks from the overhang forms large blocks at the base of the waterfall. These are slowly broken up by erosion. The loose rocks are swirled round at the base of the waterfall. As the rocks are swirled they cut into the softer rock, and erode a deep **plunge pool** (Fig 4).

▲ **Fig 3** Waterfall in Yosemite National Park, USA.

Q4 Where do waterfalls occur?

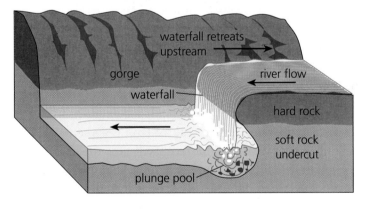

Fig 4 Formation of a waterfall and gorge.

Gorges

Over many years a gorge will form in front of the waterfall. Each time the rock overhang collapses, the waterfall retreats slightly up the valley. Over many years a steep-sided valley, called a gorge will be created.

Key words

overhang – an unsupported band of rock at the top of a waterfall

plunge pool – a deep pool which is eroded at the base of a waterfall

spur – a steep hill formed on the inside of a river bend

weathering – the breakdown of rocks by weather, plants and animals

SUMMARY

- Upland river valleys are V-shaped.
- Interlocking spurs develop as a river flows from side to side.
- Waterfalls form in areas of hard and soft rock.
- A steep-sided gorge is formed as a waterfall retreats upstream.

SUMMARY activity

Draw three labelled diagrams to show the formation of a waterfall and gorge. Research some facts about large waterfalls around the world.

16 Lower valley river landforms

In this section of the book you will investigate the following things:
- ■ What shape are river valleys in lowland areas?
- ■ How do meanders and ox-bow lakes form?
- ■ How is a flood plain created?
- ■ Why do some rivers have deltas?

In its lower course, a river flows over low-lying land with gentle slopes. There is more water in the river and its channel is wider and deeper. The river's load has been eroded so it is smaller and rounder. Because the channel is larger, and the load smaller, the river is able to flow faster. The river is still eroding downwards, but it is now also eroding sideways (laterally). Sideways erosion makes the river valley wide and flat. In places, the river is both eroding and depositing material. New landforms are created, such as meanders, ox-bow lakes, flood plains and deltas.

Meanders

A meander is a curve, or a loop, in the river. A river begins to bend from side to side in upland areas. When it reaches lowland areas, the curves can become very large. The river's flow is fastest on the outside bend of the meander. The outside bend is eroded and undercut to form a **river cliff**. On the inside bend, the river flows slowly and deposits material. The material builds up to form an area of shallow land, called a **slip-off slope**.

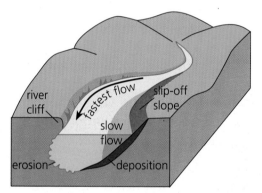

▲ **Fig 1** Cross-section of a meander.

Q1 How has the river's load changed in its lower course?

Q2 Why do rivers flow faster in their lower course?

Ox-bow lakes

During a flood, the narrow neck of land between a meander can be eroded. The river will take the shortest route possible, and form a new channel. The old meander becomes cut-off as material is deposited by the river. A lake in the shape of a horse shoe will be formed. Over time the lake will become a marshy area, and in the end will dry up completely (Fig 2).

Q3 Why does a river deposit material on the inside bend of a meander?

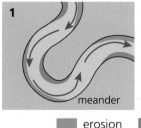
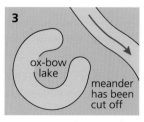

erosion   deposition   ⟶ fastest flow

◀ **Fig 2** Formation of an ox-bow lake.

Flood plains

A flood plain is the flat valley floor on either side of a river (Fig 3). Flood plains are formed by both erosion and deposition. The river erodes sideways as it meanders downstream. This sideways erosion wears away interlocking spurs and carves out a wide valley. The valley is flooded each year when the river bursts its banks. During the flood the river deposits layers of stones and mud. The deposited material builds up in layers to form a flat valley floor. Flood plains are excellent places for farming because the soil is very **fertile**.

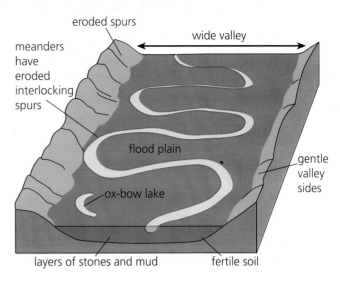

▲ **Fig 3** Flood plain.

Q4 Give two reasons why flood plains are good for farming.

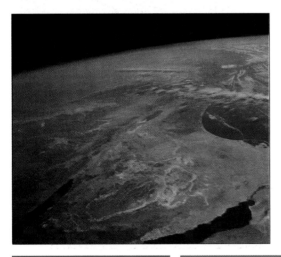

Deltas

When a river reaches the sea it deposits its load. The heaviest material is deposited first, and the lightest last. If the sea is shallow, and does not have strong tides, the deposited material can build up to form a delta. A delta is a low-lying area of land formed at a river's mouth (Fig 4). Often the main river splits into many smaller rivers. The smaller rivers are called **distributaries**.

◀ **Fig 4** Satellite photo of Egypt and the Nile delta.

Key words

distributary – a small river which has split away from the main river

fertile – rich in plant nutrients

river cliff – steep, undercut area on the outside of a river meander

slip-off slope – gently sloping area formed on the inside of a river meander

SUMMARY

- Lowland river valleys are wide, flat and gentle.
- Meanders develop as a river curves from side to side.
- Ox-bow lakes form when meanders are eroded in times of flood.
- Flood plains are formed by erosion and deposition.
- A delta is an area of low-lying flat land, formed by deposition at the river mouth.

SUMMARY *activity*

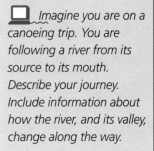

Imagine you are on a canoeing trip. You are following a river from its source to its mouth. Describe your journey. Include information about how the river, and its valley, change along the way.

17 River floods

In this section of the book you will investigate the following things:

- **Where is the River Rhine?**
- **What caused the River Rhine to flood in 1995?**
- **What were the effects of the flood?**
- **How can floods be prevented?**

The Rhine

The River Rhine is a major European river. The **source** of the Rhine is in the Alps, in Switzerland. The Rhine flows for 1320 km before it reaches the North Sea, on the Netherlands coastline. In the Netherlands the river is called the Waal. The Rhine is joined by several major **tributaries** from nine different countries (Fig 1).

In February 1995, the River Rhine flooded a large area of northern Europe. The Netherlands, Germany, Belgium and France were affected.

> **Q1** Name the countries that the River Rhine and its tributaries flow through.

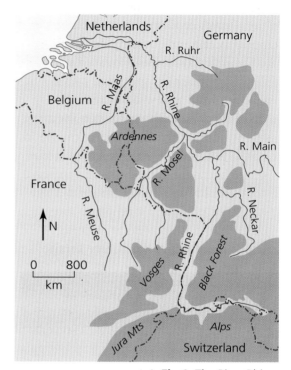

▲ **Fig 1** *The River Rhine.*

Causes of the flood

The floods of 1995 were caused by unusual weather. However, the actions of people may have made the floods worse. During January 1995, there was a period of unusually wet weather. Over three times the average rainfall fell. The weather was also warmer than usual. This meant that snow in the Alps melted. The extra rainfall, and melted snow water, soaked into the ground. When the ground was completely **saturated** the water ran quickly over the ground into the tributaries of the Rhine. The Rhine soon began to rise.

The Rhine has been greatly altered by people. To stop it from flooding, large embankments, called **dykes**, have been built at the side of the river. Some dykes are ten metres high. The river has also been straightened to make it shorter and easier for barges to navigate. Straightening the river and trapping it between two dykes has reduced the amount of water that can be held in the river. This means the river will rise more quickly.

> **Q2** How have people increased the risk of the Rhine flooding?

 Environment Agency http://www.environment-agency.gov.uk/

Effects of the flood

At the beginning of February 1995 the Rhine had risen to dangerously high levels. In some places in the Netherlands dykes began to give way. A huge operation began to reinforce the dykes. In other places temporary dykes were created out of soil, sand and sandbags. In case the dykes collapsed, a quarter of a million people were evacuated from their homes (Fig 2). Farmers also moved over 300 000 pigs and cattle away from the danger area. Luckily, most of the dykes did hold firm. In the areas where the river did flood, farmers lost their crops and houses were damaged by water and mud. The damage caused by the flood ran into millions of pounds.

▲ **Fig 2** *Area threatened by flooding, 1995.*

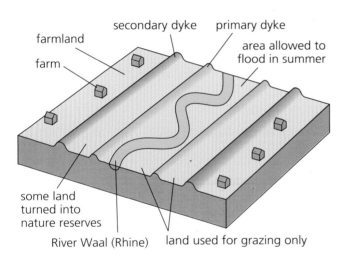

farmland
farm
secondary dyke
primary dyke
area allowed to flood in summer
some land turned into nature reserves
River Waal (Rhine)
land used for grazing only

▲ **Fig 3** *Flood control in the Netherlands.*

Flood control

Since the floods of 1995 the Dutch government has promised to spend £1 billion on improving flood defences. Dykes are being repaired and in places made higher. In some places stones and steel are being used to make the dykes stronger. The government is also buying farmland close to the river. The farmland is being turned into nature reserves which are allowed to flood in the winter (Fig 3). Although this method reduces the risk of flooding, farmers are not happy because they do not want to give up their land.

Q3 Do you think farmers should be forced to sell their land to the Dutch government to help stop flooding?

Key words

dyke – an embankment next to a river channel
saturated – waterlogged soil and rock
source – the beginning of a river
tributary – a river joining a larger river

SUMMARY

- The 1995 European floods were caused by natural and human factors.
- The floods had a large impact on people, livestock and property – but could have been worse.
- There are conflicts between farmers and the government over new flood control measures.

SUMMARY *activity*

💻 *Imagine you work for the Dutch government. Write an article for a newspaper to convince people that the flood was caused by nature. You must also explain the steps the government are taking to prevent the river from flooding again.*

 Netherlands flood http://www.hvu.nl/flood/

18 Coastal erosion

In this section of the book you will investigate the following things:
- How are waves produced?
- How do waves erode the coastline?
- Why do headlands and bays form in some areas?
- How are caves, arches and stacks formed?

The coast is an exciting area that is constantly changing. Landforms are created, and destroyed, by the power of waves. Destructive waves erode the land to create headlands, bays, caves, arches and stacks. Constructive waves deposit sand and stones, to form beaches and spits.

Waves are formed by wind blowing across the surface of the sea. The stronger the wind, the more powerful the waves. The distance that the wave travels is also important. The distance travelled by a wave is called the **fetch**. A wave that has a large fetch has more power. The more power a wave has, the greater the amount of erosion it can cause.

The rate of erosion at the coast will also depend on the type of rock. A coastline with hard rocks, such as granite or limestone, takes a long time to wear down and has high, steep **cliffs**. An area of clay is eroded more quickly, and has lower, more gentle cliffs.

> **Q1** Why are waves from the Atlantic Ocean more powerful than those in the English Channel?
>
> **Q2** Why are granite cliffs higher than cliffs made from clay?

Erosion

Waves erode the coastline in four different ways.

- Hydraulic action – the force of the waves crashing into the cliffs. Air trapped inside cracks in the cliff is compressed, and blows the rock apart.
- Abrasion – stones and pebbles are picked up by the waves and smashed against the base of the cliff. This wears away the rock to form a **wave-cut notch**.
- Corrosion – some rocks, such as chalk and limestone, are slowly dissolved by sea water.
- Attrition – stones and pebbles collide, knocking pieces off each other. In this way they become smaller, smoother and rounder. Eventually they become particles of sand.

> **Q3** How is sand formed?

Headlands and bays

Headlands and bays occur in areas with different types of rock. The Swanage area, in Dorset, has four different rock types (Fig 1). Waves have eroded the sandstone and clay more quickly to form bays. Limestone and chalk are more resistant and have not been eroded as quickly. The areas of limestone and chalk form points sticking out to sea, called headlands. The headlands have high, steep cliffs.

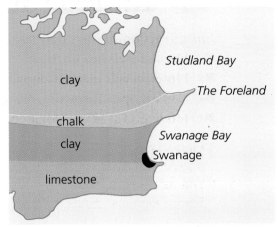

▲ **Fig 1** Geology of Swanage area.

Caves, arches, stacks and stumps

The chalk headland north of Swanage has been eroded to create landforms called caves, arches, stacks and stumps (Fig 2). Lines of weakness in the chalk, called **faults**, have been attacked by waves. Over many years the faults have opened up into caves. Eventually some caves broke through the headland to form arches. In a number of places the arches have collapsed to leave a large pillar, called a stack. A famous stack in this area is called 'Old Harry'. A second stack called 'Old Harry's Wife' was destroyed in a storm. Now all that is left is a piece of rock called a stump (Fig 3).

Q4 Describe how the landforms in Fig 2 may change over the next 100 years.

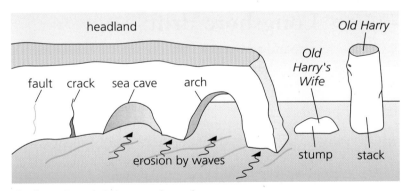

▲ **Fig 2** Caves, arches, stacks and stumps.

▲ **Fig 3** Old Harry, Swanage.

Key words

cliff – a wall of rock facing the sea

fault – a line of weakness in rock

fetch – the distance travelled by a wave

wave-cut notch – undercut area at the base of a cliff

SUMMARY

- Waves are caused by wind.
- The rate of erosion depends on the type of rock.
- Headlands and bays are formed in areas of different rock.
- Caves, arches and stacks are formed on headlands.

SUMMARY activity

Produce an information leaflet about coastal landforms in the Swanage area. The leaflet must describe the landforms and explain how they were formed. Include maps and diagrams where possible.

 Southampton University – Geology of the Dorset Coast http://www.angelfire.com/wy/westian/index.html

19 Coastal deposition

In this section of the book you will investigate the following things:
- How are beaches formed?
- How is beach material moved?
- How are spits formed?
- How are sand dunes formed?

Beaches

Many areas at the coast have a beach. A beach is a collection of pebbles, sand or mud. Beaches are formed by waves which erode, transport and then deposit pieces of rock on the sea shore. Most of the material on a beach comes from the land at the coast. Powerful waves erode the land, breaking it into pieces. The pieces of rock are then moved up and down the beach by waves. This wears the rock pieces down, by **attrition**, until they form small particles of sand. Stones, sand and mud carried out to sea by rivers are also deposited on beaches. Beaches are extremely good at absorbing wave energy. This means a wide beach will protect the cliffs behind from wave erosion.

Q1 Describe a beach you have visited.

Q2 Where do the pebbles, sand and mud on a beach come from?

Longshore drift

Sand and pebbles on a beach are constantly shifting. They are moved up and down, but also along the beach. The movement of sand and pebbles along the beach is known as longshore drift (Fig 1). Longshore drift happens when waves approach the beach at an angle. When a wave breaks it carries sand and pebbles up the beach at an angle. As the wave returns to the sea it drags the sand and pebbles straight back down. When this happens many times, the sand and pebbles move along the beach in a zig-zag pattern.

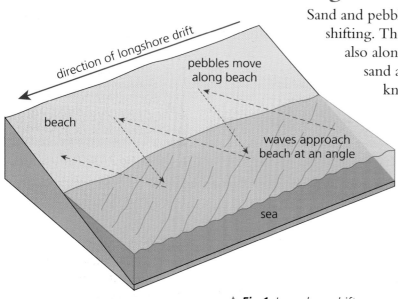

▲ **Fig 1** Longshore drift.

Q3 Draw a labelled diagram to explain longshore drift.

 NASA – images of the coast from the Space Shuttle
http://daac.gsfc.nasa.gov/CAMPAIGN_DOCS/OCDST/shuttle_oceanography_web/oss_4.html

Spits

A spit is a very special coastal landform. Spits occur where there is a break in the coastline, often at a river mouth. An example of a spit is Spurn Head, at the mouth of the Humber (Fig 2). A spit is formed by the deposition of sand and pebbles, moved by longshore drift. Over many years the sand and pebbles build up to form a long, curved beach which extends out to sea (Fig 3). A spit will develop a 'hooked end' if the wind sometimes blows from the other direction. In the sheltered area behind the spit, mud is deposited and a **salt marsh** develops. Salt marshes provide a **habitat** for several rare plants and animals.

Q4 Where do spits form?

▲ **Fig 2** Spurn Head.

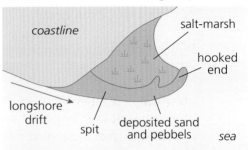

▲ **Fig 3** Formation of a spit.

Sand dunes

Sandy beaches which are exposed to the wind can develop sand dunes. Sand dunes are hills made from sand. Wind blows sand from the beach inland, where it is trapped by plants such as Marram grass. The sand builds up to form large mounds. The Dune de Pilat, in the south of France, is an example of a very large dune. It is 114 metres high, 500 metres wide and 3 kilometres long (Fig 4). Sand dunes are fragile landforms which can easily be damaged by careless tourists.

▲ **Fig 4** Dune du Pilat, France.

Key words

attrition – erosion of beach material by wave action

habitat – area suitable for plants and animals to live in

salt marsh – a marshy wetland behind a spit

SUMMARY

- Beaches are landforms created by the deposition of pebbles, sand and mud at the coast.
- Beach material is moved in a 'zig-zag' by longshore drift.
- Spits are formed by deposition, where there is a break in the coastline.
- Sand dunes form on sandy beaches with a strong onshore wind.

SUMMARY activity

Describe the method you would use to investigate whether longshore drift was happening at a beach.

 Coastal landforms http://www.angliacampus.com/tour/sec/geog/coastal/index.htm

20 Coastal defences

In this section of the book you will investigate the following things:
- Why do people live in coastal areas?
- Why are coastal defences needed in some areas?
- What different coastal defences can be used?
- What problems do coastal defences create?

Millions of people around the world live on the coast. In Britain, many coastal **settlements** began as fishing villages. Today, tourism is a very important industry at the coast. Tourists bring money into an area, but they expect a safe, clean beach.

> **Q1** What other reasons are there for people living on the coast?

Living on the coast has many benefits, but can also be hazardous. In areas where waves are eroding the coast, farmland and houses are at risk of falling into the sea. In low-lying areas, coastal flooding is also a threat. These hazards may become worse in the future if sea levels rise because of **global warming**. Many cities built on low-lying land, such as London and Amsterdam, are at risk.

Coastal defences

Coastal erosion and flooding are expensive problems. Local authorities must make a decision. Is it cheaper to build coastal defences, or pay compensation to people who have lost property?

There are a number of different types of coastal defence which can be used (Fig 1).

- Groynes – wooden barriers built on the beach. Groynes trap sand and pebbles to build up the beach. The beach absorbs the impact of waves.
- Concrete sea walls – a curved wall built at the back of a beach. Sea walls deflect waves and prevent flooding.
- Rock armour – large boulders are placed at the base of cliffs to stop undercutting.
- Drainage – coastal cliffs often collapse when they become soaked with rainwater. Improving drainage on the cliffs can make them safer.

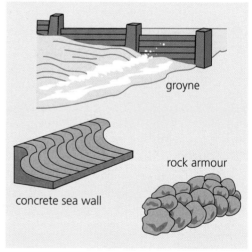

groyne

rock armour

concrete sea wall

▲ **Fig 1** Coastal defences.

Q2 How might building coastal defences affect tourism?

Q3 Do you think people who choose to live close to the sea should receive compensation if their houses are lost because of coastal erosion?

Holderness coast

The Holderness coastline has one of the fastest rates of coastal erosion in the world (Fig 2). On average it loses between one and two metres of land a year. The coast is being rapidly worn away because of the rock type. The rock, called **till**, is soft clay containing small stones. When waves crash against the bottom of the cliffs the rock crumbles, the cliffs collapse, and the pieces are washed away (Fig 3).

Coastal erosion in this area is nothing new. Twenty-nine small villages have been lost to the sea in the past one thousand years. However, in 1990 the local authority decided to try to save the village of Mappleton. They decided that it would be cheaper to spend £2 million on coastal defences than re-route the coastal road that runs through Mappleton. Two rock groynes were built out to sea and boulders were placed at the foot of the cliffs. The groynes have trapped sand and pebbles and built up a beach. The beach now absorbs the wave energy and erosion has been stopped (Fig 4).

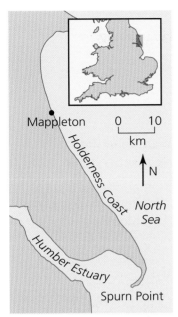

▲ **Fig 2** *The Holderness coast.*

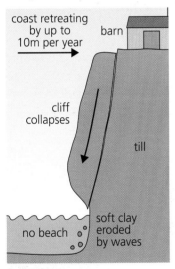

▲ **Fig 3** *Erosion of the Holderness coast.*

However, the defences at Mappleton have caused problems further south. In the past, sand and pebbles were moved along the coast by **longshore drift**. Today they are trapped by the groynes. This means that cliffs further south are no longer protected by a beach. At high tide the waves reach the base of the cliffs and erosion has increased to 10 metres a year. Farmers have lost land and even their homes.

Q4 Why does the Holderness coastline have such a high rate of natural coastal erosion?

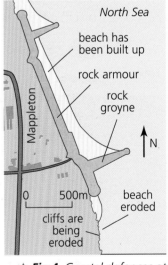

▲ **Fig 4** *Coastal defences at Mappleton.*

Key words

global warming – global increase in temperature caused by an increase in carbon dioxide in the atmosphere

longshore drift – the movement of sand and pebbles along a beach

settlement – a place where people live

till – soft rock which is mainly clay

SUMMARY

- People live in coastal areas for economic and personal reasons.
- Many coastal areas are at risk from erosion and flooding.
- A range of techniques may be used to control erosion and flooding.
- Coastal defences in one area may cause problems in another.

SUMMARY *activity*

Draw a labelled map to show why coastal erosion has increased south of Mappleton. Do you think the local authority made the correct decision to build coastal defences at Mappleton?

 Safeguarding our coast – Holderness coastline http://www1.npm.ac.uk/lois/Education/case.htm

21 Landslides

In this section of the book you will investigate the following things:
- **What causes landslides?**
- **What are the consequences of landslides?**
- **How do people respond to landslides?**

Landslides are dramatic events which happen when rock moves suddenly down a slope. Landslides are becoming more hazardous in many places around the world. Population growth means more people are having to live in areas at risk from landslides. This is especially true in poorer countries. Many **squatter settlements** are built on hillsides which are unstable and at risk of collapsing.

Q1 Why are landslides becoming more hazardous?

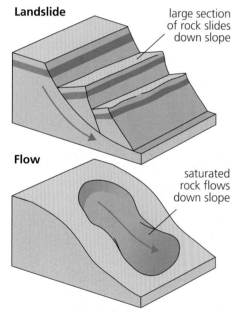

Landslide

large section of rock slides down slope

Flow

saturated rock flows down slope

◀ **Fig 1** Landslides.

Causes of landslides

Landslides are caused when rock or soil on a slope can no longer support its own weight. Landslides may be caused by nature or people. The most common natural cause is water. Heavy rainfall can **saturate** rock and weaken it. Eventually the rock may collapse and slide, or flow, down the slope (Fig 1). Unfortunately, many landslides are caused by the actions of people. Building on slopes adds weight to the rock. At the same time the slope is often made steeper. Both these things make the slope more likely to collapse. Before building on, or close to, a slope it is important to assess the risks. The softer the rock, and the steeper the slope angle, the more chance there is of a landslide.

Q2 How does rain cause landslides?

Q3 How do people cause landslides?

The Aberfan disaster

In 1966, a disastrous landslide occurred at Aberfan in South Wales (Fig 2). Aberfan was a coal mining village. For 90 years waste rock from the coal mines had been piled up to form huge **spoil heaps**. Some people were worried that these man-made hills were not stable. However, the National Coal Board insisted they were safe. Spoil heap

▶ **Fig 2** The aftermath of the Aberfan disaster.

 Australian landslide information http://www.agso.gov.au/geohazards/landslides/

number 7 was only 250 metres away from Aberfan. On 21 October, following heavy rain, spoil heap 7 collapsed. The rain had saturated the rock, and a small river had eroded the base of the spoil heap making it steeper. Two million tonnes of rock flowed downhill destroying a farm, 20 houses and a school (Fig 3). The landslide took the lives of 116 children and 28 adults. The National Coal Board were blamed for the tragedy and had to pay compensation. Today there are strict regulations in the UK to ensure that spoil heaps are safe.

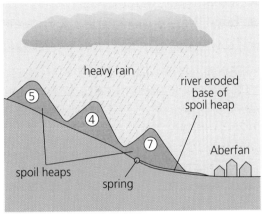

▲ **Fig 3** *Causes of the Aberfan landslide.*

Bolivia

Bolivia is a country in South America. The majority of people in Bolivia are farmers who struggle to make a living. One way for a farmer to escape from poverty is to become a gold miner. However, mining for gold is a very dangerous job (Fig 4). Mining is not regulated the way it is in the UK. This means that safety is often ignored. On 8 December 1992, a huge landslide occurred at a mine in Llipi. The steep slopes dug out by the miners were saturated by heavy rain. The rock was weakened and collapsed, killing almost 1200 people. Despite the dangers, people continue to mine for gold in the hope that they may become rich.

Q4 Who was responsible for the landslide in Llipi?

▶ **Fig 4** *Gold mining can be a dangerous job.*

Key words

saturate – soaked with water

spoil heap – a large mound of waste rock

squatter settlement – an area of very low-quality housing

SUMMARY

- Landslides are a rapid movement of rock down a slope.
- Rain often triggers a landslide.
- The actions of people are increasing the number of landslides.
- Poorer people are more at risk from landslides.

SUMMARY *activity*

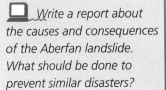 Write a report about the causes and consequences of the Aberfan landslide. What should be done to prevent similar disasters?

 Aberfan disaster http://www.nuff.ox.ac.uk/politics/aberfan/home.htm

22 Water cycle

In this section of the book you will investigate the following things:
- What is the water cycle?
- How do people interrupt the water cycle?

Earth is sometimes called 'the Blue Planet'. This is because 70% of its surface is covered by water. Ninety-seven per cent of the Earth's water is stored in the seas and oceans. Two per cent is stored as snow and ice, mainly in the Arctic and Antarctic. The final one per cent is found in the atmosphere, or on the land as rivers and lakes.

The water on the Earth today is the same water that was around when dinosaurs roamed the planet. Water is neither created, nor destroyed, but is cycled round over and over again. This endless recycling of water is called the water cycle.

Q1 Why is Earth known as 'the Blue Planet'?

Q2 ⌨ Draw a graph to show where the Earth's water is stored.

The water cycle

Water in the sea is warmed by heat from the sun. The water **evaporates** and turns into **water vapour**. The warmer the air the more water vapour it can hold. Warm air rises, carrying the water vapour upwards. As the air rises it cools. When the water vapour cools, it **condenses** into very small droplets. We see these tiny droplets as clouds. Droplets in the clouds bump into each other and grow bigger. Eventually, when they are big enough, they fall as rain drops. Eighty per cent of rain falls straight back into the sea, but some clouds are blown inland.

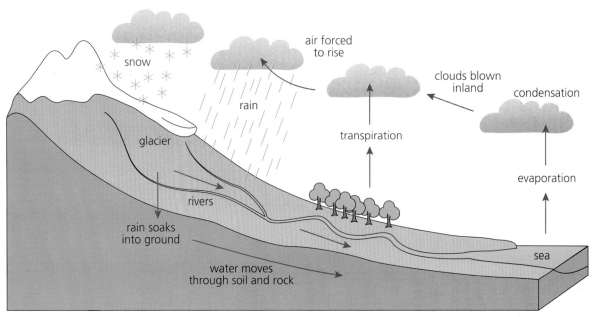

▲ **Fig 1** The water cycle.

Water also evaporates from the land. Trees and other plants release water vapour from their leaves (transpiration). This water vapour rises and joins the clouds blown in from the sea. Clouds are forced to rise by hills and mountains. This cools them further, causing the clouds to rain. Before the rain drops hit the ground, they may be caught by trees, plants or even buildings. This is called **interception**. When the rain reaches the ground it will soak into the soil and porous rock below. Once the ground is saturated the rain will flow over the surface into rivers. Rivers return the water back to the sea, where it began its journey (Fig 1).

Q3 Why does the water cycle happen more quickly at the Equator than in the Arctic?

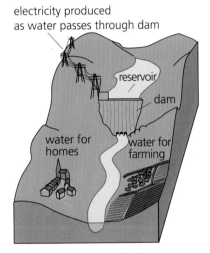

electricity produced as water passes through dam

reservoir

dam

water for homes

water for farming

▲ **Fig 2** A HEP dam.

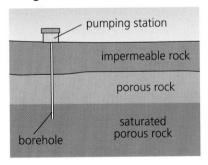

pumping station

impermeable rock

porous rock

saturated porous rock

borehole

People and the water cycle

Fresh water is a vital resource needed for people to survive. People interrupt the water cycle to obtain water in a number of ways.

Dams are built across rivers to form large lakes called reservoirs. Water is taken from reservoirs to provide water for homes, farming and industry. Dams are also used to produce hydro-electric power (Fig 2).

Boreholes are drilled into the ground and fresh water is pumped up from the porous rocks below. This water may be several thousand years old (Fig 3).

Cloud-seeding is a new technique which has been tried in the USA. Rockets are fired into the air which explode into thousands of tiny pieces. The tiny pieces cause water droplets to form creating clouds. This technique may be useful in areas which are short of water.

Q4 Why might water pumped from boreholes run out in the future?

◀ **Fig 3** A borehole and pumping station.

Key words

condense – water vapour cools and becomes a liquid

evaporate – liquid is heated and becomes a gas

interception – raindrops landing on plants, trees and buildings

vapour – a gas

SUMMARY

- The water cycle is the constant cycling of water between the sea, the atmosphere and the land.
- People interrupt the water cycle to obtain water for use in their homes, for farming and for industry.

SUMMARY activity

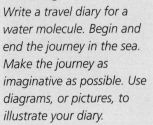

Write a travel diary for a water molecule. Begin and end the journey in the sea. Make the journey as imaginative as possible. Use diagrams, or pictures, to illustrate your diary.

23 Weather

In this section of the book you will investigate the following things:
■ What is weather?
■ How is weather measured and recorded?
■ How does weather affect people?

Weather is something we all experience every day. It is the condition of the air around us, at a certain place and time. Weather includes temperature, precipitation, air pressure, wind and clouds. All weather is powered by energy from the Sun, and it is highly changeable. It changes from place to place and from hour to hour.

Q1 What is weather?

Types of weather

Temperature describes how hot or cold the air is. Temperature is measured with a thermometer. It is recorded in degrees Centigrade.

Precipitation is the word used to describe any type of water falling from the **atmosphere**. It includes rain, snow, hail, fog and dew. Precipitation is measured using a rain gauge. A rain gauge is a cylinder which catches the rain. The water is then poured into a measuring glass and recorded in millimetres (Fig 1).

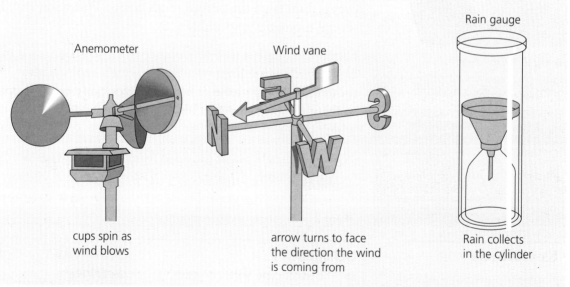

Anemometer

cups spin as wind blows

Wind vane

arrow turns to face the direction the wind is coming from

Rain gauge

Rain collects in the cylinder

▲ **Fig 1** Weather recording instruments.

Air pressure is the weight of the air. Warm air rises, causing low air pressure. Cool air sinks, causing high air pressure. Air pressure is measured using a barometer. A barometer is a small sealed cylinder which expands and contracts as air pressure changes. Air pressure is recorded in millibars. The average air pressure is 1013 millibars.

The Met. Office http://www.met-office.gov.uk/

Wind is the movement of air from one place to another. It is caused by differences in air pressure. Air flows from an area of high pressure to an area of low pressure. The greater the difference in air pressure the faster the wind. Wind speed is measured using an anemometer, which is spun round by the wind (Fig 1). Wind speed is recorded in kilometres per hour, or using the Beaufort scale (Fig 2). The direction of the wind is measured using a wind vane. Wind direction is described as the direction the wind has come from.

Clouds are tiny visible water droplets, or ice crystals, high in the air. Cloud cover is measured by sight and recorded in oktas. An okta is an eighth of the sky, so if half the sky is cloudy it is described as four oktas.

Force	Wind
0	Calm
2	Light breeze
4	Moderate breeze
6	Strong breeze
8	Gale
10	Storm
12	Hurricane

▲ *Fig 2* The Beaufort scale.

Q2 What causes wind?

Q3 Make a copy of the Beaufort scale. Draw some pictures to illustrate it.

Weather and people

Weather has a huge impact on people's lives. Weather affects work, transport, farming, sport and even people's emotions. This means it is very important to understand how weather works, and to predict what the weather will be like. Weather data is collected by weather stations, ships, aircraft and satellites. The data is processed using computers and analysed by weather experts, called **meteorologists**. Meteorologists use the data to forecast what the weather will be like for the next three or four days. Weather forecasts are often given using weather symbols on a map (Figs 3 and 4).

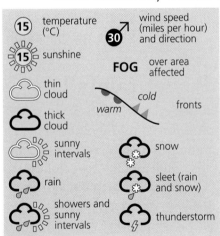

▲ *Fig 3* Weather map symbols.

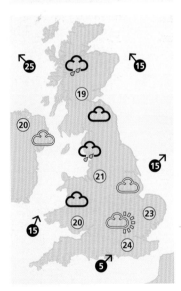

▲ *Fig 4* Weather map.

Q4 Give some detailed examples of how weather can affect people.

Key words

atmosphere – a layer of air around the Earth
meteorologist – a weather expert
weather – the condition of the air

SUMMARY

■ Weather is the condition of the air at a certain time.
■ Weather includes temperature, precipitation, air pressure, wind and cloud cover.
■ Weather affects people's lives in many ways.
■ Weather forecasts help people to plan ahead.

SUMMARY *activity*

Write a weather forecast for the UK based on the weather map in Fig 4.

 BBC Weather Centre http://www.bbc.co.uk/weather/

24 Rain

In this section of the book you will investigate the following things:
- How is rain formed?
- What are the different types of rainfall?
- What types of rainfall occur in Britain?

Water falls from the **atmosphere** in several different forms. Usually we expect water droplets to fall as rain but if it is cold enough the droplets can freeze to form snowflakes, hail or sleet. Snow is formed when water droplets freeze and form ice crystals. The ice crystals stick together and fall as snowflakes. Hail is formed when rain drops are frozen as they are swept up and down by powerful updraughts of air during a thunderstorm. Sleet is a mixture of snow and rain.

▲ **Fig 1** *Tropical rain in India.*

Rain is formed when air containing water **vapour** is forced to rise. As air rises it cools. The water vapour condenses to form clouds made of tiny water droplets. The water droplets collide and grow to form rain drops. When the raindrops are large enough they fall as rain (Fig 1). Together, rain, snow, hail and sleet are known as precipitation. Precipitation may be caused in one of three ways: there is relief rainfall, frontal rainfall and convectional rainfall. Each way involves moist air rising.

Q1 What is precipitation?

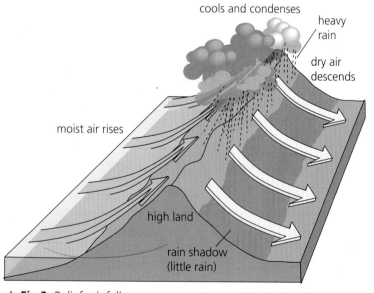

cools and condenses

heavy rain

dry air descends

moist air rises

high land

rain shadow (little rain)

▲ **Fig 2** *Relief rainfall.*

Q2 Why is the sheltered side of a hill called the 'rain shadow'?

Relief rainfall

Relief rainfall occurs when moist air is forced to rise over hills and mountains. As the air rises it cools and condenses to form clouds. The clouds release rainfall over the hills and mountains. After the air has passed over the high land it sinks back down again. As it sinks, the air warms up and any clouds are evaporated. This side of a hill or mountain is known as the 'rain shadow' because very little rain falls there (Fig 2). Britain receives relief rainfall on the west coast. This is due to moist Atlantic winds being forced to rise as they reach high land near the coast.

 The Online Guides – Meteorology http://ww2010.atmos.uiuc.edu/(Gh)/guides/mtr/home.rxml

Frontal rainfall

Frontal rainfall occurs when a warm moist **air mass** collides with a cold air mass. The air masses will not mix because they are different temperatures. Instead the cold air undercuts the warm air, and the warm air rises up over the cold air. The boundary between the air masses is called a front. Along the front, water vapour in the warm air is condensed to form clouds and rain (Fig 3). Much of the rainfall in Britain is caused by fronts, as warm moist Atlantic air collides with cold air from northern Europe.

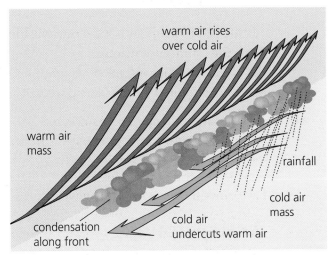

▲ **Fig 3** Frontal rainfall.

Q3 Describe what happens when a warm air mass meets a cold air mass.

Convectional rainfall

Convectional rainfall happens only where it is hot. The Sun heats the Earth's surface, causing large amounts of water to evaporate. The water vapour is lifted high into the atmosphere by rising warm air. As the air rises it cools and the water vapour condenses to form huge anvil-shaped storm clouds. Heavy rainfall results, often with thunder and lightning (Fig 4). Convectional rainfall only occurs in Britain on hot summer days.

Q4 Where in the world is convectional rainfall very common?

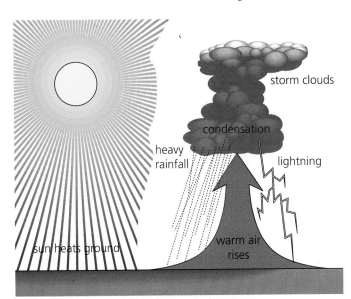

▲ **Fig 4** Convectional rainfall.

Key words

air mass – a very large body of air
atmosphere – layer of air around the Earth
vapour – a gas

SUMMARY

- Rain, snow, hail and sleet are all forms of precipitation.
- Relief rainfall occurs when air rises over high land.
- Frontal rainfall occurs when warm and cool air masses meet.
- Convectional rainfall happens when the sun causes massive evaporation.

SUMMARY *activity*

Make a 3D model out of card to show relief rainfall, frontal rainfall, or convectional rainfall. Colour and label your model to explain why it rains.

 UK Rainfall Radar Image http://www.met-office.gov.uk/datafiles/PastWx/UKRR_1200.gif

25 Anticyclones and depressions

In this section of the book you will investigate the following things:

■ What is an anticyclone?

■ What is a depression?

■ How do anticyclones and depressions affect the British Isles?

Weather is constantly changing. One day it is calm and sunny, the next windy and rainy. Moving air masses are responsible for these changes in the weather. An air mass is a very large body of air of a similar temperature. Air masses which travel overland tend to bring dry weather. Air masses which have crossed oceans will bring wet weather.

Anticyclones

An anticyclone is a cool, dry air mass. Because the air is cool it slowly sinks, creating high **air pressure**. As the air sinks towards the ground it warms up. Warm air is able to hold more water vapour. This means that any clouds are evaporated. Because there are no clouds, anticyclones bring dry, sunny weather. Winds in anticyclones are gentle. In the northern **hemisphere** the winds blow clockwise, due to the rotation of the Earth (Fig 1).

In the summer, anticyclones result in sunny days with warm temperatures (Fig 2). During the winter, anticyclones cause clear but cold days. Because there are few clouds, heat escapes upwards into the atmosphere. This means nights can be very cold with ice and frost forming. In the winter, anticyclones can often cause mist and **fog**.

Anticyclones do not affect the British Isles very often. Occasionally, dry air masses from Europe or North Africa move over Britain. Anticyclones are slow moving, which means we may have dry, bright and settled weather for several days.

Q1 What is an air mass?

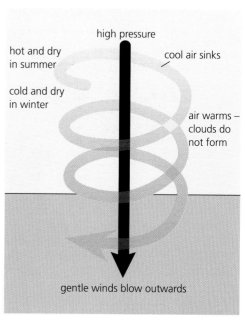

▲ **Fig 1** An anticyclone.

▲ **Fig 2** Typical weather of an anticyclone in summer.

Q2 Write down a way to remember that cool sinking air causes high air pressure.

Q3 Describe the weather caused by anticyclones in summer and winter.

Depressions

A depression is an area of low pressure, formed when a warm, moist air mass and a cool, dry air mass meet. Because the air masses are different temperatures, they will not mix. The warm air mass rises above the cool air mass. The boundary between them is called the warm **front**. Cool air then undercuts the warm air from behind, to form a cold front. Along both fronts, the cool air causes water vapour in the warm air to condense. Thick clouds form and it rains.

In the centre of the depression warm air rises. This causes low air pressure. Air is drawn in from the sides, creating strong winds. The lower the air pressure, the stronger the winds. In the northern hemisphere the winds blow in an anticlockwise direction (Fig 3).

▼ *Fig 3* *A depression.*

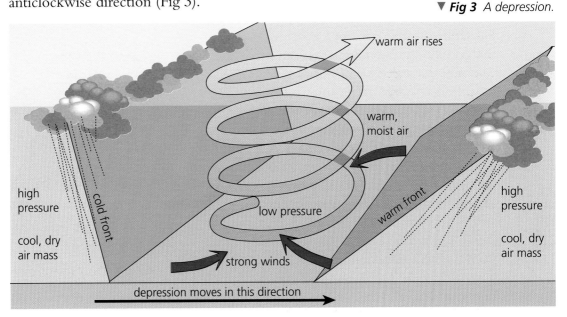

The British Isles weather is greatly affected by depressions. Warm, moist air from the Atlantic Ocean collides with cool, dry air from Europe. Large depressions are formed which take two or three days to pass over the British Isles. This means Britain experiences clouds, wind and rain for much of the year.

Q4 Why does the British Isles experience many depressions?

Key words

air pressure – the weight of the air
fog – cloud at ground level
front – boundary between warm and cool air masses
hemisphere – half of the globe

SUMMARY

- Anticyclones are areas of high pressure which bring bright, settled weather.
- Depressions are areas of low pressure which bring wind, cloud and rain.
- Britain's weather is dominated by depressions for most of the year.

SUMMARY *activity*

Use Fig 3 to describe and explain how the weather changes during the passing of a depression. Comment on temperature, air pressure, clouds, rain and wind.

Nottingham University Meteosat Images http://www.nottingham.ac.uk/meteosat/graphif.shtml

26 Hurricanes

In this section of the book you will learn the following things:
- What is a hurricane?
- What causes hurricanes?
- What are the effects of hurricanes?

A hurricane is a huge, violent tropical storm which is a hazard to people and property. Tropical storms bring winds of up to 200 kph and torrential rain. A large hurricane may be 500 km wide and can last for over two weeks. Hurricanes are called typhoons in the Pacific, cyclones in Asia and willy-willies in Australia.

Formation of hurricanes

Hurricanes begin over tropical oceans at the end of the summer when the water temperature is at its warmest. Heat from the Sun warms the sea to around 27°C. Sea water **evaporates** to form water vapour. Water vapour rises quickly, then cools and **condenses**, causing heavy rain. As the water vapour condenses it releases heat. This heat adds more power to the hurricane. An area of very low pressure forms as air is drawn upwards in a spiral. Air rushes in from the sides, developing very powerful winds. At the centre of the

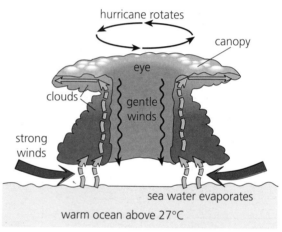

▲ **Fig 1** Cross-section of a hurricane.

hurricane is a calm area called the 'eye'. In the eye of the hurricane the air is slowly sinking, the winds are gentle and there is no rain (Fig 1).

▲ **Fig 2** Hurricane Lili over the Atlantic.

In the northern hemisphere, hurricanes move slowly westwards until they reach land. Once over land they are cut off from their power supply, the sea, and will slowly die. However, before they run out of energy hurricanes cause massive damage. Wind destroys buildings and crops, and rainfall causes flooding. Local sea levels can rise by several metres due to the low air pressure. This is called a '**storm surge**' and causes severe flooding in coastal areas.

Q1 Explain why hurricanes do not occur all year.

Q2 Give two reasons why the coast is a dangerous place to be during a hurricane.

Hurricane Lili

The beginning of Hurricane Lili was observed by the National Hurricane Centre, USA, on the 14 October 1996. A tropical **depression** had developed just east of Nicaragua in Central America. The depression grew in strength as it moved northwards. On 17 October it was classified as a hurricane (Fig 2). Warnings were issued to Cuba 30 hours before the hurricane reached land. This allowed people to prepare for the impact of the storm. On 18 October, Hurricane Lili hit Cuba with 160 kph winds and 650 mm of rainfall. The following day Lili increased in strength as it passed over the Bahamas.

Hurricane Lili then headed north east across the Atlantic, losing energy as it moved away from the tropics. When, on 28 October, Lili reached the UK it was no longer classed as a hurricane. However, winds of over 100 kph caused considerable damage as the depression passed over, on its way to Europe.

Cuba suffered enormous damage from Hurricane Lili. One million tonnes of food crops were destroyed by the winds and rain which flooded the fields. Forty-three thousand homes were destroyed and thirty thousand damaged, leaving many thousands of people homeless. However, thanks to the early hurricane warning no lives were lost. In the UK, sadly six people died as a result of the tail end of the hurricane, including two fishermen who were swept out to sea. Damage to property was not so serious but many homes lost roof tiles and had trees blown over.

▲ **Fig 3** Hurricane damage.

Date: October	Latitude (°N)	Longitude (°S)	Speed (kph)
14	12.8	80.4	45
16	16.8	83.5	55
17	18.2	84.2	100
18	21.3	82.8	130
19	23.0	78.2	160
21	31.9	60.8	140
23	33.4	53.9	120
25	34.3	49.9	150
27	44.3	30.5	100
28	52.5	15.5	100

▲ **Fig 4** Hurricane Lili's track.

Q3 Suggest why hurricanes in poorer countries cause more damage than hurricanes in richer countries.

Key words

condense – gas becoming liquid

depression – area of low pressure

evaporate – liquid turning to gas

storm surge – rise in sea level due to low air pressure

SUMMARY

- A hurricane is a tropical storm with winds of over 120 km per hour.
- Hurricanes only form in tropical areas when the sea reaches 27°C.
- Hurricanes lose power once they are over land.
- Hurricanes cause more problems in poorer countries than richer countries.

SUMMARY activity

Use the data in Fig 4 to plot the course of Hurricane Lili on a map. Use symbols and a key to show how its strength varied.

Hurricane Hunters http://www.hurricanehunters.com

27 Climate

In this section of the book you will investigate the following things:
- What is climate?
- What climate regions can be identified around the world?
- Why do climates vary?

Climate

Climate is the seasonal pattern of weather. It describes what the weather will be like in a place, month by month throughout the year. The climate of a place is based on the average weather conditions over many years. Because climate is an average it does not give details about any unusual weather that may occur.

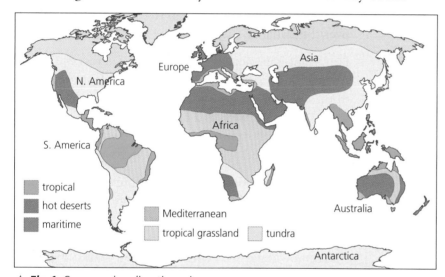

▲ **Fig 1** Some major climatic regions.

The two most important aspects of climate are **temperature** and **precipitation**. These can be shown on a climate graph. Bars are used to show total monthly precipitation, and a line is used to show the average monthly temperature. Climate graphs are useful when comparing the climates of two different places.

Different areas around the world can have very similar climates. This means it is possible to divide the world into climate regions. Fig 1 shows the location of some of the world's major climate regions. On a global scale there are five factors that affect climate.

Q1 What is the difference between weather and climate?

Factors affecting climate
Latitude

Latitude means how far north or south a place is from the Equator. At the Equator the Sun's rays are concentrated. This causes high temperatures and **convectional rainfall**. In places further north or south of the **Equator** the Sun's rays have further to travel, and they are more spread out. As a result temperatures are lower. This explains why the Arctic and Antarctic are frozen (Fig 2).

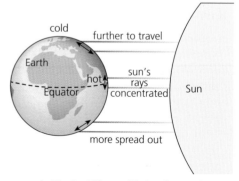

▲ **Fig 2** Effect of latitude on climate.

 World Climate Data http://www.worldclimate.com/

Altitude

Altitude is the distance above sea level. The higher a place is, the colder it will be. This is because heat from the Sun is reflected by the Earth's surface. The reflected heat warms the lower layer of the atmosphere. Temperatures fall by 6.5°C every 1000 metres (Fig 3). Higher areas also receive more precipitation due to relief rainfall.

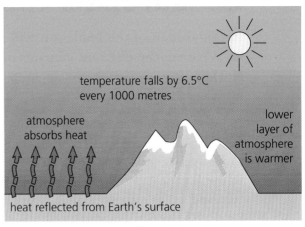

temperature falls by 6.5°C every 1000 metres

atmosphere absorbs heat

lower layer of atmosphere is warmer

heat reflected from Earth's surface

▲ **Fig 3** *Effect of altitude on temperature.*

Distance from the sea

Places close to the sea have a maritime climate. This means that they have a small annual temperature **range**. Temperatures are influenced by the sea. The sea keeps coastal areas warmer in winter, and cooler in summer. Inland areas have a much larger temperature range. Coastal areas also receive more precipitation due to moist air being blown off the sea.

Ocean currents

Currents are large flows of warm or cold water through the oceans. Warm currents flow from the tropics towards the North and South Poles. These currents warm coastal areas in winter, but also bring rain. Cold ocean currents lower temperatures in coastal areas.

Prevailing winds

Prevailing winds are the winds that blow most often. Winds can affect temperature and precipitation. Winds blowing from tropical areas bring warm weather, while winds blowing from polar areas brings cold weather. Winds blowing over oceans cause precipitation, while winds which have blown over land are dry.

Q2 Why is it very cold in the Arctic and Antarctic?

Q3 Why are high mountains covered in snow and ice?

Q4 Why are inland areas hotter than coastal areas in summer?

Key words

convectional rainfall – rainfall caused by hot air rising, cooling and condensing

Equator – imaginary line running around the middle of the Earth

precipitation – rain, snow, hail or sleet

range – difference between minimum and maximum temperature

temperature – measurement of heat

SUMMARY

- Climate is the average weather over many years.
- Many areas around the world have similar climates.
- Climates are affected by latitude, altitude, distance from the sea, ocean currents and prevailing winds.

SUMMARY activity

Draw a map of a large imaginary island. Label it to explain how its climate might vary in different places. Try to include all the factors in this unit.

 World Climates http://www.uwsp.edu/acaddept/geog/faculty/ritter/geog101/climates_Foc.html

28 Europe's climate

In this section of the book you will investigate the following things:
- What are the different climates in Europe?
- How do they vary between summer and winter?
- What causes these differences?

Europe is sandwiched between the cold polar region of the Arctic, and the hot tropical region of North Africa. To the east of Europe is the vast continent of Asia, and to the west is the huge Atlantic Ocean (Fig 1). This location results in Europe's **climate** being very varied.

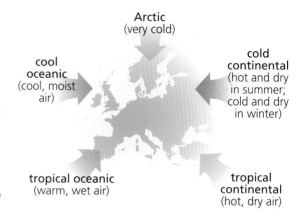

Arctic (very cold)

cool oceanic (cool, moist air)

cold continental (hot and dry in summer; cold and dry in winter)

tropical oceanic (warm, wet air)

tropical continental (hot, dry air)

▲ **Fig 1** Air masses influencing Europe.

Q1 Name the air masses which affect Europe's climate.

Europe's climate can be divided into two main regions (Fig 2).

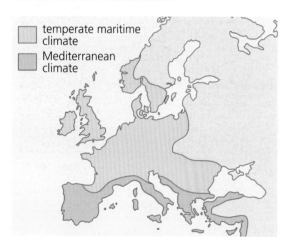

☐ temperate maritime climate
☐ Mediterranean climate

North-west Europe has a temperate maritime climate.

Temperate means moderate, and maritime means it is affected by the sea. North-west Europe has warm summers and mild winters. It has rainfall all year.

Southern Europe has a Mediterranean climate.

This means it has hot summers and warm winters. It rains in the winter, but is dry in summer.

◀ **Fig 2** Europe's climatic regions.

Temperature

Temperatures in Europe vary with the seasons. They increase in the summer and decrease in the winter. However, north-west Europe is always colder than southern Europe. There are three reasons for this:

- Northern Europe is further from the Equator. This means the Sun's rays have further to travel so they are not so powerful.
- In northern Europe the Sun's rays reach the ground at a greater angle. Therefore the heat energy is more spread out.
- The Sun's rays have to pass through more of the Earth's atmosphere in the north. Dust particles in the atmosphere reflect the rays. This means less heat energy reaches the ground.

Q2 Draw a labelled diagram to show why northwest Europe is colder than southern Europe.

 Met Office – Europe weather http://www.met-office.gov.uk/sec3/europe.html

Precipitation

North-west Europe has **precipitation** all year (Fig 3). This is because it is in the zone where cold polar **air masses** and warm tropical air masses meet. These air masses collide and form frontal depressions (unit 25), which move west across Europe. The most precipitation falls in the west and in areas with high mountains, such as the Alps.

Southern Europe does not have precipitation throughout the year. During the summer a hot dry air mass moves north from Africa, and settles over countries such as Spain, Portugal, Italy and Greece. This hot air mass is a zone of high pressure, where air is gently sinking. This means clouds rarely form and so rain is unlikely (Fig 4). However, in the winter the hot air mass moves south to North Africa. Southern Europe is then affected by frontal depressions, which bring wind and rain.

▲ **Fig 3** Scotland.

▲ **Fig 4** Spain.

Q3 Why do countries in north-west Europe have precipitation throughout the year?

Q4 Why are countries in the Mediterranean popular holiday destinations?

		Jan	Feb	Mar	Apr	May	Jun	Jul	Aug	Sep	Oct	Nov	Dec
Lisbon, Portugal	Temp Max°C	14	15	17	20	21	25	27	28	26	22	17	15
	Rainfall mm	111	76	109	54	44	16	3	4	33	62	93	103
London, UK	Temp Max°C	6	7	10	13	17	20	22	21	19	14	10	7
	Rainfall mm	54	40	37	37	46	45	57	59	49	57	64	48

▲ **Fig 5** European climate data.

Key words

air mass – a large body of air of a similar temperature
climate – the average weather over many years
precipitation – rain, snow, hail or sleet

SUMMARY

- Europe's climate is affected by five major air masses.
- Europe can be divided into two climate zones.
- North-west Europe has warm, wet summers and mild, wet winters.
- Southern Europe has hot, dry summers and warm, wet winters.

SUMMARY activity

☐ Use the data in Fig 5 to draw two climate graphs. Describe the climates of Lisbon and London.

 The Weather Channel – Europe satellite image http://www.weather.com/weather/sat/europesat_720x486.html

29 Britain's climate

In this section of the book you will investigate the following things:
- What is Britain's climate?
- How does Britain's climate vary?
- Why does Britain's climate vary?

Britain is in northwest Europe and therefore has a temperate maritime climate. This means that the climate is **moderate** and is influenced by the sea. Britain has warm, wet summers and mild, wet winters. For most of the year, Britain's weather is affected by frontal **depressions** which blow in from the Atlantic. The frontal depressions bring wind and rain. Occasionally, **anticyclones** move over Britain from Europe or North Africa. Anticyclones bring settled dry weather, which is cold in winter but warm in summer (unit 25). Although these weather conditions affect the whole of Britain, there are regional variations.

Summer temperatures

Fig 1 shows the **isotherms** for Britain in July. An isotherm is a line on a map joining all the places with the same temperature. The map shows that during the summer the warmest places in Britain are in the south, with average temperatures of 17°C. Temperatures decrease towards the north, to an average of 13°C in Scotland. The reason for this is that temperatures decrease with distance from the Equator (unit 27).

Q1 What is an isotherm?

Q2 Why is the north of Britain colder than the south in summer?

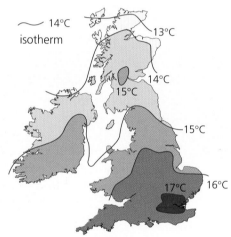

▲ **Fig 1** July temperatures.

Winter temperatures

Fig 2 shows the isotherms for Britain in January. The map shows that during the summer the warmest places in Britain are on the south-west coast, with average temperatures of 7°C. Temperatures decrease towards the north east, to an average of 4°C. Instead of running across the country, the isotherms are now at an angle. The reason for this change in direction can be explained by an ocean current. A warm current, the North

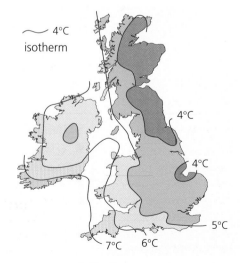

▲ **Fig 2** January temperatures.

 Met. Office – UK climate http://www.met-office.gov.uk/ukclimate/

Atlantic Drift, flows across the Atlantic from the Gulf of Mexico. When the current reaches the west coast of Britain, it warms the land. This means that palm trees can be grown on the west coast, even as far north as Scotland (Fig 3)!

Q3 Explain how it is possible to grow palm trees in Scotland.

◀ **Fig 3** Palm trees in the west of Scotland.

Precipitation

Precipitation falls throughout the year in Britain, but not all areas receive the same amount (Fig 4). The wettest areas are the west coast of Scotland and the Welsh mountains. These areas can receive over 2000 mm of precipitation per year. This is the same amount as an average rain forest! The driest areas are in the south east, where some places receive only 600 mm of precipitation per year (areas with less than 250 mm per year are classed as deserts). Most precipitation falls in the west due to relief rainfall (unit 24). Moist air, which has blown over the Atlantic, is forced to rise when it reaches high land on the west coast of Britain. As it rises, the air cools, condenses and then rains heavily. As the air descends on the other side of the hills, it warms and clouds evaporates. This means that much less rain falls in the east of Britain.

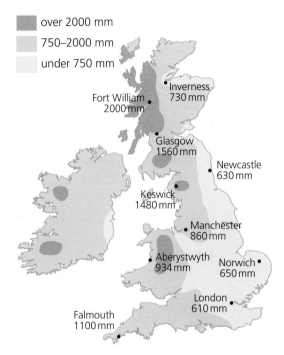

over 2000 mm
750–2000 mm
under 750 mm

Fort William 2000 mm
Inverness 730 mm
Glasgow 1560 mm
Newcastle 630 mm
Keswick 1480 mm
Manchester 860 mm
Aberystwyth 934 mm
Norwich 650 mm
London 610 mm
Falmouth 1100 mm

▲ **Fig 4** Average annual precipitation.

Q4 Why do Scotland and Wales receive so much rainfall?

Key words

anticyclone – area of high air pressure

depression – area of low air pressure

isotherm – line on a map joining places of the same temperature

moderate – not extreme

SUMMARY

- Britain has a temperate maritime climate.
- In the summer it is warmest in the south and coolest in the north.
- In the winter it is warmest in the south west and coolest in the north east.
- Precipitation is heaviest on the high land in the west.

SUMMARY activity

Imagine you work for a travel agent. Write an entry about Britain's climate which is to be included in a travel brochure for American tourists.

 Met. Office – UK weather http://www.met-office.gov.uk/sec3/sec3.html

30 Microclimate

In this section of the book you will investigate the following things:
- What is a microclimate?
- How are microclimates affected in urban areas?
- How are microclimates affected in rural areas?

A microclimate is the climate of a small area. Even over a very short distance there can be surprising changes in temperature, wind and rainfall. In **urban** areas (towns and cities) temperatures can be hotter, winds calmer and rainfall heavier, compared with nearby countryside (Fig 1). In **rural** areas (countryside) farmers must understand the microclimate so they can make the best decisions for their crops or animals. They must know where the sunniest slopes are, where frost is likely and which areas are sheltered from the wind.

Q1 What is a microclimate?

▲ **Fig 1** New York, USA – urban areas are warmer and wetter than the countryside.

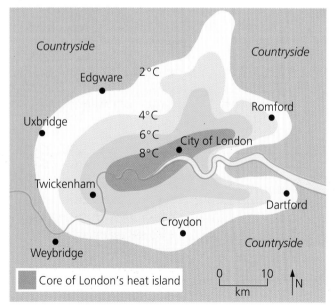
▲ **Fig 2** London's microclimate.

Core of London's heat island

Urban microclimates

Cities are always at least 1°C warmer than the countryside. During the day, dark tarmac roads and buildings absorb heat from the Sun and store it. The more buildings there are, the more heat can be absorbed. At night the roads and buildings slowly release the heat, warming the air. At the same time man-made heat is released from cars, centrally-heated buildings and power stations. All this heat warms up cities so that at night they are at least 4°C or 5°C warmer than the countryside (Fig 2).

Winds in urban areas are generally not as strong as in the countryside. Tall buildings

 BBC Weather Centre – The Heat Island Effect http://www.bbc.co.uk/weather/features/notebook/heat-islands.shtml

act as windbreaks, slowing the wind. However, in some places wind is funnelled between the buildings creating extremely strong **gusts** (Fig 3). In cities with many skyscrapers, such as New York, people can be blown over by these gusts!

Cities have up to a third more rainfall than rural areas. Heat rising from the city causes convectional rainfall (unit 24) which brings thunderstorms. However, because cities are warmer, they receive less snow than the countryside.

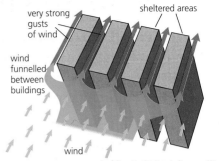

▲ *Fig 3* Wind funnelling.

Rural microclimates

Temperatures in the countryside are affected by the shape of the land. South-facing valley slopes are much warmer because they face the sun. North-facing slopes are in shade and are more exposed to cold northerly winds. Farmers consider this when deciding what to farm. South-facing slopes may be used for growing crops, while north-facing slopes are used for animals (Fig 4). The valley floor is usually used for growing crops. However, at night cold air sinks down the valley sides and can cause severe frosts on the valley floor. Fruit farmers in California, USA, use huge fans to blow the cold air away.

Winds can be very strong in open countryside. Farmers often plant hedges and trees along the sides of their fields. The hedges and trees act as windbreaks, which slow the wind down. Animals are given protection from cold winds and crops are less likely to be blown over.

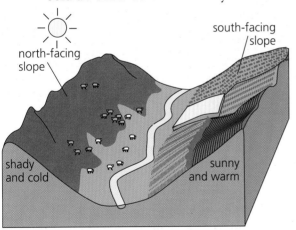

▲ *Fig 4* Rural microclimate.

Q2 Why are cities warmer than the countryside at night?

Q3 Explain why some parts of a city can be very windy.

Q4 Draw a labelled diagram to show why valley floors are at risk from frost.

Key words

gust – sudden blast of wind
rural – countryside
urban – town or city

SUMMARY

■ Climate can vary over a very short distance.
■ The microclimate of urban areas is affected by buildings and people.
■ The microclimate of rural areas is affected by vegetation and the shape of the land.

SUMMARY
activity

Use a thermometer to record the temperature at a number of places around your school. Mark the temperatures on to a base map. Join places of the same temperature with a line (isotherm). Try to explain the temperature pattern.

31 Ecosystems

In this section of the book you will investigate the following things:
- What is an ecosystem?
- Where are different ecosystems located?
- How are ecosystems affected by human activity?

Ecosystems

An **ecosystem** is a community of trees, plants, animals and insects living in a particular **environment**. All living things in an ecosystem are linked together and depend on the land, water and air for their survival (Fig 1). Because all parts of an ecosystem are closely linked, changing one part of an ecosystem can cause changes in another part. Ecosystems can range in size from a small pond to a huge area of forest which stretches across a **continent**. Many people think of the Earth as one giant ecosystem.

Q1 What are the living and non-living parts of an ecosystem?

Q2 Explain how the Earth could be seen as one ecosystem.

▲ **Fig 1** A woodland ecosystem.

Global distribution of ecosystems

Over millions of years, trees, plants, animals and insects have adapted to different climatic conditions around the world. Global differences in temperature, rainfall and sunlight have resulted in the **evolution** of eight different types of ecosystem. Each ecosystem has its own natural **vegetation**.

■ **Tropical rainforest** – hundreds of different species of tree; some trees are over 50 metres tall.

■ **Tropical grassland** – drought-resistant trees with waxy leaves and thorns; grasses up to 5 metres tall.

■ **Desert** – drought-resistant plants, such as cacti, with very long roots to reach water supplies deep underground.

■ **Mediterranean** – evergreen woodland, such as cork and pine; thorny shrubs with thin waxy leaves.

 The World's Biomes http://www.ucmp.berkley.edu/glossary/gloss5/biome/index.html

■ **Temperate grassland** – grasses up to two metres tall; some trees, such as willow.

■ **Deciduous woodland** – trees which shed their leaves in winter, such as oak and ash; shrubs and short grasses.

■ **Coniferous forest** – dense evergreen trees, such as fir and pine; few other species.

■ **Tundra** – short plants, such as moss, heather and lichen; some stunted trees.

These ecosystems are shown in Fig 2. Notice how the same types of ecosystem are found on similar lines of latitude.

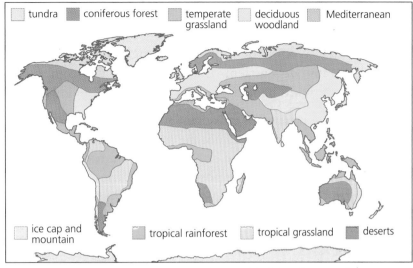

tundra	coniferous forest	temperate grassland	deciduous woodland	Mediterranean

ice cap and mountain	tropical rainforest	tropical grassland	deserts

▲ **Fig 2** Global distribution of ecosystems.

Q3 How could the amount of rainfall affect the type of vegetation?

Q4 Give two reasons why the map in Fig 2 is different to the real world.

▲ **Fig 3** A logging truck.

Human activity

Almost all ecosystems around the world have been affected by human activity. People need land to grow crops and graze animals, and land is needed to build settlements and roads. People can also make money by selling timber from forests (Fig 3). For these reasons, in some areas, little remains of the original ecosystem. In Europe and North America most of the deciduous forests have already been cut down. In Africa tropical grasslands have been overgrazed by cattle and goats. In the Mediterranean deforestation, grazing and fire means little natural woodland survives. Today, large areas of untouched tropical rainforest ecosystem are under threat from deforestation.

Key words

continent – a large land mass
ecosystem – community of plants and animals
environment – land, water, air and living creatures
evolution – adaptation of plants and animals to the environment
vegetation – trees, shrubs and plants

SUMMARY

■ Ecosystems vary in size.
■ All parts of an ecosystem are linked.
■ There are eight major types of ecosystem.
■ Most ecosystems have been affected by people.

SUMMARY activity

For each major ecosystem, name two countries where it is found. Present your answer as a table. What is the natural ecosystem in Britain?

32 Energy and nutrients

In this section of the book you will investigate the following things:

■ How does energy move through an ecosystem in a web?
■ How do nutrients move through an ecosystem in a cycle?
■ How do people interfere with these chains and cycles?

All the parts of an ecosystem are linked together. Plants get energy from the Sun, and **nutrients** from the soil. Some animals eat the plants, and then those animals may be eaten by other animals. When plants and animals die their remains **decompose** and the nutrients are returned to the soil. This can be described as the 'circle of life'. People can interfere with this circle, often upsetting the balance of the ecosystem.

Food webs

All living things need energy to survive. Plants absorb energy from the Sun and use it to grow. Plants also store energy in their stems, leaves and seeds. Animals cannot absorb energy from the Sun, so to get energy they must eat plants. Animals that eat only plants are called **herbivores**. In turn, herbivores are then eaten by meat-eating animals, called **carnivores**. Some animals will eat both plants and other animals. They are called **omnivores**. In this way, energy is passed along in a food chain (Fig 1). Because animals eat more than one thing, food chains are connected to make a food web (Fig 2). Food webs are finely balanced. For example, if pesticides are used by farmers to kill insects, then birds may die from lack of food.

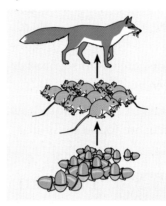

One fox must
eat lots of mice
to get enough energy

One mouse must
eat lots of acorns
to get enough energy

▲ **Fig 1** A food chain.

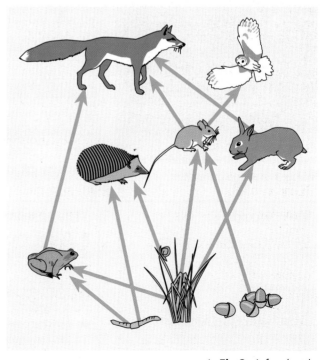

Q1 Where does energy come from?

Q2 Why are plants the most important part of a food web?

▲ **Fig 2** A food web.

Nutrient cycles

As well as energy, plants and animals need nutrients. Nutrients are chemicals which are used by living things to grow. Nutrients are released from rock as it is weathered underneath the soil. Trees and plants absorb nutrients through their roots. Animals get nutrients either by eating the plants, or by eating other animals. When the plants and animals die, their remains are broken down by bacteria and fungi. This allows the nutrients to be washed back into the soil. The nutrient cycle then begins again (Fig 3). Sometimes people add nutrients to ecosystems, such as a farmer spraying fertiliser on his field. However, nutrients will be removed when the crop is harvested.

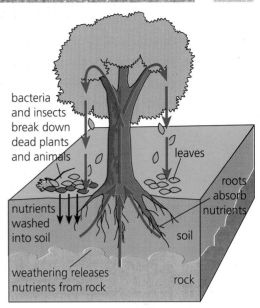

bacteria and insects break down dead plants and animals

leaves

roots absorb nutrients

nutrients washed into soil

soil

weathering releases nutrients from rock

rock

▲ **Fig 3** *A nutrient cycle.*

Q3 What are nutrients?

Q4 Why does a farmer need to use fertiliser?

▲ **Fig 4** *Cane Toad.*

Cane toads

People can easily upset the delicate balance of an ecosystem. Sometimes the results can be disastrous. In 1935 giant Cane Toads were introduced into North Queensland in Australia (Fig 4). It was hoped that the toads would eat beetles which were destroying sugar cane crops. Unfortunately, the Cane Toads ignored the beetles, but ate everything else, including lizards, frogs and mice. To make matters worse, Cane Toads are poisonous. Most birds or animals that eat a Cane Toad die within 15 minutes. Cane Toads have had a huge impact on the wildlife of Australia. Cane Toads reproduce very quickly. Female toads can lay 30 000 eggs a month. They have now spread as far as the Northern Territory and New South Wales, and they show no sign of stopping!

Key words

carnivore – a meat-eating animal

decompose – broken down by bacteria and fungi

herbivore – a plant-eating animal

nutrient – a chemical needed for living things to grow

omnivore – an animal that eats both plants and animals

SUMMARY

■ Energy moves through an ecosystem in a web.

■ Nutrients move through an ecosystem in a cycle.

■ People can affect the food webs and nutrient cycles of an ecosystem.

SUMMARY *activity*

Draw a simple food web. Explain what would happen to the web if there was a drought and many of the plants died.

Australian Museum – Cane Toads http://www.austmus.gov.au/is/sand/canetoad.htm

33 Deciduous woodlands

In this section of the book you will investigate the following things:
- Where are deciduous woodland ecosystems?
- How are deciduous woodlands related to climate and soil?
- How do people affect deciduous woodland ecosystems?

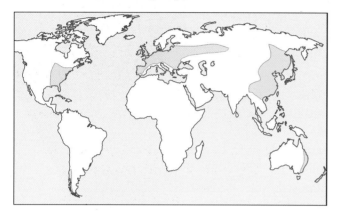

Deciduous woodlands are the natural ecosystem of Britain. However, they are also found in many other places around the world. Deciduous woodlands grow in Europe, eastern North America, northern China, Japan and New Zealand (Fig 1).

◀ **Fig 1** Location of deciduous woodland ecosystems.

Climate

Deciduous woodlands have four seasons during the year. This is because of the changing position of the Sun. Temperatures are mild in winter, averaging 4°C. Summers are warm, with an average of 16°C. Deciduous woodlands occur in the zone where polar and tropical air masses meet. This causes frontal rainfall throughout the year. Some places can receive over 2000 mm of rainfall per year (Fig 2).

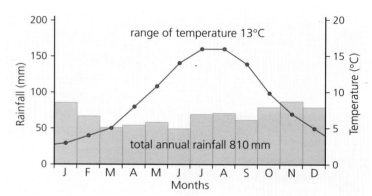

▲ **Fig 2** Deciduous woodland climate.

Soil

Deciduous woodlands have a brown soil. Brown soils can be quite deep and are **fertile**. **Nutrients** in the soil are re-cycled quickly because there are lots of insects to help break down any decaying matter. Brown soils can be slightly acidic, or slightly alkaline.

Q1 Why are nutrients re-cycled quickly in deciduous woodland ecosystems?

Vegetation

The vegetation in deciduous woodlands can be divided into four layers: the tree layer, the shrub layer, low-growing plants and fungi. In Europe, the tree layer includes oak, ash, chestnut, beech and elm. Beech trees prefer an acidic soil and ash trees an alkaline soil. Deciduous trees are broad-leaved. This means they are able to absorb as much sunlight as possible. During the winter deciduous trees lose their leaves. This protects

 National Trust http://www.nt-education.org/

them against losing too much water. When it is cold it is difficult for the roots to absorb water and nutrients. The next layer includes shrubs such as hazel, holly and hawthorn. Beneath the shrubs are plants such as grasses, brambles, bracken and bluebells. On the woodland floor species such as fungi, moss and lichen grow (Fig 3).

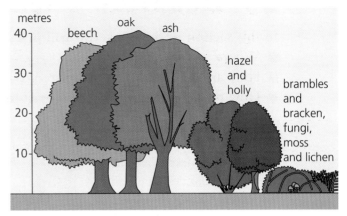

▲ **Fig 3** *Vegetation in a deciduous woodland.*

Animals

Deciduous woodlands contain large numbers of animals, birds and insects. There is a well-developed food web. Herbivores include worms, beetles, mice, shrews, rabbits, squirrels and deer.

Q2 How does the type of soil affect the vegetation in deciduous woodlands?

Q3 How are the trees adapted to the climate in deciduous woodlands?

Carnivores include foxes, weasels, badgers, owls and hawks. In North America there is another carnivore, the black bear. Animals have adapted to living in deciduous woodlands in different ways. Some animals store food for the winter, others go into **hibernation**. Some birds migrate to warmer regions for the winter.

Human activity

There is almost no natural deciduous woodland left in Europe. Most woodland has been cleared to provide land for farming and to build settlements. The woodlands that remain have been altered by the actions of people. In the past deciduous trees were coppiced. This means they were cut down to ground level. The trees then re-grew as a number of stems. The stems were cut and used to make fences and furniture. Recently, organisations such as the National Trust have begun to manage deciduous woodlands in this way again. Woodlands are seen as important areas for wildlife and as places where people may enjoy recreation.

Q4 Why is there almost no natural deciduous woodland left in Europe?

Key words

deciduous – lose leaves in winter
fertile – rich in nutrients
hibernate – to become dormant in winter
nutrient – chemical needed for living things to grow

SUMMARY

- Deciduous woodlands are made up of trees, shrubs and plants.
- The vegetation is adapted to a mild, wet climate.
- Deciduous woodlands contain a large number of animals.
- Very little original deciduous woodland ecosystem is left.

SUMMARY *activity*

Design an information board about deciduous woodlands, to be placed at the entrance to a woodland managed by the National Trust.

Forestry Commission http://www.forestry-gov.uk/home.html

34 Deserts

In this section of the book you will investigate the following things:
- Where are desert ecosystems?
- How are desert ecosystems related to climate and soil?
- How do people affect desert ecosystems?

The largest hot desert in the world is the Sahara, in north Africa. Other deserts around the world include the Kalahari (southern Africa), the Atacama (South America), the Gobi (Asia) and the Australian Desert (Fig 1).

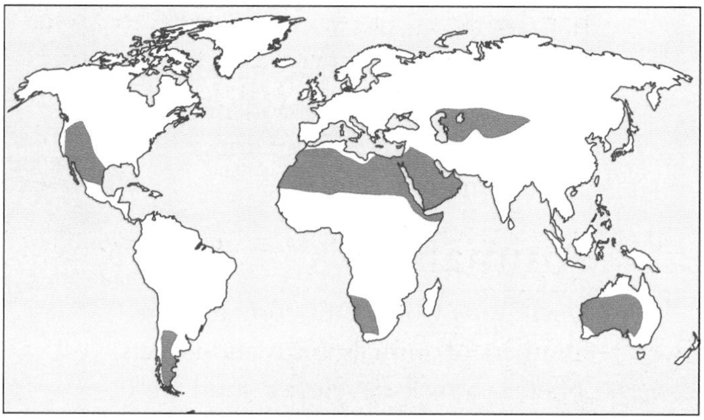

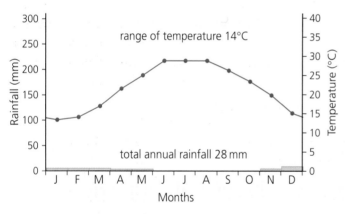

▲ **Fig 1** *Location of desert ecosystems.*

Climate

Deserts are very dry, and very hot. During the day, average temperatures are 30°C, but sometimes temperatures of over 50°C have been recorded! During the night, the temperatures drop sharply to around freezing. This happens because there are no clouds to keep the heat in. Deserts have less than 250mm of rainfall per year (Fig 2). However, this is an average figure and it may not rain for several years. Deserts form in areas of high pressure. Because air is sinking, water vapour evaporates and clouds rarely form. This is why deserts are so dry.

Q1 Why is there a large temperature difference between day and night in deserts?

Q2 Why do deserts have so little rain?

▲ **Fig 2** *Desert climate.*

(chart) range of temperature 14°C — total annual rainfall 28 mm — Rainfall (mm) / Temperature (°C) — Months J F M A M J J A S O N D

Soils

Desert soils are grey in colour. They are thin and have little **organic** matter. Because water is evaporated so quickly, salt builds up on the surface of the soil. Desert soils are not very fertile.

Vegetation

Desert plants have adapted to the very hot, dry climate (Fig 3). In the Australian Desert, Spinifex grass grows in small clumps. The grass has long roots which grow

▲ **Fig 3** *Australian desert.*

Deserts http://www.ucmp.berkeley.edu/glossary/gloss5/biome/deserts.html#hot

deep and wide to absorb scarce water. The clumps of grass are spaced out, so that there is enough water for each of them. Spinifex grass leaves are tightly folded, to form hard, sharp spikes. This protects the plant from losing too much water, and also stops animals from eating it (Fig 4). The Australian Mulga tree is shaped like a funnel. When it rains, the water runs in towards the centre of the tree. The rain water then soaks into the soil, close to the tree roots.

Q3 Explain why deserts cannot support much vegetation.

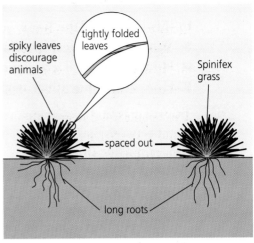

▲ **Fig 4** *Spinifex grass.*

▲ **Fig 5** *A red kangaroo.*

Animals

The Australian desert supports a surprising amount of wildlife. Animals include termites, spiders, lizards, bilbies, kangaroos, dingoes and camels. The bilby is a rare desert **marsupial**. During the day it keeps cool in deep burrows underground. At night it comes out to search for seeds, fruit and insects (Fig 5). Red kangaroos also feed at night, to prevent them from losing water during the day. Camels, brought to Australia by settlers, now live wild in the desert. Camels have large padded feet which make it easier to walk across sand. They also store fat in their humps, which means they can go for many days without food.

Human activity

Aboriginal people have lived in the Australian desert for at least 40 000 years. They have survived by hunting animals and gathering fruit, nuts and plants. Their deep knowledge of the desert ecosystem means they do not damage it. However, modern farming practices have altered the ecosystem at the edge of the desert. Overgrazing by sheep has caused soil erosion, and **irrigation** has made the soil salty. As a result, the desert is increasing in size.

Key words

Aborigine – first inhabitants of Australia
irrigation – artificial watering of crops
organic – plant and animal material
marsupial – an animal that carries its young in a pouch

SUMMARY

- Deserts contain a variety of drought-resistant trees, shrubs and plants.
- The vegetation is adapted to a hot, dry climate.
- Deserts contain a range of specialised animals.
- Deserts are becoming larger as a result of human activity.

SUMMARY *activity*

Draw a picture of a desert plant and a desert animal. Label each picture to explain how they are adapted to the harsh conditions.

 Deserts USA http://www.desertusa.com/index.html

35 Tropical grasslands

In this section of the book you will investigate the following things:
- Where are tropical grassland ecosystems?
- How are tropical grassland ecosystems related to climate and soil?
- How do people affect tropical grassland ecosystems?

Tropical grassland ecosystems are found between the Tropic of Cancer and the Tropic of Capricorn. They are areas showing the change between tropical rainforests and deserts (Fig 1). Tropical grasslands occur in South America, Australia and Africa. In Africa, tropical grasslands are called **savanna**.

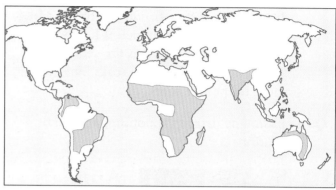

▲ **Fig 1** Location of tropical grassland ecosystems.

Climate

Tropical grasslands are hot all year, because they are close to the Equator. The average monthly temperature is always around 25°C. Unlike deserts, tropical grasslands have a wet season and a dry season. During the wet season, the sun is overhead. Heat from the sun causes convectional rainfall (unit 24). During the dry season there is very little rainfall and hot dry winds. Tropical grasslands receive around 1000mm of rainfall per year (Fig 2).

Q1 Why are tropical grasslands hot all year?

Kano, Nigeria	Jan	Feb	Mar	Apr	May	Jun	Jul	Aug	Sep	Oct	Nov	Dec
Temperature (°C)	22	24	27	31	31	28	26	26	26	27	25	22
Precipitation (mm)	0	0	5	10	70	120	210	310	140	30	0	0

▲ **Fig 2** Tropical grassland climate.

Soil

The soil in tropical grasslands is a red clay. A hard layer of minerals forms just under the surface of the soil. This makes it difficult to plough and farm. The soil is not very fertile.

Q2 Why are tropical grasslands difficult to farm?

Vegetation

The vegetation of tropical grasslands ranges from woodland, on the edge of rainforests, to patches of grass, on the edge of deserts. The area in-between contains scattered trees and tall grasses

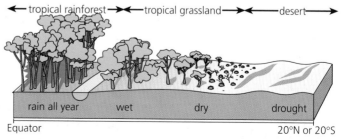

▲ **Fig 3** Transition between tropical rainforest and desert.

 Grasslands http://www.ucmp.berkeley.edu/glossary/gloss5/biome/grasslan.html

(Fig 3). The trees and plants of a tropical grassland ecosystem have adapted to the local soil and climate. In the African savanna, Acacia trees have developed long roots. The roots grow deep into the soil, but also spread outwards, to absorb as much water as possible. Acacia trees also have waxy leaves, which they lose during the dry season to conserve water (Fig 4).

▲ **Fig 4** *Tropical grassland vegetation.*

Grasses grow quickly to make the most of the rainy season. They reach a height of between three and five metres! Although the grasses die back during the dry season, their seeds lie **dormant** on the surface, waiting for next year's rain.

Animals

The African savanna supports thousands of animals, and has a large food web. Herbivores include elephants, zebra, wildebeest, rhinos, giraffe and antelope. Carnivores, such as lions, cheetahs and hyenas, hunt the herbivores. These animals have adapted to the environment in several ways. Most animals are forced to **migrate** each year during the dry season. Herbivores follow the rains to find fresh grazing land, and the carnivores follow the herbivores. Lions and cheetahs prefer to hunt at dusk when it is cooler. They spend the days sheltering from the sun in the shade of Acacia trees.

Q3 When would be the best time of year to visit the savanna to see wildlife?

Human activity

Crops such as millet, tobacco and maize can be grown on the African savanna. But because the rain is unreliable, crops sometimes fail, resulting in famine. The savanna is most suitable for grazing cattle or goats. Traditionally, farmers moved around with their animals to find areas of fresh grassland. However, tropical grasslands are delicate ecosystems and many places have been overgrazed. Once the vegetation has been removed the soil is easily blown or washed away. As a result many areas of tropical grassland are becoming desert. This process is called **desertification**.

Q4 Why are many areas of savanna at risk of desertification?

Key words

desertification – the spread of desert-like conditions

dormant – inactive

migrate – move from one area to another

savanna – tropical grasslands in Africa

SUMMARY

■ Tropical grasslands contain a range of vegetation from trees to grasses.

■ The vegetation is adapted to a hot climate with a wet and dry season.

■ Tropical grasslands support a large food web.

■ Tropical grasslands are turning to desert in areas where vegetation has been removed or overgrazed.

SUMMARY activity

Draw a climate graph for Kano, Nigeria. See Fig 2. Label the graph to explain how the savanna vegetation changes through the year.

 Tropical Savannas http://www.runet.edu/~swoodwar/CLASSES/GEOG235/biomes/savanna/savanna.html

36 Tropical rainforests

In this section of the book you will investigate the following things:
- Where are tropical rainforest ecosystems?
- How are tropical rainforest ecosystems related to climate and soil?
- How do people affect tropical rainforest ecosystems?

Tropical rainforests are amazing ecosystems. They contain 90% of all known species of plants and animals. Tropical rainforests are found in regions which are on or near the Equator. They occur in South America, West Africa, Southeast Asia and northern Australia (Fig 1).

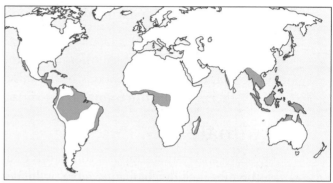

▲ **Fig 1** Location of tropical rainforest ecosystems.

Climate

Tropical rainforests are always hot and **humid**. This is because the Sun is overhead for most of the year. The average monthly temperature is around 27°C. It rains every day in tropical rainforests. In the morning, the sun evaporates water from rivers, swamps and trees. Large storm clouds form, and in the afternoon there are heavy rain storms with thunder and lightning. Rainforests receive over 2000 mm of rainfall per year (Fig 2). Tropical rainforests are not as hot as deserts, because they are cloudy in the afternoon. However, because rainforests are so humid, they feel very hot and sticky.

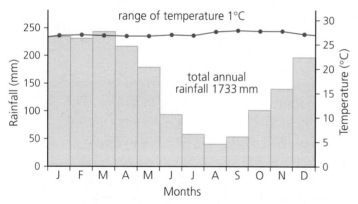

◀ **Fig 2** Tropical rainforest climate.

Q1 Why are tropical rainforests always hot?

Q2 Why does it rain during the afternoon?

Soils

The soil in a tropical rainforest is red clay. Rock is weathered quickly in hot, wet climates, so rainforest soils can be up to 20 metres deep. Although the soil is very deep, it is not very fertile. Nutrients in the soil are washed away by the heavy rain. Most of the nutrients are stored in the trees and plants.

Vegetation

A hectare of Brazilian rainforest may contain 500 different species of tree and over 1000 different types of plant. Rainforest vegetation can be divided into five layers (Fig 3). The tallest trees, called **emergents**, form the highest layer at 50 metres. The **canopy**

 Rainforest Alliance http://www.rainforest-alliance.org/

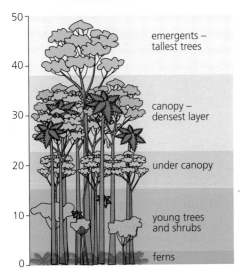

▲ **Fig 3** *Five layers of vegetation.*

Diagram labels:
- emergents – tallest trees
- canopy – densest layer
- under canopy
- young trees and shrubs
- ferns

layer below is made up of the crowns of trees, such as mahogany, that grow to around 30 metres. The canopy forms the densest layer of vegetation in the rainforest, and absorbs most of the sunlight.

Trees and plants in rainforests have adapted to the environment. Trees grow tall so they can gain as much sunlight as possible (Fig 4). They are able to grow tall because they have wide buttress roots to support them. Trees have long trunks and a wide crown of branches and leaves. The leaves are shiny and have pointed 'drip tips' to help them shed the heavy rainfall. Their bark is thin because it never gets cold. Rainforest trees grow all year.

Q3 Describe how rainforest trees have adapted to the environment.

Animals

Rainforests contain thousands of species of insects, birds and animals. Most of the wildlife lives in the canopy layer, 30 metres above the forest floor. There is a complex food web including creatures such as centipedes, spiders, beetles, frogs, squirrels, bats, parrots, monkeys and snakes. Many of these creatures live their whole lives in the tree tops.

◄ **Fig 4** *Rainforest trees and plants.*

Q4 Why do you think most of the wildlife lives in the forest canopy?

Human activity

In Brazil large-scale **deforestation** of the Amazon rainforest is taking place. Deforestation has a huge impact on the ecosystem. Many hundreds of plants and animals are becoming extinct, and the thick soils are being washed away by the heavy rainfall. As the trees are cut down and the soil eroded, places at the edge of forests are becoming deserts.

Key words

canopy – dense layer of tree tops
deforestation – cutting down forests
emergents – the tallest rainforest trees
humid – moist air

SUMMARY

- Tropical rainforests contain the most species of trees and plants.
- The vegetation is adapted to a hot, wet climate.
- Tropical rainforests contain a huge variety of animals.
- In many areas tropical rainforests are being cut down.

SUMMARY *activity*

Write a story about visiting a tropical rainforest in Brazil. What would you see? What would you hear? What would you feel?

 Amazonia http://www.amazonia.net/

37 Biodiversity

In this section of the book you will investigate the following things:
- **What is biodiversity?**
- **Why is biodiversity threatened?**
- **Why is biodiversity important?**
- **What can be done to protect biodiversity?**

Biodiversity is the huge variety of living things on the planet; the result of 3000 million years of evolution. Nobody knows the total number of species of trees, plants, animals and insects. Estimates vary from 5 to 100 million! So far around 1.7 million different species have been identified. Of these, 250 000 are plants and 13 000 are mammals and birds. These huge numbers become even more amazing when we think that almost every individual living thing is unique in some way.

Q1 What is 'biodiversity'?

Threats to biodiversity

Living things become **extinct** naturally as part of **evolution**. Environmental changes mean that other species, which adapt more quickly, are able to take over. However, today species may be becoming extinct 1000 times faster than the natural rate. This is because of the actions of people. The World Wide Fund for Nature estimate that one quarter of all species could become extinct (Fig 1).

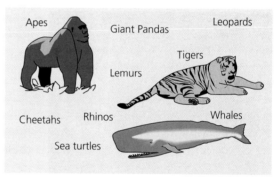

▲ **Fig 1** *Species at risk of extinction.*

4 species of cat

5 species of horse and zebra

5 species of wolves and foxes

17 species of bear

▲ **Fig 2** *Species which have become extinct this century.*

The main threat to biodiversity is the loss of **habitat**. Global population growth is increasing the demand for land for farming, industry, roads and houses. The demand for resources is also increasing. Forests are being cut down to provide timber for building and fuel wood for burning. Large open mines are being dug to extract minerals. Pollution of air, water and land is also damaging the environment. As habitats are lost or damaged, both plant and animal species may become extinct (Fig 2). Hunting and trade in wildlife is also causing a decline in biodiversity (Fig 3). The illegal trade of tiger and rhino parts has brought these species to the edge of extinction.

Q2 How do species of plants and animals become extinct naturally?

Q3 Why is the rate at which species are becoming extinct increasing?

World Wide Fund for Nature http://www.panda.org/

▲ **Fig 3** *Skins from endangered species.*

Importance of biodiversity

Biodiversity is incredibly important for many reasons:

■ We have a moral responsibility to respect life, and to conserve the biodiversity of the planet for the next generation. This is known as **stewardship**.

■ All the food we eat comes from farming wild plants and animals. Genetic diversity is vital to improve crop yields and resistance to pests and diseases.

■ It is thought there are around 30 000 medicinal plants. Over 40% of medicines come from natural resources. New discoveries may hold the cure for diseases such as cancer and AIDs.

■ People gain pleasure from looking at the natural world of trees, plants and animals.

Q4 What action could *you* take to conserve biodiversity?

Protecting biodiversity

In 1992, at the Earth Summit in Rio, Brazil, 168 countries signed the 'Convention on Biological Diversity'. The Convention is an international agreement that requires countries to conserve their biological diversity. They agreed to use their biological resources in a **sustainable** way and to share any benefits equally. This agreement is very important, but it will only work if people change their lifestyles. We need to slow down the rate at which we are using resources, and reduce pollution of the environment.

▶ **Fig 4** *Rhino – an endangered species.*

Key words

biodiversity – the number and variety of all living things

evolution – a change in the characteristics of plants and animals over time

extinct – died out

habitat – area where plants and animals live

stewardship – looking after resources in a sustainable way for the future

sustainable – using resources in a way which means they will not run out

SUMMARY

■ The Earth contains immense biodiversity.

■ Biodiversity is being lost due to the actions of people.

■ Biodiversity is vital for human survival.

■ To conserve biodiversity changes in lifestyle are needed.

SUMMARY *activity*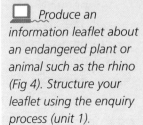

⬚ *Produce an information leaflet about an endangered plant or animal such as the rhino (Fig 4). Structure your leaflet using the enquiry process (unit 1).*

 Library of ecology and biodiversity http://conbio.rice.edu/vl/

38 Population distribution and density

In this section of the book you will investigate the following things:
- How are people distributed across the world?
- Why are some places more crowded than others?

Population distribution

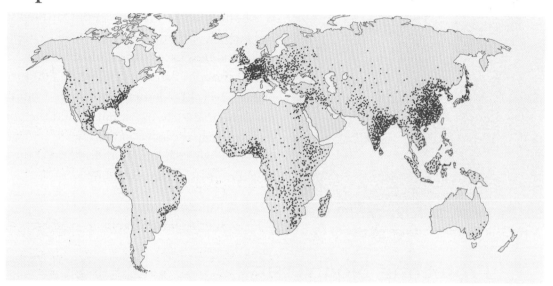

▲ **Fig 1** World population distribution.

The number of people living in the world, or an area such as a country, is called its population. **Population distribution** describes how people are spread out. The population of the world is spread out very unevenly. Most people live on only one-third of the world's land surface. Population distribution is often shown using a dot map. Fig 1 shows that most people live in Western Europe, India and China. The fewest people live in Canada, Brazil, northern Africa, Russia and Australia.

Q1 What is meant by population distribution?

Q2 What is meant by population density?

Population density

Population density describes how crowded an area is. It is the average number of people per square kilometre. It is worked out by dividing the total population of a place, by its area (Fig 2). An area which is crowded has a high population density. An area with few people has a low population density. The average world population density is 43 people per km^2. Population density is usually shown using a shaded (choropleth) map. Fig 3 shows the population density of the United Kingdom. The average population density is 237 people per km^2, but people are not evenly distributed.

$$\frac{\text{Population}}{\text{Area (km}^2)} = \text{Population density (km}^2)$$

▲ **Fig 2** How to calculate population density.

No. of people per km²

over 100

20–100

less than 20

▲ **Fig 3** *Population density of the UK.*

Influences on population distribution and density

There are many factors which help explain population distribution and density. Positive factors encourage people to live in an area, and negative factors discourage people.

Positive factors

- Land which is flat or gently sloping.
- A climate with no extremes – warm with enough rain.
- Areas of open grassland and woods.
- Deep fertile soils.
- Plenty of resources, such as coal, minerals and timber.
- Areas with good access, such as the coast.
- Good transport links – roads and railways.
- Plenty of industry and jobs.

Q3 Describe the population density of the UK.

Q4 Design a diagram to illustrate some of the positive and negative factors affecting population distribution.

Negative factors

- Land which is mountainous or very steep.
- An extreme climate – very hot, very cold and too dry.
- Areas of dense forest, or wetlands.
- Thin, infertile soils.
- Few natural resources.
- Areas with poor access, such as the middle of continents.
- A lack of industry and jobs.
- Poor transport links.

Country	Population (millions)	Area (km²)
UK	58	245 000
France	58	545 000
Brazil	162	8 400 000
Australia	18	7 618 000
USA	266	9 100 000
China	1 300	9 326 000

▲ **Fig 4** *Population data for selected countries.*

Key words

population distribution – how people are spread out over an area

population density – how crowded an area is

SUMMARY

- Population is the number of people in an area.
- The world's population is distributed very unevenly.
- Population distribution and density are influenced by a large range of physical and human factors.

SUMMARY activity

Calculate the population density of the countries in Fig 4. Draw a graph to show your results. Which country has the highest population density?

39 World population growth

In this section of the book you will investigate the following things:
- How has the world's population grown?
- Why has it grown so much?

The world's six billionth person was born on 12 October 1999 (United Nations estimate). The world's population is growing very rapidly, but this has not always been the case (Fig 1). For most of human history the world's population remained steady. Two thousand years ago the population was about 300 million. It took until 1800 for the world's population to reach 1 billion. It then took 123 years for the population to double to 2 billion. However, it took only 12 years for the population to increase from five billion to six billion. This rapid growth in world population is called the '**population explosion**'. Every year a further 78 million people are being added to the planet. Experts predict that the population will stabilise at 10.4 billion people, around the year 2200.

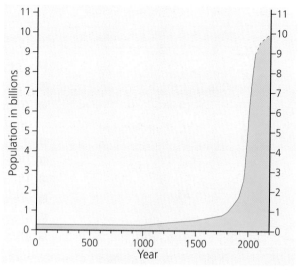

▲ **Fig 1** Global population growth.

Q1 Use Fig 1 to describe how the world's population has changed over the past 2000 years.

Q2 Why is it impossible to really know when the six billionth person was born?

Population explosion

Why did the world's population increase so quickly? Imagine you were given a free supply of Jelly Babies for a month (Fig 2). But, you had to double the number you ate every day. On the first day you ate one, on the second day you ate two, the third day you ate four, on the fourth day, you ate eight, and so on. How many Jelly Babies would you have to eat on day 30?

The increase in the number of Jelly Babies is the same as a woman having an average of four children. In parts of Africa the average number of children per woman is over five.

▲ **Fig 2** Population explosion.

 US Census Bureau – world population information http://www.census.gov/ipc/www/world.html

Birth rates and death rates

The 'population explosion' happened because more people are being born than are dying. The number of babies born per thousand people a year is called the **birth rate**. The number of people dying per thousand people per year is called the **death rate**. When the birth rate is higher than the death rate the population increases (Fig 3). This is called a **natural increase**. The population growth rate of a country is shown as a percentage. This is so different countries can be compared. The global population growth rate is 1.3% per year.

Q3 What would happen to the world's population if the death rate was higher than the birth rate?

Population increases because the birth rate is higher than the death rate

Population decreases because the death rate is higher than the birth rate

▲ **Fig 3** *Birth rates and death rates.*

▲ **Fig 4** *A crowded planet.*

Q4 Why was there a population 'explosion' after 1950?

Factors affecting birth and death rates

Before the 1800s, although people had lots of children, many died young. This meant that the world's population increased only very slowly. During the Industrial Revolution, living standards began to improve in European countries. Improvements in healthcare, diet and sanitation meant that fewer people were dying. As the death rate fell, population growth increased. Gradually, as life became less risky, people began to have fewer children. Population growth in the richer industrialised countries slowed and steadied. Today, in some richer countries, the population is decreasing.

During the 1950s, living standards improved in poorer countries. Improvements in healthcare meant that death rates fell very quickly. However, people continued to have lots of children. Populations increased dramatically, causing a world 'population explosion'. Today, although birth rates are falling in most poorer countries, population growth remains very high.

Key words

birth rate – number of babies born per thousand people per year

death rate – number of people dying per thousand people per year

natural increase – the difference between the birth rate and the death rate

population explosion – rapid increase in world population after 1950

SUMMARY

■ The world's population grew very slowly until around 1800.

■ Since 1950 there has been a 'population explosion'.

■ The 'population explosion' was caused by a fall in death rates.

■ Death rates fell due to improvements in medicine and diet.

SUMMARY *activity*

Every year, the world's population increases by 78 million people. Draw up a table to show roughly how many people are added to the world's population every: second, minute, hour, day, week, month and year.

40 Differences in population growth

In this section of the book you will investigate the following things:

■ How does population growth vary in different countries?

■ Why is the population of Japan falling?

■ Why is the population of India rising?

The number of people in the world grows by about 150 people every minute. This growth is not spread equally between countries. Out of every 100 babies born, 95 of them are born in poorer countries (Fig 1). This means that the population growth rate in poorer countries is much higher than in richer countries. In fact, in many of the richer countries the population is falling.

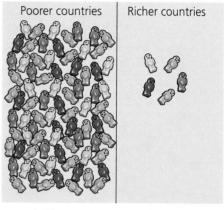

▲ **Fig 1** Uneven population growth.

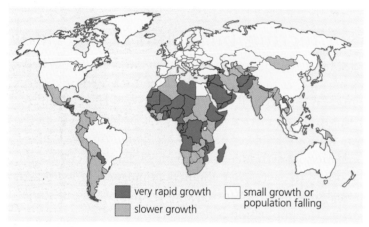

| very rapid growth | small growth or population falling |
| slower growth | |

▲ **Fig 2** Global population growth and decline.

Q1 Why is the population of the UK falling?

The areas with the highest population growth, are sub-Saharan Africa, Central America and South Asia. The areas with the lowest, or falling, population growth are Europe, North America and Japan (Fig 2). Women need to have an average of 2.1 children for a population to remain steady. The average number of children per woman in the UK is 1.7. This means that the population of the UK is slowly falling.

Japan

The population of Japan is 126 million, but the number is falling (Fig 3). On average, Japanese women have only 1.4 children. This means that in 50 years time the Japanese population will have decreased by 21 million. The Japanese government have calculated that if this pattern continues, there will only be 500 Japanese people left in the year 3000!

Japanese families are having fewer children for a number of reasons.

■ Women are choosing to work and to delay getting married until they are in their mid-twenties. This leaves less time for children.

▲ **Fig 3** Japan's population is falling.

Census of India http://www.censusindia.net/

- Children are expensive. It costs around £100 000 to raise a child to their eighteenth birthday.
- The Japanese people have a healthy diet and good health care, so most children survive to adulthood.
- **Contraception** is easily available.

Q2 Do you think the prediction about the Japanese population is likely to come true?

India

The population of India is one **billion**, and increasing (Fig 5). There is a baby born somewhere in India every two seconds. As a result, India will soon take over from China as the most populated country in the world. By 2050, the United Nations calculate that the population of India will be 1.5 billion. Although India's population growth rate is beginning to slow down, it will take at least 50 years to stabilise.

▲ *Fig 4* Japan and India.

Indian families continue to have lots of children for several reasons.

- Women marry at a young age.
- Children are valuable because they can work on a farm or in a factory.
- Children are needed to look after their parents in their old age.
- Women do not have the same rights as men. They cannot always choose whether to have children or not.
- In rural areas, having lots of children improves a person's status.
- Many children die from illness. It is important to have several children to make sure some survive.
- Many people, especially women, are uneducated – 465 million people cannot read or write.
- Contraception is not always available. It is also unpopular with two-thirds of the population.

▲ *Fig 5* India's population is rising.

Q3 Would providing free contraception lower the birth rate in India?

Key words

billion – one thousand million

contraception – family planning

SUMMARY

- Population growth is not spread equally across the world.
- Richer countries have a falling population.
- Poorer countries have rapidly increasing populations.

SUMMARY *activity*

Write an article for a magazine about differences in population growth. Include an interview with a Japanese woman and an Indian woman about the number of children they have. What could the governments of Japan and India do to solve their population problems?

 How much will it cost to raise a child? http://www.calcbuilder.com/cgi-bin/calcs/BUD7.cgi/Kiplinger

41 Population structures

In this section of the book you will investigate the following things:
- What is a population structure?
- How are population structures shown on a graph?
- Why are population structures useful?

Governments need to know how many people are living in their countries. They also need to have other information about the population, such as age, sex and occupation. This information is collected through a **census**. Most countries have a census every ten years. Information about people's age and sex is used to work out the population structure of a country.

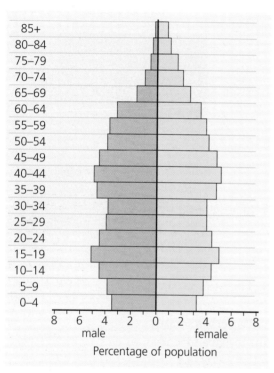

▲ *Fig 1* *Population structure of Japan.*

The population structure of a country can be shown as a graph. The population is divided into five-year age groups. A horizontal bar is drawn to show the percentage of the population in each age group. The percentage of males are drawn on the left, and the percentage of females on the right. Because of the shape of the graph, it is often called a '**population pyramid**'. Population pyramids show the birth rate, the death rate and the life expectancy of the population. Population pyramids for richer and poorer countries are very different.

Japan

The population pyramid for Japan has a narrow base (Fig 1). This shows that the birth rate is falling. The sides of the pyramid do not narrow significantly until people reach their sixties. This shows that Japan has a low death rate. The top part of the pyramid remains quite wide, showing that the Japanese have a long life expectancy.

The population structure of Japan shows that the population is becoming older. By the year 2020, one person in four will be over 65 years old (Fig 2). The Japanese government have to begin planning for this now. Because less of the population will be working, there will be less money available to pay pensions. More hospitals and rest homes will be needed. At the same time, some schools will have to close as there will not be enough children to fill them.

◀ *Fig 2* *Grandparents in Japan.*

 US Census Bureau – population pyramids http://www.census.gov/ipc/www/idbpyr.html

Q1 What percentage of males and females are over 65 in Japan?

Q2 How is the population of Japan changing?

India

The population pyramid for India has a wide base (Fig 3). This shows that the country has a high birth rate. The sides of the pyramid narrow rapidly. This shows that India has a high death rate. The top part of the pyramid is very narrow, showing that the people of India have a short life expectancy.

The population structure of India shows that 40% of the population are aged under 15. This means that the population will continue to grow for at least another 50 years as these people grow up and have children of their own. The Indian government faces many problems in having such a young population. There is not enough money to provide healthcare and education for all the young people. Many children have to work to support their families, but with so many people, finding a job can be difficult.

Q3 Are more girls or boys born in India?

Q4 What problems are created by having a young population?

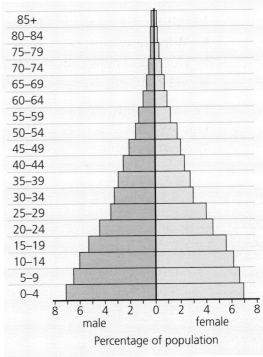

▲ **Fig 3** Population structure of India.

Age	Percentage of males	Percentage of females
0–9	6	6
10–19	8	8
20–29	7	7
30–39	6	6
40–49	6	6
50–59	6	6
60–69	4	5
70–79	4.5	5.5
80+	1	2

▲ **Fig 4** Population structure of the UK.

Key words

census – a survey of the population

population pyramid – a graph showing the age and sex of a population

SUMMARY

- A population structure is the percentage of males and females in different age groups.
- Population structures are shown as population pyramids.
- Richer countries have an ageing population.
- Poorer countries have a young population.

SUMMARY activity

Use the data in Fig 4 to draw a population pyramid for the UK. Describe what the pyramid shows about the population.

42 Population control

In this section of the book you will investigate the following things:
- Why do countries try to control their population growth?
- How has China reduced its population growth?
- What have been the effects of population control in China?

In most countries, people are allowed to choose the number of children they have. However, there has to be a balance between the population and resources of a country. Governments must ensure there is enough food, water, housing, energy, education and healthcare available for its citizens.

Rapid population growth in many poorer countries has meant that there are not enough resources to go round. As a result, millions of people have a very low quality of life. Governments have made **policies** to try to slow population growth. Most policies use advertising to persuade people to limit their families to two children. **Family planning** advice and health care for children is often offered free, or at reduced prices. These policies can be very successful, but take many years to have an effect.

Q1 Why do governments need population policies?

China

The government of China have taken a more drastic step to control population growth. In 1979 a 'one child per family' policy was announced. At the time, the population was approaching 1 billion people. The government had calculated that if population growth did not slow down, the population would reach 1.8 billion by 2025. This would mean that there would not be enough food to go round, and millions could starve (Fig 2).

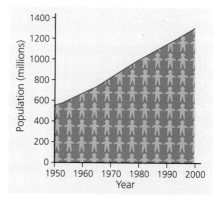

▲ **Fig 1** China.

Q2 Why did the Chinese government introduce a one-child policy?

Population policy

The Chinese policy aimed to stabilise the population at 1.2 billion by the year 2000. A number of strict rules and regulations were introduced:

- Couples must have permission from government officials to marry.
- Women must be at least 25 before they marry.
- Couples must sign an agreement, promising to have only one baby (Fig 3).

▲ **Fig 2** Population growth in China.

 United Nations Population Fund UNFPA http://www.unfpa.org/index.htm

- Women must ask officials for permission to try for a baby.
- Family planning advice is given at work.
- Couples with one child receive free health care, a monthly allowance, priority for housing and an improved pension when they retire.
- Couples who have two children must pay back all the benefits they have received, as well as a large fine.
- Workmates and neighbours are encouraged to tell the officials if they think someone is pregnant.
- Forced abortions and sterilisations have been carried out.

▲ *Fig 3* China – a one-child policy.

Consequences

China's population policy has been partly successful. Birth rates have fallen (Fig 4) and the population is expected to peak at 1 477 million in 2050, before beginning to fall.

However, the policy has caused problems (Fig 5). When women marry, they go to live with their husband's family. This leaves their ageing parents with no children to help them. As a result, boy babies are more highly valued. There are reports of girl babies being aborted, or abandoned. The Chinese population is becoming unbalanced. There are more males than females, which may cause social problems in the future. The population is also ageing. A growing number of elderly people will have to be supported by a shrinking number of young people.

1957	6.4
1960	4.0
1963	7.5
1970	5.8
1979	2.7
1980	2.5
1994	1.9

◀ *Fig 4* China – number of babies per woman.

China child policy 'disaster'

CHINA'S policy of one child per family is collapsing, with disastrous consequences, according to population experts.

The traditional preference for boys and the pressures of the one-child policy, the abortion of females and the killing of infant girls will lead to 110 men of marriageable age for every 100 women within 25 years.

The increasing shortage of women will lead to much older marriages, and a decisive advantage for rich men who will be able to offer more money to prospective brides.

▲ *Fig 5* Newspaper article.

Q3 Describe how the structure of a Chinese family would be different to yours.

Key words

family planning – contraception

policy – a plan of action

SUMMARY

- Governments try to influence population growth rates.
- The Chinese government have a 'one-child' policy.
- The Chinese policy has slowed population growth, but has caused social and economic problems.

SUMMARY *activity*

Explain how the Chinese government tries to ensure couples only have one child. What is your opinion about what they have done?

43 Migration

In this section of the book you will investigate the following things:
- What are the different types of migration?
- Why do people migrate?
- What are the effects of migration?

Types of migration

Migration is the movement of people from one place to another (Fig 1). Internal migration is when people move within a country. International migration involves a move to another country. People migrate for different lengths of time. Permanent migration is when people move to another place and stay there for good. Temporary migration is for a fixed time, such as a two-year job contract. Most people make their own decision about whether to migrate. This is known as voluntary migration, and the people are called **migrants**. Unfortunately, sometimes people are forced to migrate due to a natural disaster, or war. These people are called **refugees**.

Internal – same country	**International** – between countries
Permanent – stay for good	**Temporary** – return home later
Voluntary – own choice	**Forced** – no choice

▲ **Fig 1** Types of migration.

Q1 What is the difference between internal and international migration?

Causes of migration

People migrate for many different reasons. These reasons can be divided into 'push' and 'pull' factors. **Push factors** are things that encourage or force people to leave an area. Push factors include a low standard of living, wars and natural disasters. Pull factors are things that attract people to an area. **Pull factors** include a high standard of living and political freedom (Fig 2). Push and pull factors work together to encourage migration

Q2 What are push and pull factors?

Rural to urban migration

In poorer countries many people migrate from the countryside to the cities. This is called rural–urban migration. People wish to leave rural areas because there is often a lack of paid jobs, poor healthcare and few schools. They are attracted by the possibility of jobs in factories, higher wages, access to hospitals and more schools in urban areas.

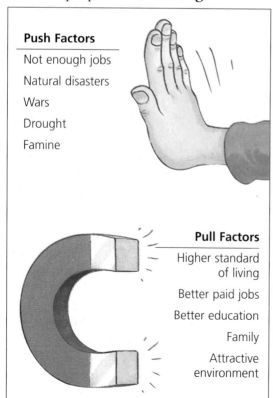

Push Factors

Not enough jobs

Natural disasters

Wars

Drought

Famine

Pull Factors

Higher standard of living

Better paid jobs

Better education

Family

Attractive environment

▲ **Fig 2** Reasons why people migrate.

 Institute of migration http://www.iom.ch/

Some migrants do improve their quality of life in the city, but for many life is very hard. They are forced to live on the streets or in shanty towns. If too many people migrate, the countryside may not have enough people to grow food. For these reasons, governments try to discourage rural–urban migration.

Q3 How does rural to urban migration affect the countryside?

Q4 Why is international migration likely to increase in the future?

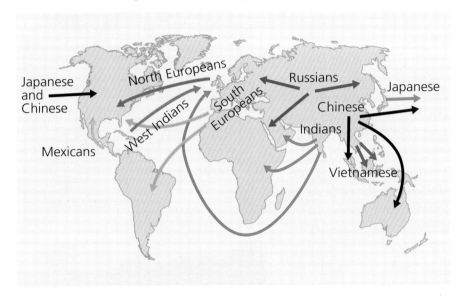

◀ **Fig 3** *Important international migrations.*

International migration

The United Nations estimate that 100 million people are living in a different country to the one they were born in (Fig 3). For thousands of years people have migrated across the world in search of a better life. The population of the UK has been affected by many migrations. Most recently people from the West Indies, Southern Asia and China have migrated to the UK. Generally, migration is becoming more difficult because most governments put limits on the number of immigrants. Immigrants may put a strain on the jobs, housing, schools and health care of a country. This can lead to outbreaks of racism. In the future, it is likely that richer countries with falling populations will allow more immigration. Skilled migrants, such as doctors and nurses, will be especially welcome. All immigrants can enrich a country by bringing with them parts of their culture, such as food, music and dress.

Key words

migrant – person who has migrated

pull factor – something which makes a place attractive

push factor – something which makes a place unattractive

refugee – a migrant forced to leave their home

SUMMARY

■ Migration is the movement of people from one area to another.

■ The reasons for migration can be divided into push and pull factors.

■ Rural to urban migration is happening mainly in poorer countries.

■ International migration can bring both positive and negative effects.

SUMMARY activity

Use Fig 1 to draw up a questionnaire about migration. Survey your friends and family. Present your findings on a map. Use a key to show the type of migration.

 Refugees and migration http://www.oneworld.org/guides/migration/index.html

44 International migration

In this section of the book you will investigate the following things:
- Why do Mexicans migrate to the USA?
- What are the effects of this migration?
- Is there a solution to the problems caused by migration?

International migration is the movement of people from one country to another. The border between the USA and Mexico is one of the busiest areas of international migration in the world (Fig 1). Each year, over one million Mexicans cross into the USA in search of work and a better life. Many Mexicans entering the USA do not have permission to do so. They are **illegal migrants**. The US government spends millions of dollars trying to keep them out. The US **Border Patrol** has the difficult job of guarding the 2000 km long border. In many places along the border, huge metal fences have been built, or deep ditches dug. The Border Patrol use 4x4 vehicles, horses and even helicopters with night-vision cameras to catch illegal migrants (Fig 2).

Q1 Why are so many Mexicans able to cross the border illegally?

Q2 Why do you think most migrants cross the border at San Diego and El Paso?

▲ **Fig 1** The USA-Mexico border.

▲ **Fig 2** Illegal migrant caught by the US Border Patrol.

Push and pull factors

The quality of life in Mexico and the USA can be very different. Fig 3 shows that, on average, Americans earn more, have better access to heath care and education, and live longer than Mexicans. This makes it very tempting for Mexicans to migrate to the USA. In the USA, many Mexicans get jobs working on large farms or in food processing factories. Although the wages are low, they can still be ten times more than they would earn in Mexico.

	USA	Mexico
GDP (Gross Domestic Product)	$29 000	$8 370
People per doctor	470	1 240
Young people at school	97%	54%
Adult literacy	99%	90%
Life expectancy (years)	76	72
Food (calories per day)	3 645	3 132

▲ **Fig 3** Quality of life in Mexico and the USA.

Q3 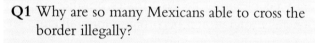 Use the data in Fig 3 to draw pictograms comparing the quality of life in Mexico with that in the USA.

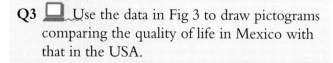

Effects of migration

People disagree about the effects of migration (Fig 4). Some people welcome Mexican migrants, while others want to send them all back to Mexico.

Arguments in favour of migration

■ Mexican migrants take the harder, dirtier, less skilled and less well paid jobs, that Americans do not want.

■ Migrants work for low wages. This makes American companies more profitable.

■ Legal Mexican migrants pay taxes. Taxes are used to fund schools and hospitals.

■ Mexicans have strong family values, and have a rich culture. Many Americans enjoy Mexican music and food.

Arguments against migration

■ Mexicans take jobs from Americans because they will work for less money.

■ It costs American tax payers hundreds of millions of dollars to keep illegal migrants in jail.

■ Young, unemployed Mexican migrants form street gangs in cities such as Los Angeles.

■ The countryside in Mexico has a shortage of young people.

> Migrants cause trouble. They use US health care, but don't pay taxes!

Pete Wilson

> Migrants are great for the USA. They pay over $12 billion a year in taxes.

Jack Kemp

▲ *Fig 4* Disagreement about Mexican migrants between US politicians.

Solutions

The American government wants to stop illegal Mexican migrants from entering the USA. Each year they spend millions of dollars on building new fences, digging new ditches and employing more Border Patrol agents. Despite all their efforts, they have had limited success. Some people suggest that the money could be used to develop industry in Mexico instead. If the quality of life in Mexico improved, Mexicans might be less likely to migrate to the USA.

Q4 Do you think Mexican migrants benefit or harm the USA?

Key words

Border Patrol – US organisation responsible for guarding the border

Gross Domestic Product (GDP) – the total amount earned by a country, divided by its population

illegal migrants – migrants without permits to live in the USA

international migration – migration between countries

SUMMARY

■ The quality of life is higher in the USA compared with Mexico.

■ At least one million Mexicans migrate to the USA each year.

■ Migrants have positive and negative impacts on the USA.

■ The US government spends millions of dollars trying to keep the illegal Mexican migrants out.

SUMMARY *activity*

Draw a labelled diagram to show the push and pull factors affecting migration between Mexico and the USA.

45 Refugees

In this section of the book you will investigate the following things:
- What causes people to become refugees?
- What caused the Rwandan refugee crisis in 1994?
- What were the effects of the Rwandan refugee crisis?

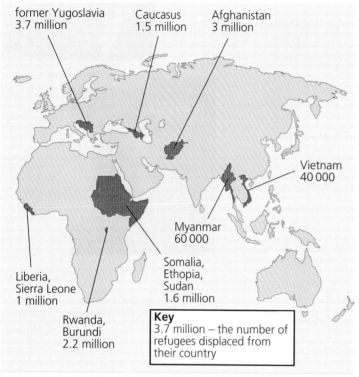

former Yugoslavia
3.7 million

Caucasus
1.5 million

Afghanistan
3 million

Vietnam
40 000

Myanmar
60 000

Somalia,
Ethopia,
Sudan
1.6 million

Liberia,
Sierra Leone
1 million

Rwanda,
Burundi
2.2 million

Key
3.7 million – the number of
refugees displaced from
their country

▲ **Fig 1** The world's major refugee situations.

Refugees are people who have been forced to leave their home country because of war, **persecution** or natural disasters. The number of refugees in the world has increased dramatically since the end of the Second World War. The United Nations estimates that there are over 13 million refugees spread throughout 140 countries (Fig 1). Eighty per cent of refugees are living in poor countries. It is difficult for the governments of these poor countries to look after the refugees as well as their own people.

The quality of life of refugees is very low. Many end up living in large refugee camps. They lack food, water, shelter, clothing and access to education and healthcare. They have few basic rights. The United Nations High Commissioner for Refugees (UNHCR) is the agency which is responsible for looking after refugees, and eventually helping them to return home.

Q1 What is a refugee?

Q2 Why are refugees not always welcomed by other countries?

Causes

War is the most important reason why people become refugees. People may be forced out of their country during a civil war, or by an invading army. In some countries people are persecuted because of their race, or their political or religious beliefs. They may have to flee the country if their lives are at risk. Every year people become refugees after natural disasters such as floods, droughts, earthquakes and volcanic eruptions. The impacts of natural disasters are likely to increase as the world's population increases.

Q3 Give three reasons why someone might become a refugee.

Rwanda 1994

Rwanda is a country in Africa (Fig 2). During 1994, over two million Rwandans fled their homes as the result of the civil war. This was one of the fastest and largest migrations ever known. People belonging to the Hutu ethnic group had massacred thousands of their enemies, the Tutsis. The Tutsis formed an army and begun to fight back. As a result the Hutus fled across the border and became refugees in Zaire, Tanzania and Burundi.

Life in the refugee camps was very hard (Fig 3). The camps were overcrowded and there was not enough food or water. There was no **sanitation**, and in the first few days over 50 000 people died from **cholera**. Overcrowding and tension led to crime and violence in the camps. The refugees had a huge impact on the environment. They cut down trees to build shelters and for firewood. Removing the trees caused soil erosion.

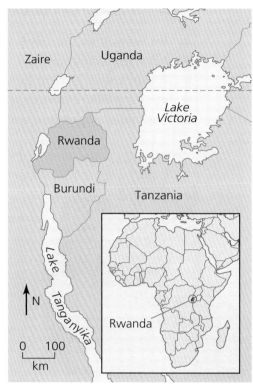

▲ **Fig 2** Rwanda.

▲ **Fig 3** Rwandan refugee camp in Zaire.

The work of the UNHCR saved many thousands of Hutu lives. But the UNHCR were criticised for helping Hutus who had massacred the Tutsis in Rwanda. In 1996, most of the Hutus returned to Rwanda. Their future remains unsure.

Q4 In what ways do refugee camps harm the environment?

Q5 Do you think the UNHCR should have helped the Hutu refugees?

Key Words

cholera – a disease caused by dirty water
persecution – threats and harassment
sanitation – safe toilet facilities

SUMMARY

■ The number of refugees world-wide has been increasing since the Second World War.
■ Refugees have a very poor quality of life.
■ Refugee movements are caused by human and natural reasons.
■ The Rwandan crisis was one of the largest refugee migrations ever seen.

SUMMARY *activity*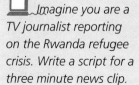

Imagine you are a TV journalist reporting on the Rwanda refugee crisis. Write a script for a three minute news clip.

 Rwanda – the triumph of evil (PBS) http://www.pbs.org/wgbh/pages/frontline/shows/evil/

46 Population and resources

In this section of the book you will investigate the following things:

■ What are resources?
■ Is population growth linked to resource depletion?
■ How is global resource use unequal?
■ How does population growth cause conflicts over resources?

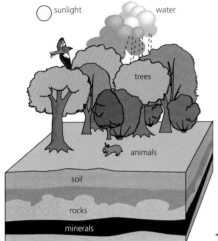

◄ Fig 1 *Natural resources.*

Resources

Resources are any part of the environment which are used by people to live. Resources include rocks, soil, minerals, metals, trees, plants, animals, air and water (Fig 1). The use of these resources has increased due to world population growth and improvements in standards of living. As a result, some resources are being **depleted**, and the environment is being polluted. The world's population is expected to grow by 3000 million in the next 50 years. This will increase the pressure on the Earth's resources.

Q1 What are resources?

Resource and environment depletion

The United Nations identified some major areas of concern in its report 'Global Environment Outlook 2000'.

■ Air – air quality is falling in cities in poorer countries, although it is improving in many richer countries. The amount of carbon dioxide in the atmosphere has increased by four times since 1950. Carbon dioxide is causing 'global warming'.

■ Water – a third of people in poorer countries do not have access to clean water. The UN predict that by 2025 two-thirds of the world's population will have a water shortage (Fig 2). The **pollution** of water with nitrogen, from fertiliser and sewage, is a growing problem.

■ Land – deforestation and forest fires are reducing the world's forest reserves (Fig 3). Also, one billion people live in areas at risk from soil erosion.

Year	Population (billion)	Water use (km³)
1910	1.75	900
1920	1.86	1000
1930	2.07	1100
1940	2.30	1300
1950	2.52	1700
1960	3.02	2500
1970	3.70	3500
1980	4.44	4300
1990	5.27	5500
2000	6.06	7200

▲ Fig 2 *Population growth and global water use.*

▲ Fig 3 *Fighting forest fires in Indonesia.*

 Negative Population Growth http://www.npg.org/

Alternative view

Some population experts argue that the Earth is able to support a much higher population. They believe that technology can be used to provide enough resources for everyone. Technological advances, such as **genetic modification** of crops, will ensure enough food is grown. Electronic technology, such as satellites, will locate new energy reserves. If any resources do begin to run out, alternatives will be found and used, for example, cars running on gas rather than petrol. They believe that environmental problems are not caused by population growth, but by a wasteful use of resources.

> **Q2** Give another example of one resource being replaced by another.

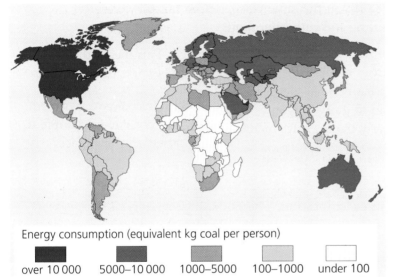

Energy consumption (equivalent kg coal per person)

over 10 000 | 5000–10 000 | 1000–5000 | 100–1000 | under 100

▲ **Fig 4** Unequal energy use.

> **Q3** Explain why demand for resources is likely to increase.
>
> **Q4** Give an example of an international conflict over resources.

Inequality and conflicts

The use of resources is very unequal. It is estimated that the richest 20% of countries use 80% of the Earth's resources (Fig 4). This means that the richest countries also cause the most environmental damage. Between them, Europe and the USA produce 60% of the gases causing global warming. Demand for resources, and pollution of the environment, will increase as the standard of living in poorer countries improves. It is predicted that as resources become more scarce, international conflicts will increase. Wars will be fought over access to resources such as oil and water.

Key words

depleted – run out
genetic modification – alteration of plants and animals to improve quality
pollution – environmental damage

SUMMARY

■ Resources are needed by people to survive.
■ World population growth is causing resource depletion.
■ The richest countries use most resources.
■ More conflicts over resources are likely in the future.

SUMMARY *activity*

Use the data in Fig 2 to draw a graph showing the link between population growth and water use. Why is fresh water likely to become more scarce in the future?

47 Settlement site and situation

In this section of the book you will investigate the following things:
- Why did people begin to build settlements?
- What factors were important when deciding the site for a settlement?
- Why did some settlements continue to grow?
- What factors led to the growth of Paris?

History of settlement

A **settlement** is a place where people live. Settlements range in size from a single isolated house to a city with millions of people. Settlements began 10 000 years ago when people learned how to domesticate wild animals, and to grow crops. These discoveries allowed people to stay in the same place. Before this they were constantly on the move, hunting and gathering food.

As farming techniques improved, food surpluses were created. This meant that food could be traded for goods from other settlements. Transport networks developed so trade could take place more easily. Settlements in good trading locations began to grow bigger. Eventually, many of these early trading settlements grew into the modern cities we know today.

> **Q1** What discoveries made it possible for people to settle in one place?

Site

The **site** of a settlement is its exact location. The physical geography of an area was very important to early people when they were deciding on the site for a new settlement (Fig 1). They had a number of factors to consider:

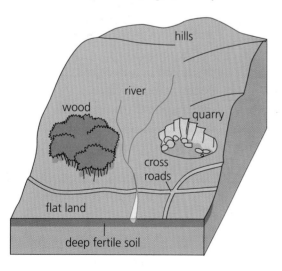

◀ **Fig 1** Site factors.

- Water supply – a clean supply of water was needed for drinking, cooking and cleaning. Water could be taken from a river or a well.
- Relief – the area needed to be high enough to be safe from flooding, but low enough to be sheltered from strong winds.
- Defence – a hilltop, or the inside of a river meander, would provide protection from attackers.
- Transport – a site at a crossroads, on a river or at the coast gave easier access to other settlements.
- Soil – deep fertile soil made it easier to farm crops and rear animals.
- Resources – a source of timber or rock was needed for building. Wood was needed as a fuel for heat and cooking.

> **Q2** Why are many of the original reasons for the location of a settlement no longer important?

Situation

The **situation** of a settlement is its location in relation to the surrounding area. If a settlement had good access to natural resources, and to other settlements, it would grow in size. Many settlements with a good site and situation have grown into large cities.

▶ **Fig 2** *L'Isle de la Cité, Paris*

Q3 What is the difference between the site and the situation of a settlement?

Paris

Paris is the capital city of France. It is the largest city in Europe and has a population of 10 million people. Paris began in the third century BC. It was sited on a small island in the River Seine (Fig 2). The site was good for defence, but was also a crossing point across the river. The fertile soil of the River Seine's floodplain was also excellent for farming. Under Roman rule, Paris grew and became the centre of a network of roads stretching across Europe.

The situation of Paris has made it one of the most important cities in Europe (Fig 3). It is the focus of many major roads and railway lines. Paris has also become the centre for many international air routes.

Q4 What were the benefits of the original site of Paris?

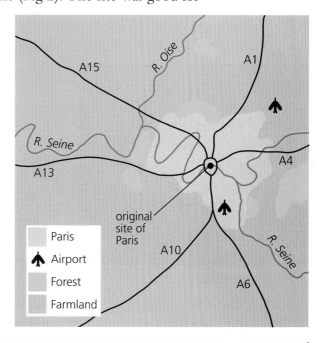

▶ **Fig 3** *Site and situation of Paris.*

Key to map:
- Paris
- Airport
- Forest
- Farmland

Labels on map: A15, R. Oise, A1, R. Seine, A13, A4, original site of Paris, A10, A6, R. Seine

Key words

settlement – a place where people live

site – the exact location of a settlement

situation – the location of a settlement in relation to the surrounding area

SUMMARY

- Settlement began as people discovered how to cultivate crops.
- Physical factors were very important in deciding the location of early settlements.
- The situation of a settlement influences whether it grows larger.
- The excellent site and situation of Paris have made it one of the most important European cities.

SUMMARY activity

Draw a sketch map of a local settlement. Label it to explain its original site, and its situation today.

 NASA – Pictures of Earth http://earth.jsc.nasa.gov/

48 Settlement patterns and functions

In this section of the book you will investigate the following things:
- What different patterns of settlement are there?
- What is a settlement function?
- Why do settlement functions change?

Settlement patterns

When early settlements began to grow there were no planning regulations. People built houses where they wanted to. Some houses were built far apart from each other (**dispersed**). Other houses were built close together, making villages. Villages began to grow outwards and the shape of the settlements changed. Some settlements became long and narrow (**linear**), others stayed clustered together (**nucleated**). Today, in the UK, people must have permission from the local authority to build houses. Settlements now grow in a planned way.

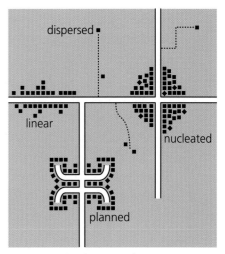

▲ **Fig 1** Settlement patterns.

▲ **Fig 2** A nucleated settlement in Sumatra.

Dispersed settlements are usually farms. They are spread out because of the space taken up by fields. Other dispersed settlements are found in mountainous areas where it is difficult to live.

Linear settlements sometimes follow the shape of the land. It is easier to build on the floor of a valley than on the steep sides. Linear settlements also follow features such as roads, railway lines or rivers.

Nucleated settlements are where buildings are clustered round a central point (Fig 2). The centre of the settlement may be a crossroads, a church, a water supply, or a market place. Nucleated settlements also occur on hill tops.

Planned settlements often have a regular pattern. They may have a square shape, or a crescent shape for example. Brasilia, the capital of Brazil, is a planned settlement in the shape of an aeroplane (Fig 3).

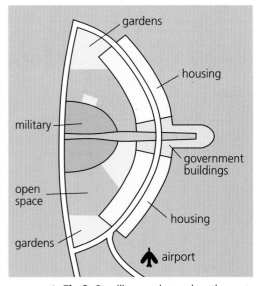

▲ **Fig 3** Brasilia – a planned settlement.

Q1 Draw a labelled diagram to show dispersed, linear and nucleated settlements.

Q2 Use a local Ordnance Survey map to name an example of each type of settlement in your local area.

Settlement functions

The **functions** of a settlement are the things that happen there (Fig 4). The function of most early settlements was farming. As settlements grew, the functions increased to include things such as markets and inns. Today settlements have many functions, which continue to change over time.

■ Residential – the main function of many settlements today is to give people places to live. People may live in one settlement and work in another.

■ Administrative – local authority offices run the local services, such as road maintenance and waste disposal.

■ Industrial – goods are manufactured in factories. Today many factories are located in business parks on the outskirts of settlements.

■ Commercial – shopping centres and recreation facilities, such as sports centres and cinemas, provide services for people.

■ Services – settlements contain public services, such as schools, hospitals and libraries.

■ Tourism – some settlements are attractive to tourists. Many coastal settlements in Spain have changed from fishing villages into large tourist resorts.

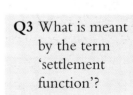

▼ **Fig 4**
Settlement functions.

Q3 What is meant by the term 'settlement function'?

Key words

dispersed – spread out
function – the activities of a settlement
linear – in a line
nucleated – clustered together
settlement pattern – shape of a settlement

SUMMARY

■ Settlements have grown to form different patterns.
■ Settlement patterns depend on physical and human factors.
■ The activities in a settlement are known as functions.
■ Settlement functions change over time.

SUMMARY *activity*

Shade an outline map to show the functions of your local settlement. What is its main function?

49 Changing village

In this section of the book you will investigate the following things:
- How have villages changed?
- Why have villages changed?
- How are different groups of people affected by these changes?

Change

Until the 1800s most people in the UK lived in villages. Villages usually grew around a central point, such as a crossroads or a well. At the centre of most villages there was a church and a village green. People lived in farmhouses, or terraced cottages. Most people worked as farmers, or in service jobs such as bakers and blacksmiths. During the nineteenth century, the **Industrial Revolution** led to many people leaving the villages. They migrated to cities to find jobs in mines and factories.

Since the 1970s, people have begun to move back to villages from cities. Villages are growing again. This change is happening for several reasons:

- People feel that the countryside offers a better quality of life.
- Roads have improved and more people own cars. It is possible to live in a village and commute to towns and cities to work.
- Many jobs are now in business parks, located in countryside areas.
- Information technology, such as personal computers, faxes and e-mail, means people can work from home.

Q1 Why did the number of people living in villages fall in the nineteenth century?

Q2 Why are villages growing again now?

Decline in services

The recent growth of villages has changed their character. New housing estates have been built on surrounding farmland. These houses are often large and expensive. Villages have become **suburbanised**. This means they are more like small towns. Although the number of people and houses in villages has increased, the number of **services** has declined (Fig 1). Shops, post offices, pubs, banks and doctors surgeries have closed. This is because commuters with cars are able to use services in town, and shop in out-of-town superstores.

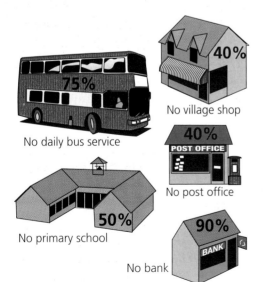

75% No daily bus service

40% No village shop

40% No post office

50% No primary school

90% No bank

▲ *Fig 1* *Villages without services.*

Q3 Why have the number of services in villages declined?

 The Countryside Agency http://www.countryside.gov.uk/

Thurston village

Thurston is a village in East Anglia, about four miles from Bury St Edmunds (Fig 2). Look at the OS map extract on page 232. Thurston grew around a crossroads and a church. Over the past 200 years, Thurston has experienced many changes.

In 1801 the population of Thurston was only 354 (Fig 3). Most people worked on farms. In 1846 a railway line was built through the village. The railway attracted more people to come and live in Thurston. New homes were built to house them and the village expanded. In the 1960s, the A45 to the south of Thurston became a dual carriageway. This meant commuting was now even easier and more people moved to the village. New houses had to be built on the heath. Today the population is over 3000, but very few of these people work in Thurston. Most people work in Bury St Edmunds or Ipswich, and also do their shopping there. As a result the village shop has closed. This means that the people without cars find shopping much more difficult.

▶ **Fig 2** *An aerial view of Thurston.*

Year	Population
1801	345
1821	377
1841	599
1861	740
1881	695
1901	600
1921	566
1951	720
1971	1419
1991	2612

▲ **Fig 3** *Population change in Thurston*

Q4 Why might both young and old people living in Thurston feel isolated?

Key words

Industrial Revolution – rapid growth of manufacturing industry
service – a facility used by people
suburbanisation – growth of residential areas on the outskirts of urban areas

SUMMARY

- During the nineteenth century the population of villages decreased.
- Since the 1970s the population of villages has increased rapidly.
- Villages have become suburbanised.
- Many villages' services have closed down.

SUMMARY *activity*

⬜ Carry out an enquiry into how the place where you live or a village nearby has changed over time. Try to include maps and graphs to show the changes.

50 Changing city

In this section of the book you will investigate the following things:
- How do cities develop?
- What problems were caused by the growth of Paris?
- What has been done to tackle the problems of Paris?

Urbanisation

During the nineteenth century some settlements in Europe grew into cities. People migrated from the countryside in search of jobs in mines or factories. This is called **urbanisation**. **Terraced houses** were built for the workers to live in and the settlements expanded to form cities. Today, most factories in city centres have closed. They have been replaced by a **Central Business District** of shops and offices. Much of the old housing has been improved, or knocked down and replaced with blocks of flats. New housing estates have been built on the city outskirts. In the UK, around 70% of the population now live in towns or cities.

Urbanisation began later in poorer countries, but is happening very quickly now. This is because of high population growth rates, and large numbers of people migrating to cities in search of a better life. There are now over 300 cities which have a population larger than one million.

> **Q1** What is urbanisation?
>
> **Q2** When did urbanisation happen in Europe?

Paris

Paris is the capital of France, and one of the most important European cities. Paris was first settled over 2000 years ago. It has grown very large because of its excellent site and situation. It now has a population of over ten million (Fig 1).

Year	Population
1900	5.0 million
1930	6.5 million
1960	8.5 million
1990	10.6 million

▲ *Fig 1* Population of Paris.

By the 1950s Paris had developed problems. Many of its old buildings were run-down and unhealthy to live in. The public transport system could not cope with all the people. The factories in the city centre were old and difficult to reach. The air had become very polluted.

> **Q3** Use Fig 1 to draw a graph to show the growth of Paris.
>
> **Q4** What were the problems of Paris by 1950?

Redevelopment

In the 1960s the government made plans to solve its problems (Fig 2). The old housing was either improved or knocked down. At the same time, hundreds of tower blocks were built in the **suburbs**. The tower blocks have not been popular with everybody. Many people miss the 'sense of community'. They are also not well designed for the elderly, or people with children.

 Encarta – Paris http://encarta.msn.com/find/Concise.asp?2=1&pg=2&ti=02859000

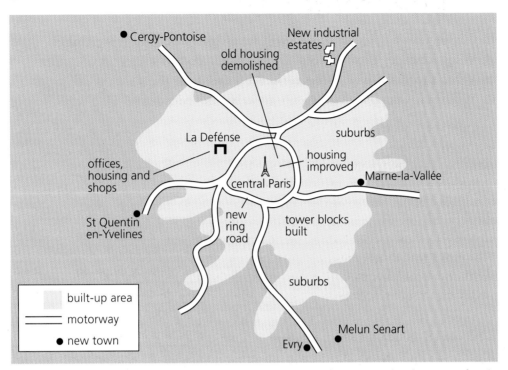

▲ **Fig 2** *Redevelopment of Paris.*

▲ **Fig 3** *La Defénse, Paris.*

Other parts of the plan have been more successful. A new ring road has eased congestion and restrictions on cars have improved the air pollution. New industrial estates were built on the outskirts. This allowed many companies to re-locate. Five new towns have been built within 25km of Paris. Each new town has its own industry and shops, but is connected to Paris by an express train. The most impressive change has been the building of La Defénse (Fig 3). This is a huge modern complex of offices, shops and high–quality homes in the suburbs. La Defénse has allowed businesses to expand, and improved the quality of housing in Paris.

Key words

Central Business District – city centre containing shops and offices

suburbs – residential areas on the city outskirts

terraced houses – houses which are joined together

urbanisation – increase in the percentage of people living in cities

SUMMARY

■ Cities developed in richer countries in the nineteenth century.

■ The fastest growing cities today are in poorer countries.

■ The changes in Paris since the 1950s have affected people in different ways.

SUMMARY *activity*

Explain what has been done to tackle Paris's problems. Use the following headings:

● *housing*
● *transport*
● *industry.*

 Lonely Planet – Paris http://www.lonelyplanet.com/dest/eur/par.htm

51 Urban challenges

In this section of the book you will investigate the following things:
- Why are cities growing rapidly in poorer countries?
- What problems have been caused by this growth?
- What have people done to try to solve the problems?

In 1950 there were only 80 cities in the world with over a million people. By the year 2000, this had risen to over 300 cities. Most of this growth has happened in poorer countries. People have **migrated** from the countryside to cities in search of better jobs, higher wages and better living conditions. This rapid growth of cities has caused a number of problems, to which governments are trying to find solutions.

Q1 What has caused the rapid growth of cities?

Q2 Where is the largest growth in cities taking place?

City	Population
1 Tokyo, Japan	28.7 million
2 Mexico City, Mexico	19.4 million
3 New York, USA	17.4 million
4 São Paulo, Brazil	17.2 million
5 Seoul, South Korea	15.8 million
6 Jakarta, Indonesia	14.0 million
7 Moscow, Russia	13.2 million
8 Bombay, India	12.9 million
9 Calcutta, India	12.8 million
10 Buenos Aires, Argentina	12.4 million

▲ **Fig 1** *The world's largest cities.*

Jakarta, Indonesia

Indonesia is a country in South-east Asia (Fig 2). It is made up of 17 000 islands. The capital city of Indonesia is Jakarta. Since the 1950s Jakarta has grown rapidly. It has become the largest city in South-east Asia, with a population of 14 million. This growth has been caused mainly by **rural–urban** migration. A shortage of land in the countryside, and the possibility of a paid job in the city, has encouraged millions of people to move to Jakarta.

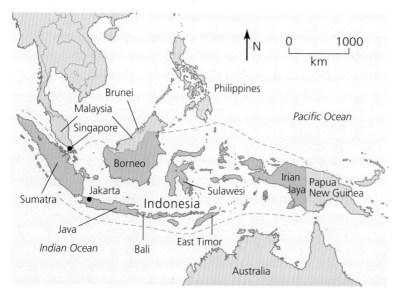

Jakarta is a city of great contrasts. It has gleaming new office buildings, and luxurious apartment blocks for the better-off. However, it also has a lot of poor-quality housing and even **shanty towns**. Shanty towns have poor-quality buildings made from scrap wood, plastic and metal by the migrants.

Q3 Draw a map of Indonesia.

◀ **Fig 2** *Indonesia.*

 Encarta – Jakarta http://encarta.msn.com/find/Concise.asp?2=1&pg=2&ti=050D600

Problems

A large number of migrants are not able to find a job in Jakarta. They may end up living in poverty on the streets. Those lucky enough to find a job in a factory may find that the pay is very low, and the work hard and dangerous. A shortage of cheap housing means that many migrants are forced to live in appalling conditions in shanty towns (Fig 3). The city authorities are struggling to supply the growing population with basic services. Piped water is unusual. Most people have to pump water up from underground by hand. This has caused the water table to fall and become polluted with sea water. Jakarta does not have a mains sewerage system. Human waste is collected in cess pits, which are emptied by special lorries. Traffic congestion is becoming worse as the number of cars, lorries and autotaxis increase. Vehicle exhaust fumes result in smog over the city. The smog can damage peoples' health.

▲ **Fig 3** A shanty town in Jakarta.

Solutions

The local government of Jakarta is trying to solve some of the city's problems. Road congestion is being tackled by building large flyovers throughout the city, and by improving the railway. New towns have been built on the outskirts, but these have merged with Jakarta to form a **mega-city**. High-rise apartments have been built, but most people cannot afford the rent. Shanty towns have been destroyed, but this leaves people with nowhere to live. A successful solution has been 'self-help schemes'. People are given land and materials, and are allowed to build their own homes.

▲ **Fig 4** High-quality housing in Jakarta.

Q4 Describe the different types of housing shown in Figs 3 and 4.

Key words

mega-city – city with over ten million people.
migration – movement from one place to another
rural – countryside
shanty town – area of very low-quality housing
urban – town or city

SUMMARY

■ The number and size of cities is increasing.
■ The largest growth of cities is in poorer countries.
■ The growth of cities is placing huge pressure on resources.

SUMMARY *activity*

Describe two problems caused by the growth of Jakarta. Explain what you think should be done to solve them.

 Lonely Planet – Indonesia http://www.lonelyplanet.com/dest/sea/indo.htm

52 Land use models

In this section of the book you will investigate the following things:

- What is 'land use'?
- What land uses are found in towns and cities?
- What are land use models?
- How does land use vary between richer and poorer countries?

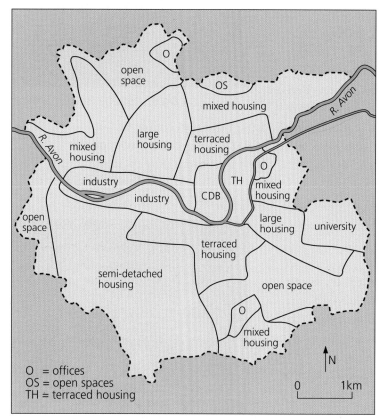

O = offices
OS = open spaces
TH = terraced housing

N

0   1km

▲ **Fig 1** *Land use in Bath.*

'**Land use**' simply means what the land is used for. As towns and cities have grown, they have developed areas of different land use. They contain areas of shops, offices, industry and housing (Fig 1). The use of land in towns and cities is often quite complicated. **Models** have been created to try to make land use easier to understand. A model is a way of simplifying something in real life. Although the models are different, they all have one thing in common. The most expensive land is always in the middle of the city. This is because it is the easiest place for most people to travel to. Moving away from the city centre, the value of the land falls.

Q1 What does 'land use' mean?

Concentric model

The simplest land use model is the concentric circle model (Fig 2). This model shows that cities grew outwards from the centre, in a series of rings. This means the oldest buildings are at the centre, and the newest on the outskirts. There used to be factories at the centre. These have now been replaced by modern offices and shops. This area is called the **Central Business District (CBD)**. Around the CBD is an area called the **transition zone**. This is where old houses are being demolished and replaced with new ones. The next zone contains mainly low-quality housing. This may be old terraced houses, or tower blocks. In places the old terraced houses have been renovated. Semi-detached houses form the next zone. The final zone, on the outskirts, contains modern estates of semi-detached and detached houses.

Q2 Why do you think houses become bigger towards the outskirts?

Sector model

The sector land use model shows that transport affects the land use in towns and cities (Fig 3). As the city grew outwards, land use followed transport routes such as roads and railways. Houses were built along main roads, making it easier for people to move around the city. Factories were built along canals and railways, making it easier to transport raw materials and products.

Central Business District
medium-quality housing
transition zone
high-quality housing
low-quality housing

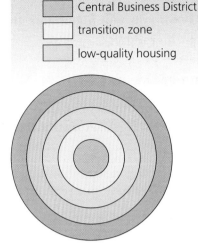

▲ **Fig 2** Concentric model.

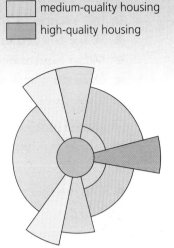

▲ **Fig 3** Sector model.

Q3 Why were factories built along railways?

Cities in poorer countries

Cities in poorer countries have very different land uses to cities in richer countries (Fig 4). At the centre there is a CBD of modern offices and shopping malls. But around the CBD there is a zone of high-quality apartments and houses. This is where the wealthy people live. The quality of the housing becomes poorer towards the outskirts. The next zone contains medium-quality housing, usually self-built by migrants. On the outskirts there are large areas of **shanty towns**. The quality of housing in the shanty towns is very low. Shanty towns may also appear on any waste land throughout the city. Factories in poorer cities tend to be built along the roads and railways.

Q4 Give two differences between cities in richer and poorer countries.

Central Business District
low-quality housing
medium-quality housing
high-quality housing
shanty towns
industry

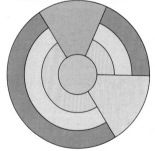

▲ **Fig 4** Urban land use model for poorer countries.

Key words

CBD (Central Business District) – an area of shops and offices
land use – the use of the land
model – a way of simplifying real life
shanty town – an area of self-built housing of very low quality
transition zone – area of demolition and rebuilding

SUMMARY

■ Towns and cities have zones of different land use.
■ Land increases in value towards the CBD.
■ Models are used to investigate land use in cities.
■ Cities in richer countries have different patterns of land use to cities in poorer countries.

SUMMARY *activity*

Map the land use of your local area. Describe the pattern. Does it fit the pattern of any of the land use models?

53 Settlement hierarchy

In this section of the book you will investigate the following things:
- **What is a settlement hierarchy?**
- **What is a service?**
- **How do services in settlements vary?**

A hierarchy is a list of people or things in order of importance. Settlements can also be arranged in a hierarchy (Fig 1). A **settlement hierarchy** is worked out by measuring three different things.

- The number of people living in a settlement.
- The number, and range, of services in a settlement.
- The distance to other settlements of a similar size.

The type of settlement at the top of a hierarchy is called a 'mega-city'. A mega-city has a population of over ten million people. It is also at the top of the hierarchy because it has thousands of services and is a long way from other mega-cities. Hamlets are at the bottom of the settlement hierarchy. A hamlet is a small group of houses with only a few people living there. A hamlet may have no services, but be very close to other hamlets.

A settlement hierarchy is drawn as a pyramid. The top of the pyramid is narrow because there are very few mega-cities. The base of the pyramid is wide because there are thousands of hamlets.

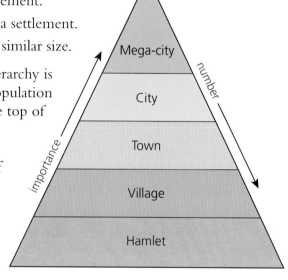

▲ *Fig 1* Settlement hierarchy.

Q1 What is a settlement hierarchy?

Q2 Why are hamlets at the bottom of a settlement hierarchy?

Services

A **service** is a facility used by people, such as shops, restaurants, schools and hospitals. The number of services in a settlement depends on its size. The larger the settlement, the more services there will be. There will also be a greater variety of goods for sale. Shops in cities sell more expensive items, which are not bought very often. These are called comparison goods, because people like to compare prices before buying. Comparison goods include things like jewellery, clothes and computers (Fig 2). Shops in villages sell cheaper items, which are bought frequently. These are called convenience goods, because people buy them at the most convenient shop. Convenience goods include things like food and newspapers (Fig 3).

Q3 What is a service?

Range and threshold

A minimum number of people are needed for a shop to be profitable. This is called the **threshold** population (Fig 4). A village shop can survive with a low threshold of around 300 people. A department store needs a high threshold of around 100 000 people. This is why department stores are only found in cities. Cities will also attract shoppers from a long way away. The distance people are prepared to travel to visit a shop is called the **range**. Because department stores sell many comparison goods they have a large range.

▲ **Fig 2** High order service.

▲ **Fig 3** Low order service.

Village shop	300
Doctor	2500
Secondary school	10 000
Shoe shop	25 000
Large supermarket	50 000
Department store	100 000

▲ **Fig 4** Threshold populations.

Q4 Why would village shops only have a small range?

Key words

settlement hierarchy – the order of importance of settlements
range – the maximum distance people will travel to use a service
threshold – the minimum number of people needed for a service to be worthwhile
service – a facility used by people

SUMMARY

- Settlements can be arranged in order of importance.
- The larger the settlement, the greater the number and range of services.
- Comparison goods are expensive, and bought infrequently.
- Convenience goods are cheaper, and bought often.

SUMMARY *activity*

Make a list of the services in a number of settlements in your local area. Draw a pyramid to show the hierarchy of these settlements.

54 House building

In this section of the book you will investigate the following things:

- Why are 4.4 million new houses needed in England?
- Where will they be built?
- What will be the impacts of the new houses?

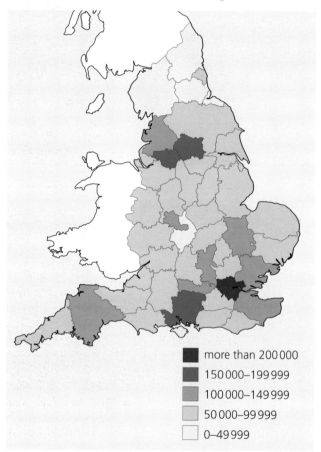

▲ **Fig 1** Number of new homes needed in England by 2016.

Legend:
- more than 200000
- 150000–199999
- 100000–149999
- 50000–99999
- 0–49999

The government has predicted that England will need 4.4 million new homes by 2016 (Fig 1). These homes are not needed because there are more people. In fact, the population of England is falling. The new homes have to be built because of changes in the way people are living. These changes are listed below.

- People are leaving home at a younger age.
- People are living longer.
- People are getting married at an older age.
- More marriages are ending in divorce.
- Some people prefer to live alone.
- People are migrating to the south of England.
- People are moving from the cities to the countryside.

Q1 How many new homes will England need by 2016?

Q2 How have changes in marriage increased the need for new houses?

Conflicts

There have been many arguments about where the new homes should be built. House developers like to build in the countryside on 'greenfield' sites (Fig 2). A **greenfield site** is land which has not been built on before. It is easier, and cheaper, to build on greenfield sites. Developers also argue that most people prefer to live in the countryside. However, the government has a policy that most new homes should be built in **urban** areas. They have set a target for 60% of homes to be built on '**brownfield**' sites. Brownfield sites are areas of wasteland in towns and cities. Building on brownfield sites is a way of re-cycling land. Environmental organisations, such as Friends of the Earth, say that 75% of new homes should be on brownfield sites.

Q3 What are greenfield and brownfield sites?

Dept. of Environment, Transport and Regions http://www.detr.gov.uk/

Greenfield sites

The government predicts that new homes on greenfield sites will cover 169 000 **hectares** of countryside by 2016. There is concern that this amount of building will damage the environment. The amount of traffic in the countryside will increase and more roads will be needed. Traffic congestion and air pollution will become greater problems. More building will be needed to provide services such as shops, schools and hospitals. There could be problems supplying enough water for all the new homes and services. Wildlife will also suffer as habitats are destroyed.

▲ **Fig 2** New homes on a greenfield site in Cambridgeshire.

Brownfield sites

Using brownfield sites for new homes will help reduce the impact on the countryside. In London, space for 100 000 new homes has been found on the sites of old buildings and factories (Fig 3). The government is trying to persuade developers to build on these sites. However, in order to persuade more people to live in cities, the government will have to tackle urban problems such as crime and public transport. Other solutions to the housing problem have been suggested. Throughout England there are 250 000 empty homes which could be renovated. There are also thought to be another 800 000 possible homes in unused offices, or flats above shops.

▲ **Fig 3** New homes on a brownfield site in London Docklands.

Q4 Can you think of any other solutions to the housing shortage?

Key words

brownfield site – land which has been built on before

greenfield site – land which has not been built on before

hectare – ten thousand square metres

urban – town or city

SUMMARY

- England needs 4.4 million new homes by 2016.
- The new homes are needed because of changes in lifestyle.
- Around 40% of homes will be built on greenfield sites.
- The government's aim is for 60% of homes to be built on brownfield sites.

SUMMARY *activity*

Write two letters to the government: one letter from a developer wanting to build a new housing estate on a greenfield site; the other from someone living in the countryside who wants to stop the houses being built.

55 Road building

In this section of the book you will investigate the following things:
- Why are more roads needed?
- Who is responsible for road building?
- How does road building result in conflicts?

Roads play a very important part in most peoples' lives. Roads allow companies to transport their goods. They also allow people to travel to the shops, to work and to leisure activities. Changing lifestyles are increasing the amount of traffic on the roads. There are now more single people, and most want their own car. More shops and services are now on the outskirts of towns and cities, and cars are needed to reach them. As a result, road traffic is expected to double by 2030. The government has to find solutions to cope with this growth.

Q1 Why is the number of cars on the roads increasing?

Map

N

0   1km

Snelsmore Common SSSI

River Lambourn

Watermill Theatre

Donnington Castle

Area of Outstanding Natural Beauty

Bagnor Conservation Area

Donnington Grove Historic Park

Rack Marsh Nature Reserve

Second Battle of Newbury site

Benham Historic Park

A34

Newbury

River Kennet

First Battle of Newbury site

Hamstead Historic Park

Newbury bypass

Redding's Copse

alternative central route

Area of Outstanding Natural Beauty

The Chase Nature Reserve

National Trust Land

Great Pen Wood

Government

The Highways Agency is responsible for 6500 miles of **motorways** and **trunk** roads in England. It spends £1.5 billion a year on maintaining roads, improving roads and building new roads. Government policy is to make the best use of existing roads, rather than building new ones. But, 37 new roads will be built over the next few years. In recent years, road building has caused conflicts. People are worried about damage to the environment. Road building results in loss of countryside and an increase in noise and air pollution.

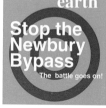

FRIENDS of the earth

Stop the Newbury Bypass
The battle goes on!

◄ **Fig 1** The route of the Newbury bypass.

Q2 Who is responsible for roads in England?

 Highways Agency http://www.highways.gov.uk/index.htm

The Newbury bypass

Newbury is a town in Berkshire which suffered from terrible road congestion. The A34, carrying traffic between the Midlands and the south coast, passed right through its centre. Combined with local traffic, 50 000 cars a day were driving through Newbury. This caused huge traffic jams which cost businesses money and increased pollution.

- **Snelsmore Common** – destruction of heath and ancient woodland.
- **Watermill Theatre** – road noise impacts on open-air theatre.
- **River Lambourn** – road passes over pure stream.
- **Rack Marsh** – meadow and wetland area: important wildlife habitat.
- **First Battle of Newbury** – one of the twelve sites of archaeological importance along route.
- **North Wessex Downs** – Bypass runs through an Area of Outstanding Natural Beauty.
- **Redding's Copse** – woodland providing wildlife habitat.

The Highways Agency decided that the solution to Newbury's traffic problem was to build a **bypass** (Fig 1). In January 1996, work began on a new road to the west of the town. The route of the new road caused much conflict because of damage to the local environment (Fig 2). Environmental organisations, such as Friends of the Earth, believed that better traffic management could have solved the traffic problems. The National Rivers Authority objected to the road crossing the River Kennet and River Lambourn. English Heritage were worried about damage to historical sites.

▲ *Fig 2* Environmental impacts of the Newbury bypass.
▼ *Fig 3* Protesters campaign against the Newbury bypass.

Protesters tried to stop the bypass from being built (Fig 3). Thirty camps were built along the new route. Some people climbed trees and others dug tunnels to try to stop the developers. Although the protesters failed to stop the road, they did slow down its construction. It took the developers 85 days to cut down 10 000 trees that were in the way. The extra security cost the government £15 million. The Newbury Bypass opened in November 1998.

Q3 Why did Newbury need a bypass?

Q4 How did the bypass damage the environment?

Key words

bypass – a road built around a town

motorway – a major road with several lanes

trunk road – a national main road

SUMMARY

- New roads are needed to cope with the increase in traffic.
- The Highways Agency is responsible for the motorways and trunk roads in England.
- New roads damage the environment.
- Road building causes conflicts between groups of people.

SUMMARY activity

What action could you take to try to prevent a new road from being built?

 Friends of the Earth – Newbury Bypass http://www.foe.co.uk/action/newbury/index.html

56 Economic activities

In this section of the book you will investigate the following things:
- What are economic activities?
- How can economic activities be classified?
- How do economic activities change over time?

Economic activities are ways that people can make a living. In the UK, most workers have a paid job. In poorer countries many people make a living by growing their own food. The work done by people can be classified into four types: primary, secondary, tertiary and quaternary. These words simply mean first, second, third and fourth.

> **Q1** What is an economic activity?

Primary

Primary workers extract, collect or grow **raw materials**. Raw materials are natural products which can be sold as they are, or processed to make something else. Primary activities include mining, fishing, farming and forestry.

▲ **Fig 1a** Primary.

Secondary

▲ **Fig 1b** Secondary.

Secondary workers **process** raw materials. This means they are changed into something different. For example, oil is refined to make petrol, fish are processed to make fish fingers, wheat is ground to make flour, and trees are sawn into timber. Secondary workers also **manufacture** things. This means different parts are put together to make a finished product. This includes making ships, cars, televisions and jobs such as building roads and houses.

Tertiary

Tertiary workers provide people, and other companies, with services. Tertiary jobs include working in shops, offices, schools, hospitals, transport, leisure and tourism. Most workers in the UK have tertiary jobs.

▲ **Fig 1c** Tertiary.

Quaternary

▲ **Fig 1d** Quaternary.

Quaternary workers research and develop the latest technology. Quaternary work includes designing new computers, writing computer software, researching new medicines and medical equipment, genetically modifying plants and animals for farming, and designing new ways of communicating using satellites and fibre optic cables.

> **Q2** Write a short description of primary, secondary, tertiary and quaternary work.
>
> **Q3** Draw a diagram, similar to Fig 2, to show the links between primary, secondary and tertiary work.

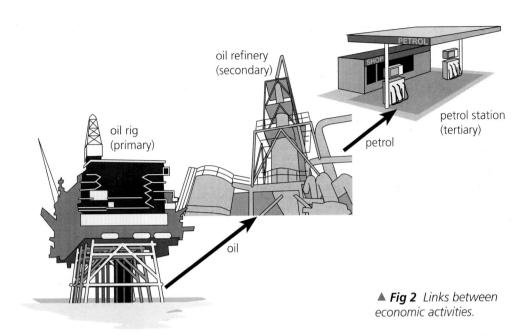

▲ **Fig 2** Links between economic activities.

Changes

Work changes over time (Fig 3). Peoples' first work was farming. The invention of machines meant fewer people were needed to work on the land. Most people began to work in factories, making things. Technology improved again and machines began to replace workers. Service jobs have now become the most important. The latest jobs are in high-tech research and development.

Work has not changed like this in all countries. In poorer countries such as India and Kenya, most people still work in farming. As these countries become richer, the type of work that their people do will change.

	1900	2000
Primary	10%	2%
Secondary	50%	27%
Tertiary	40%	69%
Quaternary	0%	2%

▲ **Fig 3** Changes in UK employment (percentage of workforce).

Q4 How does technology change the type of work people do?

Key words

economic activity – a way people make a living
manufacture – make things
process – change raw materials
raw materials – natural products

SUMMARY

- Economic activity is the work people do to make a living.
- Work can be classified as primary, secondary, tertiary or quaternary.
- The type of work changes over time.
- The type of work varies between different countries.

SUMMARY activity

Carry out a survey of the jobs of people in your local area. Draw a graph of your results. What does your graph show?

57 Farming

In this section of the book you will investigate the following things:
- ▨ **What are the different types of farming?**
- ▨ **What factors affect the type of farming?**
- ▨ **What is the global distribution of farming?**

Farming is the growing of crops and rearing of animals.
Farming is extremely important work because it provides
the world's population with food and other essential
products. Although there are many different types of
farming, it can be classified into three main types.

- ▨ **Arable** farming – the growing of crops such as
  wheat, barley, maize, rice and potatoes. Arable farming
  also includes crops such as fruit, cotton, tea and coffee
  (Fig 1).

- ▨ **Pastoral** farming – the rearing of animals for meat
  and animal products. Pastoral farming includes rearing
  cows, sheep, pigs, goats, camels and chickens (Fig 2).

- ▨ **Mixed** farming – the growing of crops and rearing of
  animals in the same area.

▲ **Fig 1** *Arable farming.*

▲ **Fig 2** *Pastoral farming.*

Q1 What are the
three different
types of farming?

Farmers have to decide what type of
crops or animals to farm. Their
decision is affected by several physical
and human factors.

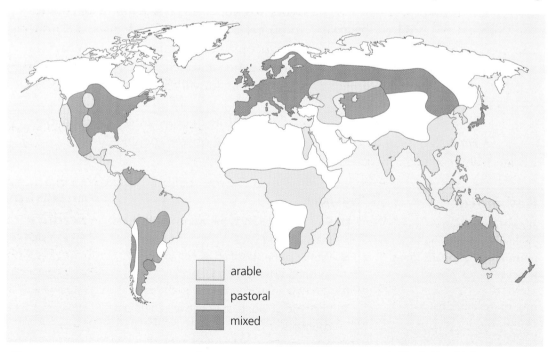

arable
pastoral
mixed

▲ **Fig 3** *World farming types.*

Physical factors

Rainfall – water is needed by all crops and animals. The amount of water which different crops need varies, but most need between 250mm and 500mm per year.

Temperature – crops need the temperature to be above 6°C to be able to grow. Some crops, such as wheat, prefer a temperate climate, other crops, such as bananas, need a tropical climate..

Relief – the shape of the land can affect the type of farming. Mountainous areas are too cold for crops. Steep slopes also make it difficult to use farm machinery. Most high areas are used for animal grazing. Lowland areas are used mainly for crops.

Soil – crops prefer deep, fertile, well-drained soils. Thin, less fertile soils are better for animal grazing.

Human factors

Labour – some crops and animals need a lot of caring for, others very little. In poorer countries much of the work is done by hand. In richer countries machines do most of the work.

Market – farmers must sell their goods to make a profit. They have to decide which crops will sell for the most money. Today farmers export their goods all over the world.

Government – governments can encourage the farming of certain products by promising farmers a minimum price for their goods. They can also place a limit on the amount farmers are allowed to produce.

Q2 Why are bananas not grown in the UK?

Global distribution

Different physical and human factors mean that many different types of farming take place around the world (Fig 3). In Western Europe, farming is mainly mixed. In the centre of the USA there are huge fields of cereal crops. In South-east Asia, rice growing is the most popular. In Australia, large areas are used for sheep grazing. Farming is constantly changing. In richer countries, too much food is being produced. Farmers are being paid not to farm their land. In poorer countries, population growth means more food is needed. New areas of land are having to be farmed.

Q3 Use an atlas to find out the main crops and animals farmed in France, Brazil and Australia.

Q4 Explain why less land is being farmed in richer countries.

Key words

arable – farming crops
mixed – farming crops and animals
pastoral – farming animals

SUMMARY

- Farming can be classified as arable, pastoral or mixed.
- The type of farming depends on a range of physical and human factors.
- There are many different types of farming around the world.
- The global distribution of farming is constantly changing.

SUMMARY *activity*

Draw two labelled diagrams to illustrate the physical and human factors which affect farming.

58 Farming in the UK

In this section of the book you will investigate the following things:
■ How is farming distributed in the UK?
■ How has the Common Agricultural Policy affected farming?
■ How has UK farming changed?

Distribution

Different types of farming are linked to particular areas in the UK (Fig 1):

■ Dairy farming of cattle is found in the western parts of England, Scotland and Wales. These areas have flat land, fertile soils and good-quality grass.

■ Arable farming is popular in the east. Wheat and barley grow well on the flat land with deep fertile soil. These crops also prefer a fairly dry climate.

▲ *Fig 2* Oilseed rape.

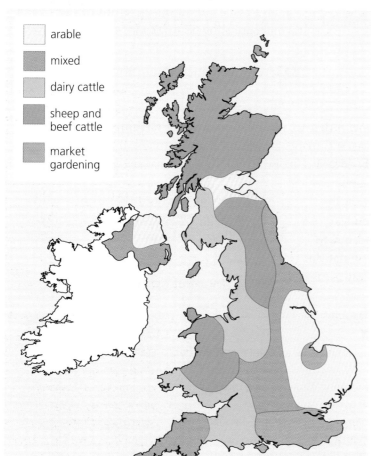

- arable
- mixed
- dairy cattle
- sheep and beef cattle
- market gardening

◀ *Fig 1* Distribution of farming types in the UK.

■ Sheep and beef cattle farming are found in the upland areas of England, Wales and Scotland. The high hills and steep slopes have thin infertile soils. These areas also have heavy rainfall and low temperatures making it difficult to grow crops.

■ Market gardening is the growing of crops such as fruit and salad vegetables. Market gardening takes place mainly in greenhouses in the south east of England.

Q1 Describe the distribution of farming shown in Fig 1.

The Common Agricultural Policy

In 1962, the UK and other European countries agreed the **Common Agricultural Policy (CAP)**. The CAP aimed to protect farmers' incomes, ensure fair prices for shoppers, and to make Europe self-sufficient in food. The CAP encouraged farmers to grow as much as possible. This meant that by the 1980s huge surpluses had built up. Now the CAP has become very expensive and the European Union (EU) is trying to cut the amount of money it pays to farmers.

Q2 What were the aims of the CAP?

Changes

Many changes are taking place in farming. Traditional crops such as wheat and barley are being replaced by crops such as oilseed rape (Fig 2) and linseed. This is because farmers can make more money from these crops. Farmers are rearing more unusual animals such as ostriches for their meat, and llamas for their wool. Many farmers have taken advantage of the 'set aside' scheme. Under this scheme, the EU pay farmers to leave their land **fallow** for five years. This is cheaper than storing surplus food. Farmers are also moving into other areas of business, such as farm shops and bed and breakfast. This is called **diversification**.

Q3 Why are oilseed rape and linseed replacing wheat and barley?

Q4 Does it make sense to pay farmers not to grow crops?

Crisis

The end of the 1990s was a crisis time for UK farming as the price of goods fell (Fig 3). In 1999 farmers' incomes dropped by 47%. This was caused by several problems. The ban on exports of British beef, because of **BSE**, meant farmers lost £500 million a year. Also, new food safety standards increased the cost of British goods. Cheaper imports from Europe resulted in over 1000 UK farmers going out of business in 1999. News reports appeared about farmers abandoning their livestock at animal sanctuaries.

	September 1996	September 1998
Wheat (£ per tonne)	102	70
Lamb (pence per kg)	119	76
Beef (pence per kg)	120	79
Pig meat (pence per kg)	141	61
Chickens (pence per kg)	65	50
Milk (pence per litre)	26	20
Eggs (pence per dozen)	45	29

▲ **Fig 3** Prices received by farmers. (source NFU website)

Key words

BSE – mad cow disease

CAP – Common Agricultural Policy

diversification – expanding into other areas of business

fallow – land which is not farmed

SUMMARY

- Farming in the UK is affected by human and physical factors.
- The CAP has a large influence on farming.
- Traditional crops and animals are being replaced by alternatives.
- Farming in the UK is experiencing huge changes.

SUMMARY activity

Use the data in Fig 3 to calculate by what percentage the prices of farmers' goods fell between 1996 and 1998. Draw a graph to show your results. Explain what caused the prices to fall.

 Ministry of Agriculture Fisheries and Food http://www.maff.gov.uk/maffhome.htm

59 Farming and technology

In this section of the book you will investigate the following things:
- How has technology changed farming?
- What are Genetically Modified Organisms?
- What are the arguments in favour of GMOs?
- What are the arguments against GMOs?

The food we eat today is the result of thousands of years of work by farmers. Ten thousand years ago people had the idea of growing wild plants, and domesticating wild animals. This meant people had a more reliable supply of food. Over the years the best plants and animals were bred, giving us the crops and farm animals of today. Farmers have always used new **technology** to improve the quality of food. Machines such as tractors and combine harvesters have made sowing and harvesting crops much easier. Pesticides and herbicides have protected crops from weeds and harmful insects. The latest farming technology is the introduction of **Genetically Modified Organisms (GMOs)**.

Q1 When did people begin farming?

Q2 Give two examples of farming technology.

▲ **Fig 1** Counties with Genetically Modified Crop test sites.

Genetically Modified Organisms

Genetically Modified Organisms are plants or animals which have had their **genes** altered. Genes are molecules containing codes which give all living things their characteristics. Genes and characteristics are normally inherited from two parents, but since the 1970s scientists have been able to modify the process. Genes may now be added, taken away or 'switched off'. Genes may even be transferred between species. For example, genes from cold water fish can be added to tomatoes to make them frost resistant (Fig 2). Although the possible benefits of genetic modification are huge, many people and organisations are worried about GMOs. In 1999 protesters destroyed fields of GM crops which were being grown in England (Fig 4).

Q3 What is a GMO?

flounder

DNA

+ tomato plant

= frost resistant tomato plant

▲ **Fig 2** Benefits of GMOs.

 Food Future http://www.foodfuture.org.uk/

118

Arguments in favour of GMOs

Agricultural companies, and some farmers, think GMOs offer many benefits:

- Genes can be added to plants to make them resistant to diseases, droughts and frost. These crops can be grown in more difficult areas.

- Plants can be made poisonous to insects. This means pesticides are not needed.

- Genes can be added to crops to make them resistant to herbicides. Farmers are then able to kill the weeds without harming their crops.

- GM foods could be used to improve peoples' health. Extra minerals and vitamins can be added to crops. In the future, vaccines might be added to fruit such as bananas.

- Plants have been developed which can be turned into bio-degradable plastic.

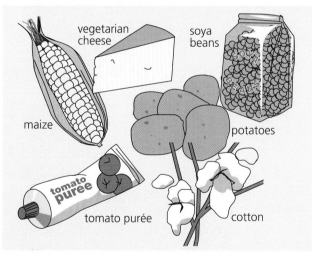

▲ *Fig 3* Genetically modified products.

Arguments against GMOs

Organisations such as Greenpeace, the Soil Association and the RSPB are worried about GMOs:

- Genes from modified crops could cross to other plants. 'Superweeds' might develop.

- Terminator genes can be added to crops. These crops produce infertile seeds. Farmers must buy new seeds every year.

- Killing more plants and insects will affect the food chain. Birds such as the skylark and thrush could disappear.

- The effects of GMOs on people's health is not yet understood.

Q4 People have described 'terminator' genes as immoral. Why do you think this is?

▲ *Fig 4* Protesters destroy GM crop.

Key words

gene – molecule which controls characteristics of living things

GMO – Genetically Modified Organism

technology – appliance of science

SUMMARY

- Farming has been improved by new technology.
- The characteristics of plants and animals can be altered by genetic modification.
- GMOs could revolutionise farming.
- Many groups are worried about the effects of GMOs.

SUMMARY *activity*

Prepare a short talk giving your opinion about Genetically Modified Organisms.

 Soil Association http://www.soilassociation.org/SA/SAWeb.nsf/!Open

60 Farming and the environment

In this section of the book you will investigate the following things:
- How is farming linked to the environment?
- How has farming damaged the environment?
- How can farming benefit the environment?

Farming and the **environment** are closely linked. If one changes, the other will be affected. Changes in farming include using more machinery and chemicals. This new technology has helped farmers to produce more food, but has often had a negative effect on the environment. Changes in the environment, such as air pollution, can affect farming by harming crops. Recently in the UK, several schemes have been introduced to encourage farming which benefits the environment.

Q1 How could changes in the environment affect farming?

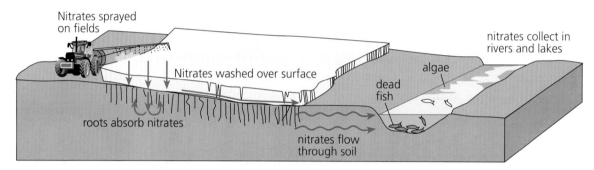

▲ **Fig 1** Nitrate pollution.

Fertiliser

Plants need **nutrients** to grow. Farmers spray their crops with **fertiliser** which contains nutrients called **nitrates** (Fig 1). Plants take up some nitrates through their roots. Unused nitrates soak down through the soil into the water table or are washed into rivers and lakes. The United Nations has said that nitrate pollution is now a major global environmental problem. Nitrates cause algae in rivers and lakes to grow very quickly. The algae use up all the oxygen and so fish die (Fig 2). Nitrates in water supplies can also damage people's health. However, the National Farmer's Union (NFU) say that water pollution from farming is decreasing in the UK.

Q2 What are nitrates?

▶ **Fig 2** Effects of nitrate pollution on rivers.

 MAFF Environment http://www.maff.gov.uk/environ/envindx.htm

Hedgerows

Hedgerows were planted by farmers in the eighteenth century. They were used to mark the boundaries of fields and to keep animals in. Since 1945, over 377 000 km of hedgerows have been cleared by farmers because hedgerows take up valuable space (Fig 3). One kilometre of hedgerow covers one hectare of farmland. Hedgerows also obstruct large farm machinery such as combine harvesters. However, hedgerows provide important habitats for wildlife. The removal of hedgerows has caused a drop in the number of insects, birds and animals. The NFU point out that between 1990 and 1993 farmers planted 4400 km of new hedgerows.

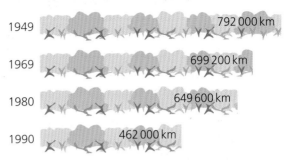

1949   792 000 km
1969   699 200 km
1980   649 600 km
1990   462 000 km

▲ *Fig 3* Hedgerows in the UK.

Q3 Why have farmers removed hedgerows?

Conservation

The role of farmers is changing. As well as producing food, they are expected to look after the countryside. Grants are available from the government, and the EU, for farmers who agree to manage their land in ways that improve the environment. By 2000, farmers had entered over 1.2 million hectares of land into conservation agreements.

The Farm Woodland Premium Scheme pays farmers to plant trees on their land. Farmers are paid up to £300 per hectare of trees, each year. The money is paid by the Ministry of Agriculture, Fisheries and Food and the Forestry Commission. Native species such as oak and beech are encouraged by higher grants. This scheme has been very successful. Between 1993 and 1998 over 46 000 hectares of trees were planted (Fig 4). The woodland has provided new habitats for plants and wildlife.

	1993	1994	1995	1996	1997	1998	Total
Trees planted (hectares)	7106	10259	7627	6712	5146	9600	46450
Number of farms	1178	1512	1222	1151	852	1524	7439

▲ *Fig 4* The Farm Woodland Premium Scheme

Q4 Describe the benefits of the Farm Woodland Premium Scheme.

Key words

environment – the air, land, water, plants and wildlife

fertiliser – substance added to soil to improve fertility

hedgerow – hedge forming a field boundary

nitrate – a nutrient which is important for plant growth

nutrient – chemicals needed by living things

SUMMARY

- Changes in farming affect the environment.
- Changes in the environment affect farming.
- Modern farming methods have damaged the environment.
- Recent changes to farming can benefit the environment.

SUMMARY *activity*

💻 *Draw a flow diagram to show the causes and effects of nitrate pollution. Include the following key words: fertiliser; nutrients; nitrates; plant roots; water table; rivers and lakes; algae; oxygen; kills fish; damages health.*

 Friends of the Earth http://www.foe.co.uk/

61 Industry

In this section of the book you will investigate the following things:

■ What was the Industrial Revolution?
■ Where were the UK's industrial regions located?
■ Why has industry in the UK declined?
■ What are the impacts of industrial decline?

▲ *Fig 1* Location of traditional industries.

The Industrial Revolution

Until the nineteenth century, most people in the UK worked as farmers in the countryside. This pattern of work changed during the **Industrial Revolution**, when steam-powered machinery was invented. Machines could now do jobs that had previously been done by people. This meant fewer farm workers were needed, but more workers were needed in the new industries. The most important new industries were iron and steel factories and textile mills. Large numbers of people migrated from the countryside to find jobs in factories and mills. Towns and cities grew as workers' houses were built.

Q1 What invention revolutionised industry?

Location

Factories and mills were built in areas close to **raw materials**. Coal was the most important raw material. It was needed to produce steam to power the machines. Because coal is heavy and difficult to transport, factories and mills were built close to coal mines. The iron and steel industry grew up around the coal fields of South Wales, the Midlands, north-east England and central Scotland. The wool industry developed in Yorkshire, and the cotton industry in Lancashire.

Q2 Why did industry develop close to coal fields?

Industrial decline

By the 1960s, traditional industries in the UK were declining. Raw materials had been used up, or had become too expensive. Also, other countries were producing goods more cheaply. Hundreds of mines, factories and mills have since closed, making thousands of people unemployed.

 Department of Trade and Industry http://www.dti.gov.uk/

The iron and steel industry in South Wales

By 1800 South Wales had become the most important metal smelting area in the world. The area had the three raw materials needed to make iron and steel (Fig 2). Coal and iron ore were mined in the valleys and limestone was quarried in the Brecon Beacon mountains. The towns of Merthyr Tydfil and Ebbw Vale became the centre of iron and steel production. Ports on the coast were used to export the finished products all over the world (Fig 3). Many of the **markets** were British colonies such as India and Australia.

By the 1960s, the iron and steel industry in South Wales had collapsed. The iron ore deposits had been used up, and the coal seams were too narrow for modern mining methods. Many markets had also gone as colonies became independent. The closure of the factories had huge impacts.

- Thousands of people became unemployed.
- Industries connected with the steel industry closed down.
- The environment was severely damaged. In the Lower Swansea valley, air pollution had killed all the vegetation.

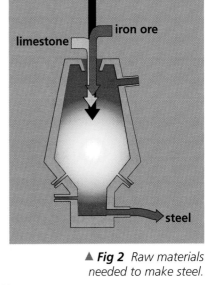

▲ **Fig 2** *Raw materials needed to make steel.*

▼ **Fig 3** *Iron and steel in South Wales.*

Today only four steelworks remain in the UK. All of them are located close to the coast so that they are able to import raw materials by ship. These modern steelworks use computer technology to make them efficient. They are able to compete with other steel manufacturers all over the world.

Q3 Why did the iron and steel industry in South Wales decline?

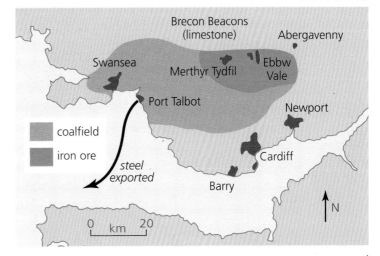

Key words

Industrial Revolution – rapid growth of manufacturing industry

market – the place where goods are sold

raw material – natural products processed to make something else

SUMMARY

- The UK was the first country in the world to have an industrial revolution.
- Industry located close to supplies of coal.
- The growth of industry caused large rural-urban migration.
- Today traditional industries have declined.

SUMMARY activity

Draw a map of South Wales. Label the map to explain the original location of the iron and steel industry.

 British Steel http://www.corusgroup.com/

62 Modern industry

In this section of the book you will investigate the following things:
- What are modern industries?
- Where are modern industries located?
- What factors affect the location of modern industries?

As traditional industries such as iron and steel declined, modern industries have taken their place. Modern industries include light manufacturing industry and high-tech industry. Light manufacturing produces things such as electrical goods, parts for cars and food. High-tech industries are involved in computing, bio-technology and communications.

Q1 What are high-tech industries?

Business parks and science parks

Modern industries are described as '**footloose**'. This means they are not tied to one place. Because they do not use bulky raw materials they are able to locate wherever they choose. Most modern industries will look for a site with good transport links and a suitable workforce. Modern industries tend to locate in **business parks** or **science parks** on greenfield sites. **Greenfield sites** are locations on the edge of towns and cities which have not been built on before. Business parks are planned developments of offices and industrial units. Sometimes they also have shops and services. Science parks are located close to universities. They contain mainly high-tech companies which have links with the university. Both business and science parks are designed to be attractive. Many have gardens with trees and lakes to make them pleasant places in which to work.

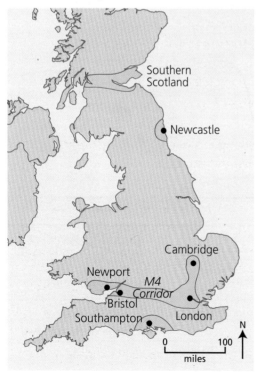

▲ *Fig 1* Location of modern industries.

Q2 Why are modern industries described as footloose?

Q3 What are business and science parks?

Distribution

Although modern industries are footloose, they are concentrated in a number of areas (Fig 1). One area is between Oxford, London and Cambridge. The industries have located along the M4 and M11 motorways. These roads give good links with head offices and banks in London, and they are close to airports for international travel. A skilled workforce is found in this area of southern England.

Other areas of modern industry are South Wales, north-east England and southern Scotland. Industries have located here for two main reasons. They are areas of high unemployment due to the decline in traditional industries. The government gives grants to businesses locating in these areas.

Milton Park

Milton Park is a business park in Oxfordshire. It is located in Didcot, which is 12 miles south of Oxford (Fig 2). Milton Park is home to 147 businesses ranging from food processing to computer design and manufacture. Milton Park is attractive to modern industries for a number of reasons.

■ It has excellent transport links. It is on the A34 which links the Midlands with Southampton, and it is close to the M4 which links South Wales with London. It is on the Intercity Bristol to London train route.

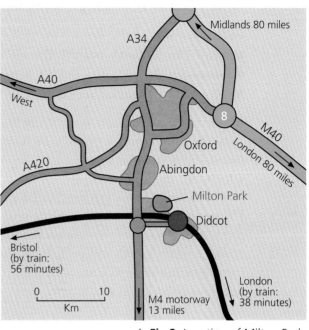

▲ *Fig 2* Location of Milton Park.

■ It is an area with access to a skilled workforce. There are a large number of other modern industries in the area.

■ The surrounding area is an attractive place in which to live.

■ Milton Park provides facilities including a fitness club, a health centre, shops, a bank, a hairdresser and a nursery.

Q4 Why are good transport links important for modern industries?

▲ *Fig 3* Milton Park.

Key words

business park – a development of offices and industrial units

footloose – not tied to a particular location

greenfield site – land which has not been built on before

science park – a development of high-tech industries close to a university

SUMMARY

■ Modern industries include light manufacturing and high-tech businesses.

■ Modern industries are concentrated in south-east England, South Wales and Scotland.

■ Modern industries often locate in business and science parks.

■ Transport links and a workforce are very important for modern industries.

SUMMARY *activity*

Compare Fig 1 with Fig 1 on page 122. Describe how the distribution of industry has changed.

 Milton Park http://www.miltonpark.co.uk/

63 Industry and the environment

In this section of the book you will investigate the following things:
- How can industry pollute the environment?
- How can industrial pollution be reduced?
- How can industrial accidents affect people and the environment?

Industry provides people with many benefits; it gives people work and money. Industries also produce goods which people buy to improve their standard of living. Industries aim to make a profit. The profits are taxed by government which uses the money to provide services for people. Countries which have well-developed industries tend to be richer and have a higher quality of life. However, industries can also create problems. The more goods industries produce, the more of the world's **resources** are used up. Many industries also produce waste, which can pollute the environment. Some industries are hazardous and if there is an accident people may be killed or injured.

Q1 How does industry improve standards of living?

Industrial pollution

Air Some industries release gases into the air. Carbon dioxide is released when fossil fuels such as coal are burned. Carbon dioxide is causing **global warming.** Other industries release **toxic** gases into the air which can damage people's health.

Water Toxic chemicals are released into rivers by some industries. The chemicals build up in the bodies of river creatures and pass up the food chain. Some fish are now too toxic to eat.

Land Mining industries 'scar' the landscape, causing visual **pollution**. Spoil tips of industrial waste can also be ugly and dangerous (unit 21: Aberfan). Some industries pollute the soil with toxic substances.

Q2 How does burning fossil fuels harm the environment?

Reducing pollution

Environmental problems caused by industry have become global concerns. In 1992, governments of 118 countries met in Rio de Janeiro, Brazil, for the Earth Summit. They agreed to use fewer resources and cause less pollution. This is very difficult, especially for poorer countries which cannot afford to restrict industrial development. The UK government fines industries who pollute the environment, and taxes those who bury their waste in landfill sites.

Q3 Can you think of any other ways of reducing industrial pollution?

 Greenpeace http://www.greenpeace.org/

The Bhopal disaster

Bhopal is a city in central India (Fig 1). In 1984 it was the site of the world's worst industrial accident. A US chemical company, called Union Carbide, owned a factory in Bhopal which produced pesticides and fertilisers (Fig 2). On 2 December 1984, there was a violent reaction in one of the chemical tanks. A large cloud of toxic gas escaped into the air. The gas quickly covered an area of over 40 km². The toxic gas killed 12 000 people, and permanently injured up to 500 000 people (Fig 3).

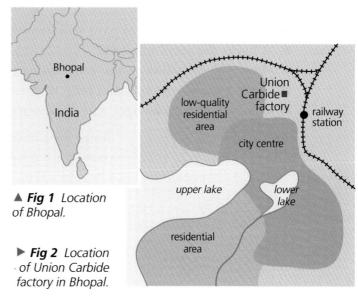

▲ **Fig 1** Location of Bhopal.

▶ **Fig 2** Location of Union Carbide factory in Bhopal.

In 1999, a demonstration took place in Delhi on the fifteenth anniversary of the accident (Fig 4). Although Union Carbide was fined $470 million after the accident, most victims have not received any compensation. Many thousands of people are still very ill, and cannot afford healthcare. Union Carbide is paying for new clinics in the area, but recent tests showed that water supplies near the factory still contain toxic chemicals.

Q4 Why do you think Union Carbide is paying for new clinics in Bhopal?

▲ **Fig 3** Victims of the Bhopal disaster.

▲ **Fig 4** Demonstration on the anniversary of the accident.

Key words

global warming – heating of the Earth's atmosphere
pollution – damage to the environment
resources – natural things used by people
toxic – poisonous

SUMMARY

- Industry increases wealth and standards of living.
- Industry can cause environmental problems.
- Governments have agreed to reduce industrial pollution.
- The effects of industrial pollution can be long term.

SUMMARY activity

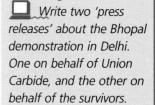

Write two 'press releases' about the Bhopal demonstration in Delhi. One on behalf of Union Carbide, and the other on behalf of the survivors.

 Union Carbide http://www.unioncarbide.com/

64 Retail industry

In this section of the book you will investigate the following things:

- What is the retail industry?
- How is the location of the retail industry changing?
- What are out-of-town shopping centres?
- What are the advantages and disadvantages of out-of-town shopping centres?

▲ **Fig 1** *Out-of-town shopping centres.*

Q1 What is the retail industry?

Shops are a service industry called **retailing**. Shops provide a service by selling people the products they need. Like other types of industry, the retail industry is changing. Shopping in the UK has become a leisure activity, and the location of many shops has changed. Traditionally, shops were located in the centre of towns and cities. This was the easiest place to get to by foot or public transport. Since the 1980s, the retail industry has been moving to out-of-town locations (Fig 1). This has happened because more people are living in the suburbs and the countryside. Also, more people own cars so out-of-town shopping centres are easier to reach.

▶ **Fig 2** *Merry Hill shopping centre, Dudley, West Midlands.*

Out-of-town shopping centres

Out-of-town shopping began in the USA in the 1950s. It caught on in the UK in the 1980s. At this time the government encouraged the building of out-of-town **shopping malls**. A shopping mall is a huge undercover shopping complex. They contain two or three major **chain stores**, around 200 other shops, restaurants, cinemas and even funfairs. Shopping malls are carefully located. They have been built in areas where a large number of people are able to reach them by car. They are usually close to motorways and have very large car parks.

Shopping malls have been very successful. Thirty per cent of all shopping now takes place in out-of-town shopping centres. However, this has been bad for the centre of towns and cities. Many shops have either moved to shopping malls, or closed down altogether. For this reason, government policy is now against building any more out-of-town shopping centres.

Q2 What is a shopping mall?

Merry Hill

Merry Hill is a large out-of-town shopping centre near Dudley, in the West Midlands (Fig 2). It is built on the site of an old steelworks. When the steelworks closed down, the site was redeveloped (Fig 3). Merry Hill was opened in 1989. Merry Hill has been very successful, but the local town of Dudley has been affected.

Size	110 000 m²
Stores	220
Restaurants	28
Visitors	20 million a year
Staff	4000
Parking spaces	7000

▲ **Fig 4** Key facts about Merry Hill.

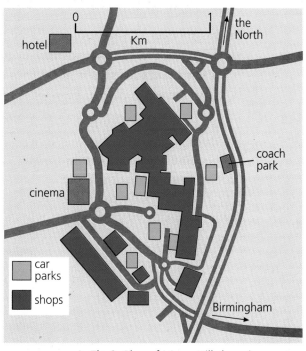

▲ **Fig 3** Plan of Merry Hill shopping centre.

Benefits of Merry Hill

- Provides over 4000 jobs.
- Huge variety of shops in one place.
- Easy, free parking.
- Attractive, pleasant environment.
- Good access for disabled people.
- Protected from bad weather.

Q3 Draw up a table to show how different groups of people have been affected by Merry Hill shopping centre.

Changes in Dudley

- Chain stores have closed down and moved to Merry Hill.
- Independent shops have closed as the numbers of customers have fallen.
- Retail jobs were lost in Dudley.
- The town centre became run-down.
- The elderly and the young, who do not have cars, have to use public transport to visit Merry Hill.

Key words

chain store – a company with many shopping outlets

retail – selling products to the public

shopping mall – a large, enclosed shopping complex

SUMMARY

- The retail industry sells products to the public.
- The retail industry has moved from town centres to out-of-town locations.
- The change in location has had negative effects on some town centres.
- Government policy is now against out-of-town shopping centres.

SUMMARY activity

Imagine a new shopping mall is to be built close to where you live. Would you be in favour of it or against it? Why?

 Merry Hill http://wavespace.waverider.co.uk/~merryh/Pages/frame.html

65 Tourist industry

In this section of the book you will investigate the following things:
- Why has the tourist industry become more important?
- What makes an area a good tourist destination?
- How have the destinations of tourists changed?

Tourism is when people visit other places for enjoyment. This could be a holiday for a few days or weeks, but must include an overnight stay. Tourism has become a very important **tertiary** industry. World–wide, there are around 635 million international tourist visits each year, and this number is increasing (Fig 1). Twenty-five million visits are made to the UK. Tourists visiting the UK spend an estimated £14 billion, which benefits the economy.

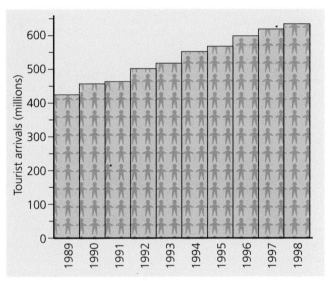

▲ **Fig 1** Growth of world-wide tourism.

The tourist industry has become more important since the 1950s. This is because of changes in the way people live and work. Working conditions have improved: wages have gone up, the number of hours worked have gone down and many people are allowed paid holiday from work. Holidays have become cheaper, and most people now expect to have some sort of break each year.

Q1 What is tourism?

Q2 Use Fig 1 to describe the growth in international tourism since 1989.

Tourist destinations

Tourist destinations are places which are attractive to tourists. Places may be attractive for different reasons.

Climate Places which are hot and dry make popular tourist destinations for people who want to relax in the sun. In the winter, many mountainous areas with reliable snowfall have become ski resorts.

Scenery Sightseeing is a favourite tourist activity. Tourists enjoy seeing spectacular natural landforms, such as mountains, lakes and waterfalls.

Culture Some people like to experience a different culture on holiday. Places which have an interesting history, special buildings, tasty food and drink or a good nightlife may become tourist destinations.

Q3 Describe a tourist destination you have visited, using the headings Climate, Scenery and Culture.

 Virtual tourist http://www.vtourist.com/

Changing destinations

Tourism in the UK took off in the 1800s. People who were wealthy enough visited seaside towns such as Blackpool (Fig 2). Unfortunately, the unreliable British weather ruined many holidays. During the 1970s the price of air travel fell. **Package holidays** to the warm and dry Mediterranean coast became very popular. Package holidays include flights, hotels and food. As more people began to travel abroad for their holidays the UK resorts declined. Meanwhile, tourism on the Mediterranean coast exploded. Fishing villages in countries such as Portugal, Spain and Greece were taken over by huge concrete hotels (Fig 3).

▲ **Fig 2** Blackpool.

▲ **Fig 3** Benidorm, Spain.

By the 1980s many Mediterranean destinations had become over-crowded. Their original beauty and culture had disappeared. People began to look for new unspoilt places to visit. Many Mediterranean resorts began to decline. Today, destinations such as the USA, Mexico and China have become popular (Fig 4). However, the tourist industry is always on the look out for new places to develop.

Country	Number of visitors 1998 (millions)
France	70.0
Spain	47.7
USA	46.4
Italy	34.8
UK	25.7
China	25.0
Mexico	19.8
Canada	18.8
Poland	18.8
Austria	17.4

▲ **Fig 4** Top ten tourist destinations.

Q4 Which country is the most popular tourist destination?

Key words

package holiday – a holiday including travel, hotel and food
tertiary – a service industry
tourism – a holiday with at least one overnight stay

SUMMARY

- Tourism has become a very important tertiary industry.
- Changes in work and lifestyle mean more people go on holiday.
- Climate, scenery and culture are important factors in tourist destinations.
- The popularity of tourist destinations changes over time.

SUMMARY activity

Carry out a survey to find out where people have been on holiday. Mark the destinations on a map. Which areas are the most popular?

66 Tourism in Kenya

In this section of the book you will investigate the following things:
- Why has tourism developed in Kenya?
- What benefits has tourism brought to Kenya?
- What disadvantages has tourism brought to Kenya?

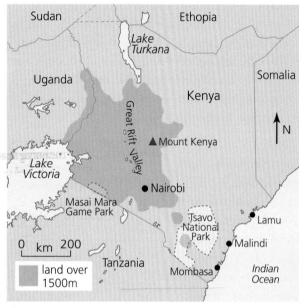

▲ **Fig 1** Kenya.

Kenya is a country in East Africa. It is a poor country and the standard of living for many Kenyans is very low compared with that of people in countries like the UK. The Kenyan government have invested in tourism as a way of earning money for the country. Kenya has a lot to offer tourists. It has a long coastline on the Indian Ocean. The beaches are made of white coral sand and are backed by palm trees. Tourists can enjoy sunbathing, swimming and snorkelling above the coral reefs.

Inland, Kenya has large areas of **savanna** grassland (unit 35) which are home to many different species of wildlife. The government has made over 50 of these areas into National Parks or Game Reserves where the wildlife is protected. Tourists are able to visit these areas on **safaris**. A safari involves driving around a game reserve in search of wildlife. Tourists like to take photographs of the animals, especially the 'big five': lions, elephants, rhinos, giraffes and leopards (Fig 2).

▲ **Fig 2** Kenyan wildlife.

Q1 Draw a map of Kenya. Label it to show its advantages for tourism.

Q2 Use the data in Fig 3 to draw a climate graph for Kenya.

	Jan	Feb	Mar	Apr	May	Jun	Jul	Aug	Sep	Oct	Nov	Dec
Temperature (°C)	27	28	28	26	25	24	23	23	26	27	25	25
Rainfall (mm)	49	36	85	153	126	32	13	18	21	48	132	75

▲ **Fig 3** Climate statistics for Nairobi, Kenya.

 Kenya tourism http://www.seekenya.com/

Benefits

Tourism has benefited Kenya in a number of ways. The tourist industry provides many Kenyans with jobs. Around 180 000 Kenyans are employed in hotels, restaurants and as guides. Another 380 000 Kenyans make a living by selling things to tourists or by supplying hotels with food. The money earned by the tourist industry is taxed by the government. These taxes are used to invest in things such as industry, schools and hospitals. In this way, the standard of living for Kenyan people can be improved.

Q3 List three ways tourism has been good for Kenya.

Problems

The rapid growth of tourism in Kenya has led to problems and conflicts. At the coast near Mombassa a National Maritime Park has been created. This means that local fishermen can no longer fish in the area. At the same time, many beaches have been privatised. Women are no longer allowed on the beaches to collect crabs. Villagers have had to move as their land was taken for hotels. Tourists are damaging the environment they have come to see. The **coral** reefs are dying because many tourist boats drop their anchors on the coral, and allow tourists to walk on the coral reefs.

In the Game Reserves, the local Maasai people have been forced to leave by the government. Traditionally the Maasai were **nomadic** herdsmen who tended cattle. Today many Maasai have either migrated to the slums in the capital, Nairobi, or have become tourist attractions. Tourists pay to see Maasai singing and dancing. The Game Reserves have also suffered soil erosion. The number of animals has increased and the land has been over-grazed leaving bare soil. Tourist vans have churned up the bare soil, and it has been blown away causing dust storms.

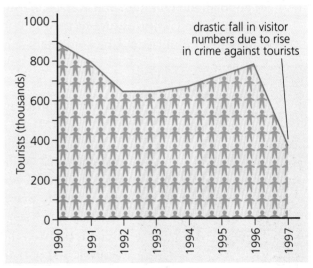

▲ *Fig 4* Number of tourists visiting Kenya.

drastic fall in visitor numbers due to rise in crime against tourists

Q4 Give three ways tourism has been bad for Kenya.

Key words

coral – underwater reefs made of tiny sea creatures

nomads – people who move from place to place

safari – a wildlife tracking holiday in the savanna

savanna – an area of tropical grassland

SUMMARY

■ Kenya needs tourism in order to develop.

■ Tourism has increased the amount of money earned by Kenya.

■ Tourism has damaged Kenya's environment.

■ There are conflicts between the tourist industry and Kenyan people.

SUMMARY activity

🖥 *Tourism in Kenya has caused many problems. Design and write a 'code of conduct' for tourists who visit Kenya.*

 Tourism concern http://www.gn.apc.org/tourismconcern/

67 Development

In this section of the book you will investigate the following things:
- What is development?
- What are MEDCs?
- What are LEDCs?

All the countries in the world are trying to increase their wealth. As people earn more money they are able to afford more things, and their standard of living improves. This process of countries becoming richer is known as 'development'. Not all countries are developing at the same rate, and the gap between the rich and poor is growing. Some countries have become very rich, while other countries remain very poor. The richer countries have only 20% of the world's population, but own 80% of the world's wealth. This means that the world's wealth is distributed very unevenly.

One way of measuring the wealth of a country is its Gross Domestic Product **(GDP)**. This is the total amount of money earned by a country, divided by its population. This gives the average amount of money per person. GDP is always written as US dollars, so that different countries can be compared.

Q1 What is development?

▲ **Fig 1** Housing in the UK.

MEDCs

Richer countries are described as More Economically Developed Countries **(MEDCs)**. MEDCs have well developed industries, often based on high-technology. Farming is for profit and uses machines and chemicals. MEDCs have many service industries, because people have spare money to spend on luxuries and entertainment. Children are entitled to free education and almost everyone can read and write. People have plenty to eat, in fact many are overweight. Clean water is supplied directly to people's homes. Healthcare is easily available and of high quality (Fig 1).

LEDCs

Poorer countries are described as Less Economically Developed Countries **(LEDCs)**. Industries in LEDCs tend to be primary, such as mining and farming. Manufacturing industry uses old machinery and has lots of workers. Many people are farmers who grow only enough food for themselves. Service industries are not well developed because people have little spare money. Not all children go to school, and fewer girls are educated. Education may not be free for all. People do not have enough to eat and are under-nourished. Millions do not have access to a safe water supply. There are too few doctors and hospitals (Fig 2).

Q2 Why are these descriptions of MEDCs and LEDCs too general?

▲ **Fig 2** Delhi slums.

United Nations Development Programme http://www.undp.org/indexalt.html

The North-South divide

In 1980 a report on world development found that most MEDCs were found in the north, and most LEDCs in the south. A line was drawn on a world map dividing the richer and poorer countries (Fig 4).

In reality, it is very difficult to divide countries into either rich or poor. Many countries come somewhere in the middle. Of course, there are also huge differences within countries. In the UK some people are millionaires, while others live on the streets.

- 1.3 billion people live on less than $1 (US) a day
- 1 billion people cannot read or write
- 840 million people do not have enough food
- 1.2 billion people do not have a safe water supply
- 500 000 women in poorer countries die each year giving birth

▲ **Fig 3** World development facts.

Q3 Name four areas in the 'rich' North, and five areas in the 'poor' South.

Q4 Which 'rich' country does not fit the North-South pattern?

▼ **Fig 4** North-South development divide.

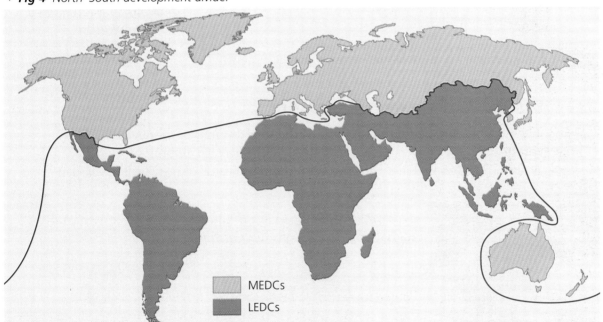

MEDCs
LEDCs

Key words

GDP – Gross Domestic Product
LEDC – Less Economically Developed Country
MEDC – More Economically Developed Country

SUMMARY

- Development is the process of becoming richer.
- The world's wealth is shared out very unevenly.
- Most MEDCs are in the North.
- Most LEDCs are in the South.
- Differences in wealth also exist within countries.

SUMMARY activity

Use the data on pages 234–5 to draw a shaded map showing the GDP for a range of countries. How does your map compare with Fig 4?

 One World http://www.oneworld.org/

68 Measuring development

In this section of the book you will investigate the following things:

- How can development be measured?
- What is the difference between social and economic development?
- What are the links between social and economic development?
- What are the problems with measuring development?

Development is very difficult to measure because it involves so many different things. A simple way of measuring development is to work out the **Gross Domestic Product (GDP)** for a country. This gives an idea of how wealthy the country is. It is an **economic** indicator of development. However, development is about much more than money. It is also about improving standards of living. Standards of living can be measured by looking at things like education, healthcare and life expectancy. These are indicators of **social** development (Fig 1). It is best to measure development by looking at economic and social indicators together.

- Infant mortality rate
- Calorie intake
- Energy consumption
- Number of people per doctor
- Access to safe water
- Number of children per woman

▲ ***Fig 1*** *Social indicators of development.*

Q1 Give three examples of social indicators of development.

Gross Domestic Product

The Gross Domestic Product (GDP) is the total amount of money earned by a country, divided by its population. This gives the average amount of money available per person. GDP can be a very useful indicator of how well developed

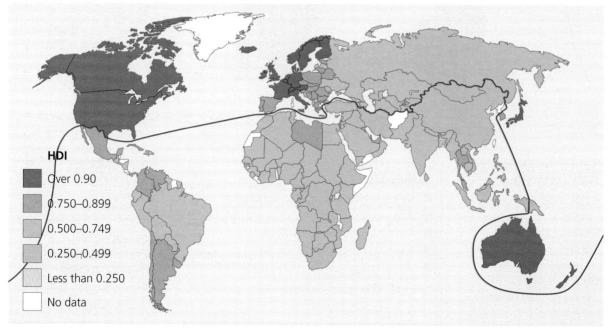

HDI
Over 0.90
0.750–0.899
0.500–0.749
0.250–0.499
Less than 0.250
No data

▲ ***Fig 2*** *Human development index (HDI).*

United Nations – Country at a glance
http://www.un.org/Pubs/CyberSchoolBus/information/e_glance.htm

a country is. For example, the GDP of the UK is $20 730 per year, and the GDP of India is $1670 per year. This suggests that people in the UK are much richer than people in India. In reality, it is not that simple. The cost of living is much cheaper in India compared with the UK. The cost of a meal in a restaurant in India can be less than £1.00. GDP also ignores standards of living.

Human Development Index

The **Human Development Index (HDI)** was created by the United Nations Development Programme (UNDP) in 1990 (Fig 2). The HDI is a way of measuring development which includes economic and social indicators. The HDI measures three indicators:

- income per person – adjusted for the cost of living
- education – percentage of adults who can read and write, and average number of years in education
- life expectancy.

These three indicators are added together, and worked out as a score between 0 and 1. The closer to 1, the higher the level of development (Fig 3). The HDI for the UK is 0.918. The HDI gives a better picture of development than GDP or social indicators alone.

Top		HDI
1	Canada	0.932
2	Norway	0.927
3	USA	0.927
4	Japan	0.924
5	Belgium	0.923

170	Burundi	0.324
171	Burkina Faso	0.304
172	Ethiopia	0.298
172	Niger	0.298
174	Sierra Leone	0.254
Bottom		

Q2 What is the HDI?

▲ *Fig 3* *The most and least developed countries.*

Links

Many of the development indicators are linked. Relationships can be shown using a scatter graph. Fig 4 shows how GDP can affect the number of people per doctor. The higher the GDP, the fewer people per doctor.

Q3 Why do you think countries with a low GDP have a large number of people per doctor?

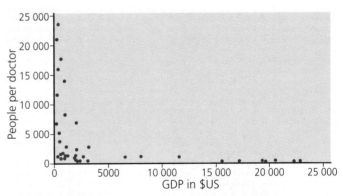

▲ *Fig 4* *Scattergraph to show relationship between GDP and number of people per doctor.*

Key words

economic – to do with money
GDP – Gross Domestic Product
HDI – Human Development Index
social – to do with people

SUMMARY

- Development can be measured using economic and social indicators.
- It is more accurate to use a combination of both social and economic factors.
- Measurements of development hide variations within countries.
- Economic and social development are closely linked.

SUMMARY ☞
activity

💻 *Use the data on pages 234–5 to draw scatter graphs to investigate relationships between development indicators. Try to describe and explain your findings.*

69 Obstacles to development

In this section of the book you will investigate the following things:
- Why have some countries developed more slowly than others?
- What is the cycle of poverty?

Although a small number of countries have become rich, the majority of people in the world live in countries that are poor. This is because the rich countries have advantages which make it easier for them to develop quickly. The poor countries have many problems which have slowed down their development. Some of the key problems faced by LEDCs are rapid population growth, debt and poor health.

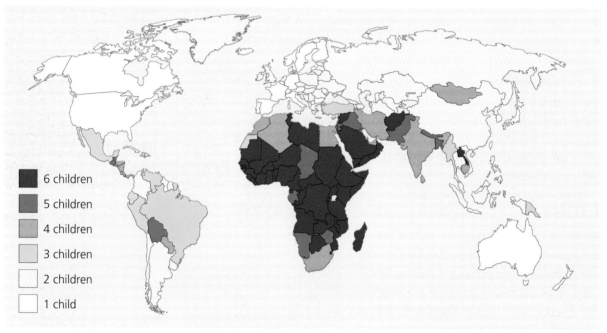

6 children
5 children
4 children
3 children
2 children
1 child

▲ *Fig 1* *Average family size.*

Population growth

Countries in Asia, South America and Africa have rapidly growing populations. People choose to have lots of children because they are poor. Children are useful to poor parents because they are able to help them with work, and may earn money for the family. In countries without pension schemes, children are needed to look after their parents in old age. It makes sense to have several children when healthcare is poor and some may not survive childhood. However, having more children puts pressure on schools and hospitals. More food needs to be grown to feed them. This means having more children can cancel out any development.

Q1 Why does having lots of children make development difficult?

Q2 Describe the pattern of births shown in Fig 1.

 UN Cyber School Bus http://www.un.org/Pubs/CyberSchoolBus/index.html

Debt

During the 1970s the richer countries had plenty of spare money. They lent it to poorer countries so they could invest in development projects. But, in the 1980s **interest** rates rose and the world's economy slowed down. The debts became too expensive and today over 50 countries are still struggling to pay. Some countries spend a third of their GDP just on loan repayments. As long as poor countries have to pay back their loans, they will not have enough money to invest in their own countries. Campaigners are now calling for the debts to be cancelled.

> **Q3** How did the poorer countries get into debt?

Health

Disease causes huge problems for poorer countries. Diseases such as **malaria** and, more recently, **AIDS** are affecting large numbers of people. Malaria, which is passed on by mosquitoes, kills around two million people each year. It is estimated that each year 1 400 000 people in Sub-Saharan Africa are infected with the AIDS virus. Also, a lack of clean water puts people at risk from disease (Fig 2). Up to 25 000 people die each day from diseases caused by dirty water. Disease and illness mean that people are unable to work. This means the country as a whole is earning less money, which makes it hard to develop.

▲ **Fig 2** *Not having access to safe water makes development difficult.*

Cycle of poverty

Many poor countries have now become trapped in the 'cycle of poverty' (Fig 3). They do not have enough money to invest in development. This means they are slow to develop. Their lack of development means they do not have enough money.

Less Economically Developed Country

few manufactured exports, many people cannot read and write, illness

not enough money to invest in industries, schools and hospitals

lack of industry, poor education and healthcare

▶ **Fig 3** *The cycle of poverty.*

Key words

AIDS – a disease transmitted by sexual contact, or infected blood

interest – money charged as a percentage of original loan

malaria – a disease transmitted by mosquitoes

SUMMARY

■ Countries with high birth rates tend to be poor.

■ Many poorer countries owe money to richer countries.

■ Disease and poor healthcare limits development.

■ Many poorer countries are locked into a cycle of poverty.

SUMMARY activity

Draw a 'cycle of poverty' diagram to show how poor health makes development difficult. What could be done to break the cycle?

70 Development in the UK

In this section of the book you will investigate the following things:
- How developed is the UK?
- What differences in wealth and standards of living can be identified?
- Why are there differences in wealth and standards of living?

	Average wages per week (£)	Average house prices (£)	Unemployment rates (%)
North-East	315	51 300	8.4
North-West	331	58 100	5.1
Yorkshire and Humberside	317	57 400	6.6
East Midlands	315	59 800	5.0
West Midlands	322	64 600	5.6
Eastern	348	74 300	4.7
London	464	94 700	6.7
South-East	367	88 300	3.7
South-West	329	68 400	4.4
Wales	317	55 400	6.4
Scotland	325	57 500	6.4
Northern Ireland	310	47 900	8.2

The UK appears to be a very wealthy country. It is ranked as the tenth most developed country in the world by the United Nations. Of course, not everybody living in the UK is rich and has a high **standard of living**. In fact, 14 million people live below the official '**poverty line**', while the richest 10% of people own half of all the wealth. This means that wealth is shared out very unequally. Wealth and standards of living vary between different areas, and between different groups of people (Fig 1).

◀ **Fig 1** Wealth and living standards in the UK.

Wealth

The highest wages are paid in London and the South-East. In London the average wage is £464 per week, and in the South-East is £367 per week. In contrast the average wage in the North is £315 per week, and in Northern Ireland only £310 per week. These figures seem to show that there is a wealth divide between the north and south of the UK. In reality, there are rich and poor people in both areas. The poorest groups of people are likely to be unemployed single parents, and pensioners (Fig 2). The richest groups of people are likely to be working couples without children. Children are expensive!

▲ **Fig 2** A homeless woman in Oxford.

Q1 Where are the wealthiest areas in the UK?

Q2 Where are the poorest areas in the UK?

 Joseph Rowntree Foundation http://www.jrf.org.uk/

Health and standard of living

The amount of money people have has a large impact on their health and standard of living. The poor are more likely to suffer from obesity and depression. They are also more likely to die in childhood, or to die early when they are adults. For example, the death rate of young boys is eight times higher in Manchester than Dorset. The poorest households are twice as likely to be burgled than average, and are likely to be more isolated because they do not have cars. Children from poor backgrounds are less likely to go on to further education.

Reasons

The poorest regions tend to be in areas where traditional industries, such as iron and steel, have closed down. When the factories closed, many people became unemployed and poverty increased. Modern industries have tended to locate in the south of the country. As a result, average wages and standards of living are higher in the south. Many reports have shown that health is closely linked to income. People earning high wages are able to afford healthy diets with plenty of fresh fruit and vegetables. Often, people on low wages are forced to buy cheaper, but less healthy, processed food.

Q3 How can poverty affect health?

Q4 Read the two opinions on poverty in Fig 3. What is your opinion on poverty in the UK?

I don't think people in developed nations are actually poor, they are only relatively poor to their richer countrymen. Try living in one of the Third World slum areas for a day and then start discussing about rich and poor.

Peddu, India

People who think there is no real poverty here in the UK must be going about with their eyes shut. To have a civilised country, we need to care about people experiencing hardship. I have been unemployed and believe me, living on benefit is not easy at all. The problem with Britain today is the greed of the rich and their arrogant attitude about it.

Peter, England

▲ **Fig 3** Two views about poverty in the UK.

Key words

poverty line – a very low level of income
standard of living – the quality of life

SUMMARY

- Compared with other countries, the UK is very rich.
- Wealth within the UK is not shared equally.
- The South tends to be better-off than the North.
- The poorest groups tend to be the elderly and single parents.
- Poverty and health are closely linked.

SUMMARY activity

Use the data in Fig 1 to draw some shaded maps to show the differences in wealth and standard of living in the UK. What do your maps show?

Government Statistical Service http://www.statistics.gov.uk/

71 Negative impacts of development

In this section of the book you will investigate the following things:
- What are the impacts of development on the environment?
- What are the impacts of development on health?
- What are the impacts of development on culture?

Development makes people richer and improves their standard of living. The more money people have, the more goods and services they can buy. This means that for most people development is a very good thing. But as well as doing good, development can do harm. Development can have negative effects on the natural environment, on health and on traditional culture.

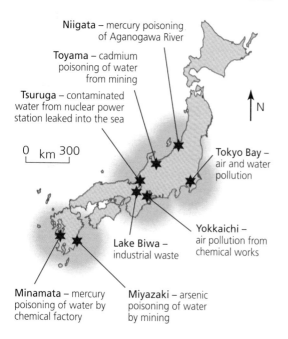

Niigata – mercury poisoning of Aganogawa River

Toyama – cadmium poisoning of water from mining

Tsuruga – contaminated water from nuclear power station leaked into the sea

0　km　300

N

Tokyo Bay – air and water pollution

Yokkaichi – air pollution from chemical works

Lake Biwa – industrial waste

Minamata – mercury poisoning of water by chemical factory

Miyazaki – arsenic poisoning of water by mining

▲ **Fig 1** *Industrial pollution in Japan.*

Environment

Development increases the pressure on the natural environment. As industries develop, more raw materials are needed. The extraction or collection of raw materials can cause environmental damage. For example, the demand for timber is causing deforestation of the rainforests, and the demand for minerals means large areas of land are being dug up. Factories, which process the raw materials and manufacture goods, produce waste. This waste may be released into the water, or air, causing pollution (Fig 1). As the world's poorer countries develop, and become richer, the demand for **resources** is going to increase. At the same time, **pollution** will become an even greater problem.

> **Q1** How did development affect the environment in Japan?

Health

Development brings improvements in diet and healthcare. People can afford to buy more food, and the number of doctors and hospitals increase. As a result, people become healthier and live longer. However, some groups of people in richer countries are becoming less healthy. Recent studies show that the number of obese people in the USA, Japan and the UK have doubled since 1982 (Fig 2). In the USA, one third of the population are now obese. **Obesity** is linked to heart disease and other health problems.

> **Q2** Why does development make some people less healthy?
>
> **Q3** What does Fig 2 tell us about the health of the UK population?

	1980	1991	1994	1996
Men (% of population)	6.0	12.7	13.2	16.4
Women (% of population)	8.0	15.0	16.0	18.4

▲ **Fig 2** *Obesity in the UK.*

 McDonalds http://www.mcdonalds.com/

The growth in obesity and heart disease has been caused by changes in diet and lifestyle. Much of the processed food in richer countries is high in salt, sugar and fat. Also, many jobs are now in offices meaning people do not get enough exercise.

Culture

Development can also bring cultural changes. As more people buy televisions they are able to see what life appears to be like in richer countries. This can affect the way people think and behave. For example, the most popular TV programme in the world is the American show, 'Baywatch'. 'Baywatch' is broadcast in 78 countries, and watched by around one billion people (Fig 3). Watching programmes like 'Baywatch' may encourage people to adopt American culture. American products such as Coca Cola and McDonalds hamburgers have become status symbols. People have abandoned their traditional dress in favour of jeans. Some countries, such as India, are fighting to keep their own **culture**. They prefer to broadcast Indian television programmes, and have not yet allowed a McDonald's restaurant to be built!

Q4 Name ten countries where 'Baywatch' is watched.

▼ **Fig 3** Countries where 'Baywatch' is broadcast.

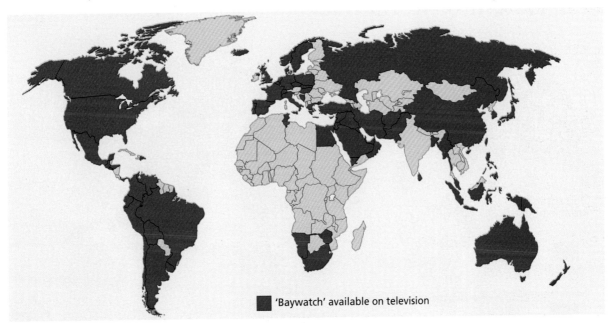

■ 'Baywatch' available on television

Key words

culture – way of life including language, dress, food etc.
obesity – significantly overweight
pollution – damage to the environment
resources – natural products used by people

SUMMARY

- Development has both positive and negative effects.
- Uncontrolled development can damage the environment.
- People in richer countries are more likely to be obese.
- Development can change traditions and cultures.

SUMMARY activity

Make a list of the ways that the UK has been affected by American culture. Do you think the effects are good or bad?

 McSpotlight http://www.mcspotlight.org/

72 International trade

In this section of the book you will investigate the following things:
- What is international trade?
- What is the pattern of world trade?
- What are the problems of being dependent on one main export?
- How can fair trade help development?

International trade is the exchange of **goods** and **services** between countries. Trade happens because no country has everything it needs. Countries buy things that they do not have, or things that are cheaper, from other countries. Things that are bought by countries are called **imports**. To pay for their imports, countries have to sell things. The things that they sell are called **exports**. The difference between the cost of the imports and exports is called the 'balance of trade'. If a country exports more than it imports, it makes a profit. Making a profit from trade is very important for development. Profits can be invested in new industries and services such as schools and hospitals.

Q1 What is trade?

Q2 What are imports and exports?

Pattern of world trade

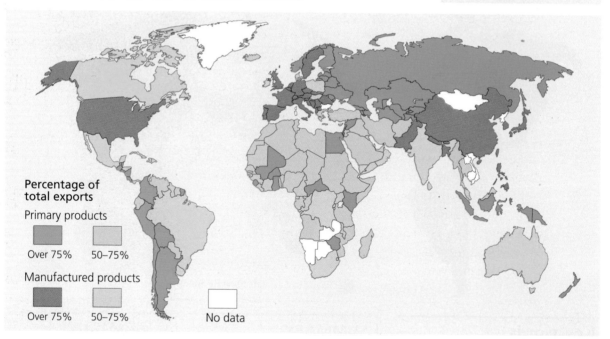

Percentage of total exports

Primary products

Over 75% 50–75%

Manufactured products

Over 75% 50–75% No data

▲ *Fig 1* World exports of primary and manufactured goods.

Trade is not always fair. The richer countries make much more money from trade than the poorer countries (Fig 1). One reason for this is that poorer countries tend to export raw materials, while the richer countries export manufactured goods. Raw materials are things such as crops, timber and metal ores. The price of raw materials is much lower than the price of manufactured **goods**. This means the poorer countries make less money. Because they make less money it is difficult for them to afford to buy manufactured goods from richer countries. Many poorer countries are now in debt to the richer countries.

 World Trade Organisation http://www.wto.org/

Problems

Some of the world's poorest countries rely on exporting only one or two raw materials (Fig 2). This makes it very hard for them to develop for a number of reasons:

- The price of raw materials has fallen compared with the price of manufactured goods. This means poorer countries can afford to buy less of the things they need.

- The price of raw materials can go up or down very quickly. If there is a **surplus** the price can fall, and the poorer countries earn even less.

- Obtaining raw materials can damage the environment. For example, many poorer countries are cutting down their forests to sell the trees as timber.

Country	Product	Percentage of exports
Nigeria	Oil	99%
Cuba	Sugar	77%
Ghana	Cocoa	80%
Zambia	Copper	87%
Botswana	Diamonds	52%
Uganda	Coffee	75%

▲ **Fig 2** *Countries that depend on one main export.*

Q3 Draw a pie chart to show where the money for a bar of chocolate goes.

Fair trade

► **Fig 3** *The cost of chocolate.*

Many of the products that we take for granted, such as tea, coffee and chocolate, come from poorer countries. These products are quite expensive in the UK, but the people who supply the raw materials only earn a small amount of money. Most of the profit is made by the manufacturers and shops (Fig 3).

Fair trade is a way of doing business that makes sure the people who produce the raw materials earn a fair wage. It also ensures safer working conditions and limits the work done by children. A number of companies, such as the Body Shop and Co-Op, now sell 'Fairtrade' products. Although 'Fairtrade' products may be a little more expensive, buying them ensures that the lives of people in poorer countries become better.

cocoa farmer **8p**
transport **10p**
other ingredients **5p**
manufacturer **34p**
retailer **28p**
tax **15p**

Total cost **100p**

Q4 What is fair trade?

Key words

exports – things which are sold to another country

goods – raw materials and manufactured products

imports – things which are bought by another country

services – supply of information or expertise

surplus – producing more of something than is needed

SUMMARY

- Trade is the exchange of goods and services between countries.
- The pattern of world trade is very unequal.
- Countries which rely on one or two raw materials find it very difficult to develop.
- Fair trade ensures improvements in standards of living for people in poorer countries.

SUMMARY *activity*

Write a letter to your local supermarket asking them about their policy on stocking 'fairtrade' products. Include your opinion about fair trade.

Fair Trade http://www.fairtrade.org.uk/

73 Transnational companies

In this section of the book you will investigate the following things:
- What are transnational companies?
- What advantages do they bring?
- What disadvantages do they bring?

The world's largest industries are called transnational companies (**TNCs**). TNCs have offices, factories, mines and plantations in many different countries. The largest TNCs are American, Japanese and European companies (Fig 1). General Motors, the largest TNC, is an American car manufacturer. Worldwide, General Motors employs over 600 000 people. In 1997, it made a profit of 6.7 billion US dollars. This is more than the **GDP** of many poorer countries. The huge amount of money earned by TNCs make them very powerful.

1	General Motors	US
2	Ford	US
3	Mitsui	Japan
4	Mitsubishi	Japan
5	Shell	UK/Netherlands
6	Itochu	Japan
7	Exxon	US
8	Wall-Mart	US
9	Marubeni	Japan
10	Sumitomo	Japan

▲ **Fig 1** The world's largest transnational companies.

TNCs locate anywhere they can make a **profit**. Many of their factories, mines and plantations are in poorer countries. People in poorer countries will work for less money, and this means more profit for the TNCs. TNCs are managed from their head offices, usually in richer countries.

Q1 What is a transnational company?

Q2 Why do transnational companies locate in many countries?

Nike

Nike is an American transnational company, which sells athletic footwear and clothing. The footwear is designed in the USA, but is made in China, Thailand, Malaysia, Vietnam and Indonesia (Fig 2). Wages in these countries are much lower than in the USA or Europe.

■ Nike goods manufactured

▲ **Fig 2** Countries where Nike goods are manufactured.

In recent years, Nike has been accused of **exploiting** workers in poorer countries. Charities have campaigned for Nike to improve working conditions in its factories. In Indonesia, workers went on strike, and there were protests against low wages (Fig 3). As a result Nike has taken steps to make factories safer. Nike has also increased the wages of its workers.

▲ **Fig 3** Indonesian protesters.

 Nike http://www.nikebiz.com

Q3 What is Nike?

Q4 How has Nike improved conditions for its factory workers?

Indonesia

Indonesia is a country in South-east Asia. Indonesia has developed rapidly over the last decade, but many of its people are still poor. Transnational companies are attracted to Indonesia because it has a large workforce who will work hard for low wages. At the same time, the Indonesian government welcomes transnational companies because they benefit the country in several ways.

- Factories provide work for local people. The money they earn has improved their standard of living.
- Wages spent by factory workers benefit local businesses.
- Workers can learn technical skills which they can use if they want to find another job.
- Taxes are paid to the Indonesian government. The government can use the taxes to improve services such as schools and hospitals.

However, there are also disadvantages with transnational companies.

- Most of the profit goes to the company shareholders in the richer countries.
- Many jobs are boring and do not involve any skill. Workers may be punished for making mistakes.
- Health and safety regulations may be ignored.
- Working conditions can be very poor: 6-day weeks and 12-hour shifts, plus overtime are normal.
- The products are too expensive for local people to buy.
- TNCs may not protect the environment because it is not their country.

Q5 Survey your friends to find out where their sports shoes and clothes were manufactured.

Country	Hourly wage (£)
Bangladesh	0.07
China	0.29
France	5.20
Germany	15.46
India	0.17
Indonesia	0.22
Italy	9.33
Thailand	0.10
UK	4.92
USA	6.37

▲ **Fig 4** Average hourly wages of spoprtswear factory workers.

Key words

exploit – take advantage of workers for financial gain
GDP – Gross Domestic Product; the total amount of money earned by a country
profit – the money made by a company
TNC – transnational company

SUMMARY

- TNCs have branches in several countries.
- TNCs locate wherever they can make the most profit.
- TNCs bring both advantages and disadvantages to poorer countries.

SUMMARY activity

Use the data in Fig 4 to draw a graph showing the wages of factory workers in different countries.

 Global Exchange http://www.globalexchange.org/economy/corporations/nike/

74 Newly Industrialised Countries

In this section of the book you will investigate the following things:

■ What are Newly Industrialised Countries (NICs)?
■ How did South Korea become a NIC?
■ What problems has rapid development caused Korea?

A small number of poorer countries have developed very quickly since the 1960s. These countries are no longer poor, but they are not yet as rich as Europe and the USA. Countries which have developed quickly are called **Newly Industrialised Countries (NICs)**. Most NICs are in south Asia (Fig 1). The four NICs which have developed most quickly are Hong Kong, Taiwan, Singapore and South Korea (Fig 2). These four are sometimes called the 'tiger economies'.

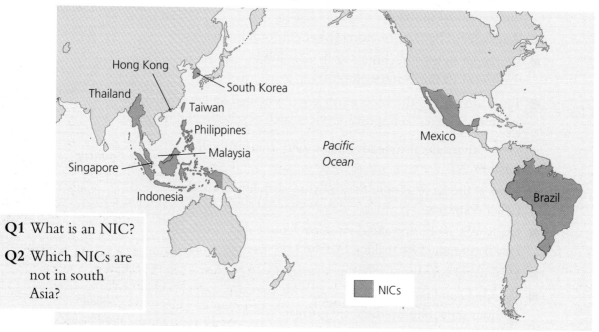

Q1 What is an NIC?

Q2 Which NICs are not in south Asia?

▲ **Fig 1** Newly Industrialised Countries.

South Korea

During the 1950s, most people in South Korea worked as farmers and had a low standard of living. Today, most people work in **manufacturing** or **service industries** (Fig 3) and their standard of living has greatly improved. There are five reasons which explain why South Korea has been able to develop in this way.

■ Labour – people are prepared to work very hard. Twelve hour shifts, for six days a week are normal.

■ Government – the government arranged cheap loans for businesses so they could develop manufacturing industries. They also restricted imports to protect South Korean industries from competition.

■ Education – people are educated to a very high standard. This has made it easier to set up high-tech industries.

Q3 How has education helped South Korea to develop?

 Network Korea http://www.han.com/

- Transport – South Korea is in a good location to export goods by sea.
- Markets – South Korea sells most of its goods to the USA, Japan and Australia.

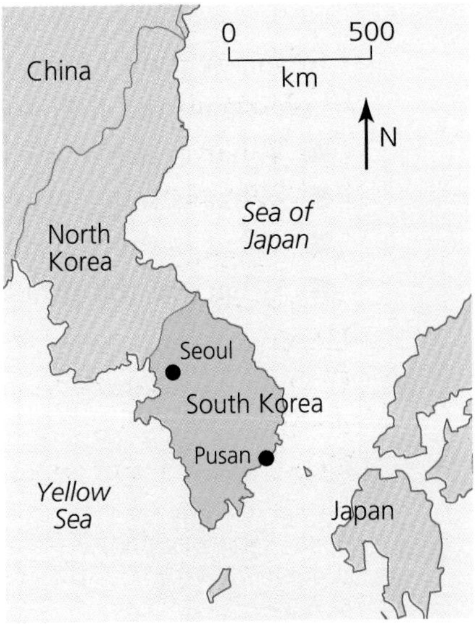

Development

In the 1960s, South Korea began to manufacture goods such as clothes and footwear. This was often for American **transnational companies**, such as Nike. During the 1970s, the profits were invested in developing steel, shipbuilding and chemical industries. These industries were successful and, during the 1980s, profits were invested in developing car and electronics industries (Fig 4). These industries have grown very fast. During the 1990s, several South Korean companies, such as Samsung and Daewoo, began setting up factories in other countries, including the UK.

▲ **Fig 2** South Korea.

Problems

The rapid development of Korea has caused problems. Firstly, waste from factories has damaged the environment. In 1991, a factory making circuit boards released a chemical called phenol into the River Nakhtong. Phenol is very poisonous. The public were very angry and new laws have now been made to protect the environment.

	1950	2000
Primary	66	20
Secondary	6	30
Tertiary	28	50

▲ **Fig 3** Changing employment in South Korea (percentage of workforce).

Secondly, in the late 1990s, there was a financial crisis. Many South Korean industries had borrowed too much money. They had problems paying their debts and many factories had to close. Thousands of people lost their jobs in South Korea, and in factories around the world.

Q4 Describe one problem caused by South Korea's very rapid development.

Daewoo – steel, cars, electronics, ships
Hyundai – cars, excavators, trucks, trains, ships, chemicals
Samsung – electronics, semi-conductors, ships, mobile phones
Lucky Goldstar – computers, electronics, ships

▲ **Fig 4** South Korean transnational companies.

Key words

manufacturing industry – making products used by people
Newly Industrialised Country (NIC) – a country which has recently developed its industry
service industry – providing information or advice
transnational company – company with branches in more than one country

SUMMARY

- Countries which are developing quickly are called Newly Industrialised Countries.
- Most NICs are located in south Asia.
- South Korea has developed by investing in the latest technology.
- Rapid development can cause environmental and economic problems.

SUMMARY activity

Draw a timeline to show how South Korea has developed since the 1950s.

Samsung http://www.samsung.com/

75 Aid

In this section of the book you will investigate the following things:
- What is aid?
- What is long-term aid?
- What is short-term aid?
- What are the problems with aid?

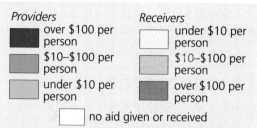

Providers
- over $100 per person
- $10–$100 per person
- under $10 per person

Receivers
- under $10 per person
- $10–$100 per person
- over $100 per person

no aid given or received

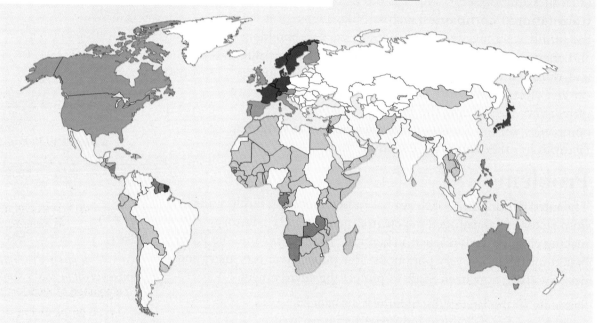

▲ **Fig 1** *Aid providers and receivers.*

Aid is when richer countries help poorer countries (Fig 1). Aid can be either a gift or a loan. It can include money, equipment, training and food. Sometimes aid is given directly from one country to another. In this case it is called **bilateral aid**. Richer countries also give aid through large international organisations, such as the United Nations and World Bank. This type of aid is called **multilateral aid**. A further way aid is given is through charities such as Oxfam or Christian Aid. These charities are also known as **Non Government Organisations (NGOs)**. NGOs raise money from the public, but are also given money by governments.

Q1 What is aid?

Q2 Use Fig 1 to name three countries which give aid, and three countries which receive aid.

How much?

The United Nations suggests that richer countries should give 0.7% of their **Gross National Product (GNP)** in aid each year. GNP is the total amount of money earned by a country each year. Very few countries manage this amount. The most generous are Norway, Denmark and Sweden (Fig 2). The UK gives around £3 billion a year. This is a huge amount of money, but only

 World Bank http://www.worldbank.org/

0.3% of the UK's GNP. The countries which receive the most aid are China, Egypt, Indonesia and India.

USA	0.16%	Canada	0.48%
UK	0.26%	France	0.62%
Japan	0.29%	Sweden	0.83%
Australia	0.32%	Denmark	0.87%
Germany	0.37%	Norway	0.92%

▶ **Fig 2** *Percentage of GNP donated by richer countries.*

Q3 Draw a graph to show the amount of aid given by richer countries.

Long-term aid

Long-term aid involves projects which will have a long-term impact. Long-term aid aims to help countries make better use of their resources. If it is successful, poor countries will become richer and standards of living will improve. Eventually aid will no longer be needed (Fig 3). Long-term aid can focus on a number of areas:

- improving healthcare and family planning;
- providing a safe water supply and sewerage;
- training teachers and building schools;
- providing tools and machinery;
- providing loans for large scale projects such as dams.

'Give a person a fish, and it will feed them for a day. Give them a net in order to fish and it will feed them for a lifetime.'

▲ **Fig 3** *The benefit of long-term aid.*

Short-term aid

Short-term aid is given to help solve immediate problems. Following a natural disaster, such as a flood or earthquake, help is needed very quickly. Lives can be saved by sending food, water, tents, blankets and medical supplies. Short-term aid is also given to refugees who have had to flee because of war. When the emergency is over the aid is withdrawn.

Q4 Explain the saying in Fig 3.

Problems

Although we expect aid to help poorer countries it is not that simple. Donations from richer countries may have strings attached. For example, the poorer country may have to use the money to buy goods from the richer country. Aid is also a loan, rather than a gift. The loan can be difficult to repay. Many large-scale aid projects, such as dams, have not benefited the poorest people living in the countryside. These kind of projects can also damage the environment.

Key words

bilateral aid – aid given directly from one country to another
Gross National Product (GNP) – the total amount of money earned by a country each year
multilateral aid – aid distributed through international organisations.
Non Government Organisation (NGO) – an independent organisation, often a charity

SUMMARY

- Aid is when resources are transferred from richer countries to poorer countries.
- Long-term aid is used to help poorer countries develop.
- Short-term aid saves lives after natural disasters or wars.
- Aid does not always benefit the poorer countries.

SUMMARY activity

Use the 'enquiry method' to research and write a report about the work of an NGO such as Oxfam, or Christian Aid.

Oxfam http://www.oxfam.org.uk/

76 Appropriate aid

In this section of the book you will investigate the following things:
- Why does aid not always benefit the poor?
- What is appropriate aid?
- How is appropriate aid being given in Zimbabwe?

Many **aid** projects in the past have failed to help the people that need them most. Loans have been spent on large-scale projects such as dams, power stations, airports and roads. These projects look impressive, but usually only benefit the better off. In fact some of these projects have made life worse for the poor. The debt repayments mean that less money is being spent on basic services, such as health and education.

Q1 Why do large-scale aid projects not always help the poor?

Appropriate aid

Today, most people believe that small-scale aid projects, which involve local people, are best. **Non Government Organisations (NGOs)** such as Oxfam, work with local people to find out what their needs are. They then help them make the best use of their resources. Projects tend to use simple technology. This means they are cheaper, and there is less to go wrong. Local materials are used where possible. This type of aid is often called '**appropriate technology**'.

Q2 How do NGOs find out the type of aid that is needed?

Q3 What is meant by the term 'appropriate technology'?

Zimbabwe

Zimbabwe is a country in southern Africa (Fig 1). Although some very wealthy people live in Zimbabwe, most of the population is poor. Zimbabwe borrowed money to help it develop, but it is now struggling to pay its debts. As a result, less money is being spent on education, healthcare and on growing food. The charity, Oxfam, has been working in Zimbabwe since 1980.

Q4 Why has the amount of money spent on health and education in Zimbabwe been falling?

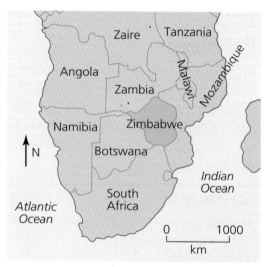

▲ **Fig 1** Zimbabwe.

Mupako nursery

Oxfam helps fund the Mupako nursery in the Masvingo province in south-east Zimbabwe. The Mupako nursery is helping local people in a number of ways. Free seedlings (baby trees) are given to people to plant. These trees help to prevent soil erosion by holding the soil together. Fallen branches can also be used as fuel.

 Oxfam – Cool Planet http://www.oxfam.org.uk/coolplanet/index.html

The nursery is also training people in new farming methods. They teach people to grow crops in 'kidney' shaped beds (Fig 2). The shape of the beds slows down the rainfall which runs over the surface. The water has more time to soak down to the roots. As a result the crops have higher yields.

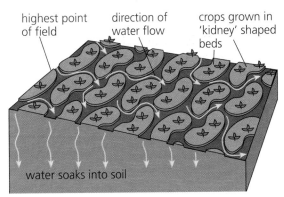

highest point of field | direction of water flow | crops grown in 'kidney' shaped beds

water soaks into soil

▶ *Fig 2* *New farming methods at the Mupako nursery, Zimbabwe.*

▲ *Fig 3* *Baskets for sale in Zimbabwe.*

Gutu basket weavers

In the Gutu district in south-east Zimbabwe, Oxfam is helping women to make a living from weaving baskets. The baskets are made from sisal, a natural fibre, wrapped with thread from re-cycled coloured plastic sacks. Oxfam has paid for an advisor to train the women in new skills, such as book-keeping and marketing. As a result the women are beginning to export their baskets. The money made from selling the baskets allows the women to help support their families (Fig 3).

❝ I am supporting my family from the money I get from it. I am able to buy groceries, pay school fees, buy clothing, and have cash for travelling… When my child becomes educated, it is with money that comes out of a basket.❞

▲ *Fig 4* *Pellagia Rubaya, basket weaver.*

Key words

aid – transfer of resources from richer to poorer countries
appropriate technology – low technology aid based on local situation
Non Government Organisation (NGO) – an independent organisation, often a charity

SUMMARY

- Large-scale aid projects rarely benefit the poorest people.
- NGOs prefer to work with local people to find out what their needs are.
- Appropriate aid uses low technology and local materials.
- Appropriate aid projects are improving standards of living in Zimababwe.

SUMMARY *activity*

☐ *Make a leaflet which could be used to raise money to support the two aid projects in Zimbabwe. Why not try to actually raise some money for these projects or for another appropriate aid project?*

 Christian Aid http://www.christian_aid.org.uk/main.htm

77 Debt

In this section of the book you will investigate the following things:

■ Why are poor countries in debt to rich countries?

■ What are the impacts of being in debt?

■ What is 'Jubilee 2000'?

Country	Debt (billion US$)
1 Nigeria	28.2
2 Vietnam	23.9
3 Ivory Coast	12.4
4 Sudan	10.7
5 Dem. Rep of Congo	9.9
6 Angola	9.3
7 Cameroon	8.1
8 Zambia	6.4
9 Tanzania	6.3
10 Kenya	6.1

▲ **Fig 1** Top ten countries in debt.

Debt is one of the largest problems faced by poorer countries. Altogether, 52 of the world's poorest countries owe $354 **billion**! (Fig 1). This money was lent by the richer countries such as the USA, Japan and the UK in the 1970s. Today the huge debt repayments make it very difficult for poorer countries to develop. Money that could be invested in education and healthcare is instead spent on paying **interest** on the loans. For example, Africa spends four times as much on debt repayments as it does on healthcare. As a result healthcare has become worse. Also fewer people in poorer countries can afford to send their children to school. Fewer children are being educated, which makes it even more difficult for the country to develop.

Q1 What do you notice about the location of the countries which are most in debt?

Q2 How does debt make development more difficult?

The debt crisis

During the 1970s the rich countries had plenty of money. The money was not earning much interest in the banks, so they decided to lend it to poorer countries. The poorer countries spent much of the money on large projects, such as building dams and power stations. These projects often did not help to reduce poverty. During the 1980s the price of raw materials fell. This meant that poorer countries earned less for their products, such as tea, coffee and cotton. At the same time interest rates went up. Poorer countries now had higher debt repayments, but less money to pay them. Most countries have had to borrow more money, to pay the interest on their original debts. They are now trapped in a 'cycle of poverty'.

Q3 Give two reasons which explain why the debt crisis occurred.

▲ **Fig 2**

Jubilee 2000

Jubilee 2000 is an organisation which is campaigning against debt (Fig 2). Jubilee 2000 was launched in the UK in 1994 and now has links with at least 80 organisations in over 40 countries. The organisation is trying to persuade the governments of richer countries to cancel the debts of 52 of the world's poorest countries (Fig 3). Famous people including Bono, Muhammad Ali and the Pope have spoken on behalf of the organisation. Jubilee 2000 argue that it would cost the UK taxpayer only £2 each to cancel all of the debt owed to the UK.

 Jubilee 2000 http://www.jubilee2000uk.org/

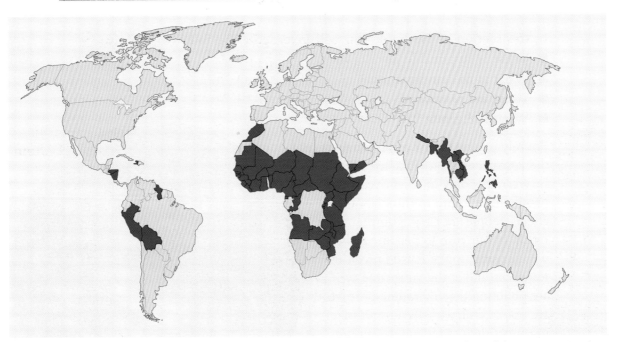

▲ *Fig 3* *Indebted countries included in Jubilee 2000 campaign.*

Progress

The campaign by Jubilee 2000 has had considerable success. During 1999 peaceful protests around the world brought the debt problem to the attention of millions of people. In September 1999, President Clinton announced that the USA would cancel 100% of the debts owed to it by poorer countries. This was followed by the UK government announcing that it would cancel the debt of 26 poorer countries. These 26 countries must first agree to spend the money on reducing poverty. The United Nations have predicted that if all the debts of the poorer countries were cancelled, the lives of 21 million children a year could be saved.

Q4 Why might it be in the interest of richer countries to cancel the debts of poorer countries?

> *Unsustainable debt is helping to keep many poor countries poor, and poor people in poverty.*
>
> President W. Clinton, USA 1999

> *It is no longer a question of people talking about what they are going to do, it is now a question of action.*
>
> Gordon Brown, Chancellor of the Exchequer, UK 1999

▲ *Fig 4* *Progress on debt relief?*

Key words

billion – a thousand million

debt – money owed to someone else

interest – money charged for borrowing money

SUMMARY

- The world's poorest countries are in debt to the world's richest countries.
- Debt repayments make it difficult for poorer countries to develop.
- Jubilee 2000 is an organisation campaigning against debt.
- A number of richer countries have agreed to cancel the debts of poorer countries.

SUMMARY *activity*

Make a list of the things you could do to persuade the governments of richer countries to cancel the debt of poorer countries.

 Netaid http://www.netaid.org/

78 Sustainable development

In this section of the book you will investigate the following things:
- What is sustainable development?
- What is the environment?
- What are resources?
- What is Agenda 21?

We rely on the Earth's **environment**, and the **resources** it provides, for our survival. It is only in recent years that people have begun to think about the effects people are having on the Earth. In our rush to become rich, we are using up the Earth's precious resources, and at the same time we are polluting the environment. If we are not careful, we will run out of resources such as oil and gas within our lifetime, and the consequences of environmental pollution, such as global warming, could be disastrous for millions of people worldwide. If these problems are to be avoided, we need to adopt a policy of '**sustainable development**'. Sustainable development means 'meeting our needs today without compromising the ability of future generations to meet their needs'. In other words, we need to use fewer resources and take more care of the planet.

▲ **Fig 1** The Earth, a limited resource.

Q1 What is meant by the term 'sustainable development'?

The environment

The environment is the land, the air, the water and the living organisms of the Earth (Fig 2). All four areas of the environment are at risk from misuse by people. Twenty per cent of the land is at risk from **desertification** and **salinisation**. The air is being polluted, causing global warming, acid rain and ozone layer damage. The seas, rivers and lakes are being polluted with chemicals. A quarter of all species of plants and animals are at risk of extinction.

Q2 What is the environment?

air

people plants animals

water   land

▶ **Fig 2** The environment.

Planet.com http://planet.channel4.com/

156

Resources

Natural resources are things provided by the Earth that people use. Resources can be divided into renewable and non–renewable (Fig 3). Non-renewable resources are in limited supply. Once they have been used up they cannot be replaced. Non-renewable resources include coal, oil, gas and minerals. The rate at which we are using up these resources is increasing.

In contrast, renewable resources should last forever if they are used carefully. Renewable resources include things such as water, trees and soil. Unfortunately, many renewable resources are being used up faster than they can be replaced.

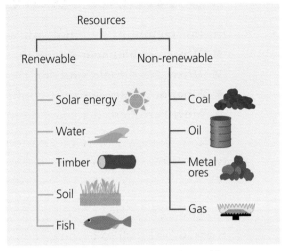

▲ **Fig 3** Renewable and non-renewable resources.

Q3 Give an example of a renewable and a non–renewable resource.

Agenda 21

Many environmental and resource problems are a global concern. For this reason, the governments of 153 countries met at the first 'Earth Summit' in Rio, Brazil, in 1992 (Fig 4). The focus of the summit was to agree how together they could achieve sustainable development.

Q4 What is the aim of Agenda 21?

One of the agreements of the Earth Summit is **Agenda 21**. Agenda 21 states that countries should set out ways to achieve sustainable development at a national and local level. In the UK, every local authority must consider sustainable development in its 'local plan'. Agenda 21 is also intended to encourage individuals to alter their lifestyles to live in a more sustainable way.

- To promote family planning
- To aleviate poverty and meet basic human needs
- To invest in alternative energy sources
- To promote less damaging farming
- To protect habitats and bio-diversity

▲ **Fig 4** The objectives agreed at the Earth Summit, Rio 1992.

Key words

Agenda 21 – sustainable development at local level

desertification – the spread of desert-like conditions

environment – the air, water, land and organisms of the Earth

resources – natural things used by people

salinisation – the build up of salt on the sutface of the soil

sustainable development – development which does not over-exploit resources or damage the environment

SUMMARY

- We depend on the Earth's environment and resources.
- The Earth's resources are being used at an unsustainable rate.
- The environment is being polluted.
- Agenda 21 aims to tackle sustainable development at a local level.

SUMMARY *activity*

Find out what is being done in your local area for Agenda 21. What could you do to live in a more sustainable way?

79 National Parks

In this section of the book you will investigate the following things:

■ What are National Parks?

■ What are the demands on the environment in National Parks?

■ How do these demands conflict?

■ How can these demands be managed?

◀ **Fig 1** National parks.

National Parks

National Parks are large areas of attractive countryside. There are eleven National Parks in England and Wales (Fig 1). National Parks were set up in 1949, to protect our most beautiful areas from uncontrolled development. Each National Park is managed by a **National Park Authority (NPA)**. National Park Authorities have two main jobs:

■ To preserve the beauty of the landscape, and the traditional way of life of people living there.

■ To encourage the public to visit the National Parks for recreation.

The job of the NPAs is difficult because they do not actually own the National Parks. Most of the land is owned by farmers and organisations such as the National Trust and Department of Defence.

Q1 What is a National Park?

Q2 Name the eleven National Parks in England and Wales.

▶ **Fig 2** Yorkshire Dales.

The Yorkshire Dales

The Yorkshire Dales are a National Park in north-east England. The Park is an area of outstanding upland scenery. It contains areas of limestone which form spectacular features such as caves and gorges. As a result over one million people visit the Yorkshire Dales every year. These visitors put pressure on the environment. They also come into conflict with the people who live and work in the National Park.

 Association of National Park Authorities http://www.anpa.gov.uk/

Tourism

Tourism is extremely important in the Yorkshire Dales. People come to sightsee, to walk, to climb or just to visit shops and cafés. Visitors bring money into the area, and many local people make their living from the tourist industry. However, the large number of tourists can cause problems. Many of the roads are winding and narrow. During the summer, traffic congestion can be very bad. In response the NPA has introduced a 'park and ride' scheme. Free guided walks are offered to people who arrive by bus, rather than by car.

Q3 How has the Yorkshire Dales NPA tried to reduce traffic congestion?

Farming

Much of the Yorkshire Dales are used for sheep farming. The farmland, with its dry-stone walls, barns and farmhouses, gives the area much of its character. Some farmers are given grants to farm using traditional methods. Although visitors enjoy the farmland scenery, they can come into conflict with the farmers. Many visitors expect to be able to walk anywhere in the Park, even though the land belongs to the farmers. Farmers complain that visitors trespass across their fields, and forget to shut gates. To help solve this conflict the NPA has clearly signposted the footpaths.

Q4 Why is there a conflict between tourism and farming?

Quarrying

Limestone quarrying is a traditional industry in the Yorkshire Dales. **Quarries** provide valuable jobs for people living in the area. But, quarries can seem very out of place in a National Park. Tourists expect peace and beautiful views. Instead, limestone quarries spoil the view, are noisy and produce clouds of dust. To reduce the impact of the quarries on the environment, they are screened behind trees. When the quarries close down, the company must spend several years restoring the area. Trees are planted and the quarry may be turned into a lake.

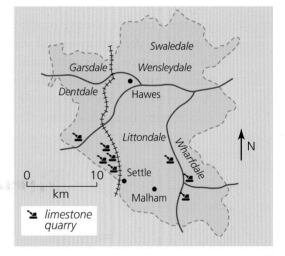

▶ **Fig 3** *Quarrying in the Yorkshire Dales National Park.*

Key words

National Park – an area of outstanding countryside which is protected from development
National Park Authority – people in charge of managing National Parks
quarry – an opencast mine for digging out stone

SUMMARY

- National Parks aim to protect outstanding countryside from development.
- There are many demands placed on National Parks, including farming, tourism and industry.
- The different demands often conflict with each other.
- The National Park Authority is responsible for managing the impacts and conflicts of different users of National Parks.

SUMMARY *activity*

Draw up a table to show the impacts that tourism, farming and quarrying have on the Yorkshire Dales. Divide the impacts into positive and negative.

80 Antarctica

In this section of the book you will investigate the following things:
- **What is Antarctica like?**
- **How is Antarctica managed?**
- **What are the demands on the environment in Antarctica?**
- **How can these demands be managed?**

Antarctica is the large continent at the South Pole. It covers one-tenth of the Earth's surface, making it twice the size of Australia. Antarctica is an ice **desert**. Temperatures in the winter fall to −50°C and winds blow at up to 300 km per hour. Although the amount of snowfall is small, it has built up over millions of years. In places the ice is 5000 metres deep. Because the environment is so hostile people have not settled in Antarctica permanently. This means it remains an unspoilt environment. It has not been affected by people.

- UK
- Chile
- New Zealand
- Argentina
- France
- Australia
- Norway

▲ **Fig 1** Countries with a claim to part of Antarctica.

Q1 Describe Antarctica.

Management

Antarctica is not owned by anybody, although seven countries have claimed parts of it (Fig 1). Instead, Antarctica is managed by international agreements. The first agreement was the Antarctic **Treaty** of 1959. This agreement focused on protecting and conserving the continent and surrounding seas. In 1998 another agreement was signed by 26 countries. This agreement suggested that Antarctica should be declared a World Park. If this happened, it would mean that Antarctica would be safe from development. At the moment, the only people allowed to live in Antarctica are scientists. There are 48 scientific research stations throughout the continent.

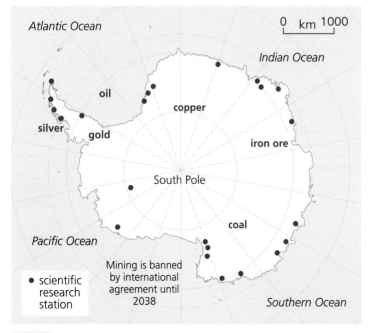

Atlantic Ocean

0 km 1000

Indian Ocean

oil
copper
silver gold
iron ore
South Pole
coal
Pacific Ocean

- scientific research station

Mining is banned by international agreement until 2038

Southern Ocean

Q2 How is Antarctica managed?

Resources

Explorations have shown that beneath Antarctica's ice, there are valuable **resources** (Fig 2). There are reserves of gold, silver, copper, coal and oil. At the moment it would be too difficult, and expensive, to mine the reserves, although, in the future, new technology may make it possible. People are very worried about the huge impacts this would have on the fragile ecosystem.

◄ **Fig 2** Antarctica's resources.

 British Antarctic Survey http://www.nerc-bas.ac.uk/

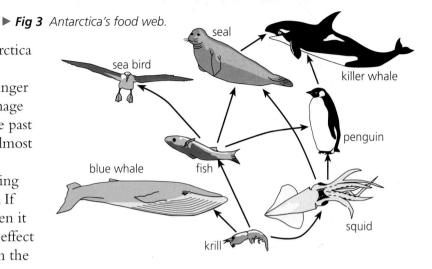

▶ *Fig 3* Antarctica's food web.

The seas around Antarctica are full of marine life. However, there is a danger that fishing could damage the **ecosystem**. In the past whales were hunted almost to extinction. Fishing concentrates on catching krill, a type of shrimp. If too many krill are taken it will have a knock-on effect on the other species in the ecosystem (Fig 3).

Q3 Why might there be pressure to mine Antarctica's resources in the future?

Tourism

The number of tourists visiting Antarctica is increasing (Fig 4). Tourists come to see the spectacular scenery and colonies of seals and penguins. Tourists stay aboard cruise ships and come on land by dinghy or helicopter. Recently, the Australians have made plans to allow tourists to stay in disused research stations. Environmental groups are worried about the impacts the tourists are having on the environment. The tourist season clashes with the wildlife breeding season. Tourists frequently go too close to the wildlife, disturbing them. Trampling of plants has also been a problem. A tourist 'code of conduct' has been written to try to reduce the impact of tourism.

Q4 Why would tourism have more impact on Antarctica if tourists were allowed to stay on land, rather than on ships?

▲ *Fig 4* A tourist in Antarctica.

Key words

desert – area receiving less than 250 mm of precipitation per year
ecosystem – a community of plants and animals living in a particular environment
resources – natural products used by people
treaty – an international agreement

SUMMARY

- Antarctica is the world's largest unspoilt environment.
- Antarctica is not owned by anyone.
- There are thought to be large reserves of resources in Antarctica.
- Tourism is putting pressure on Antarctica's fragile environment.

SUMMARY activity

Draw a map of Antarctica. Label the map to show the impacts that people might have on the continent in the future.

 Virtual Antarctica http://www.terraquest.com/va/index.html

81 Three Gorges Dam

In this section of the book you will investigate the following things:
- What is the Three Gorges Dam project?
- What is its impact on people?
- What is its impact on the economy?
- What is its impact on the environment?

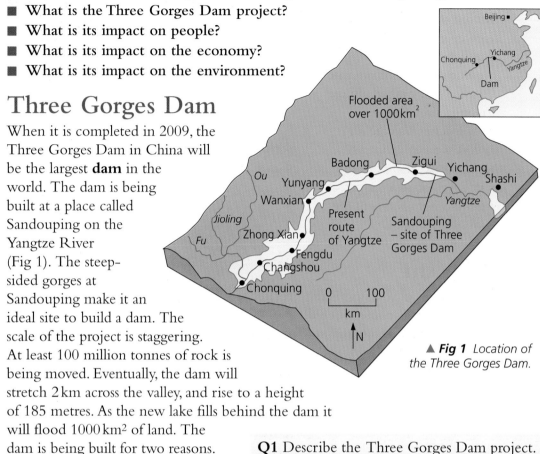

▲ **Fig 1** *Location of the Three Gorges Dam.*

Three Gorges Dam

When it is completed in 2009, the Three Gorges Dam in China will be the largest **dam** in the world. The dam is being built at a place called Sandouping on the Yangtze River (Fig 1). The steep-sided gorges at Sandouping make it an ideal site to build a dam. The scale of the project is staggering. At least 100 million tonnes of rock is being moved. Eventually, the dam will stretch 2 km across the valley, and rise to a height of 185 metres. As the new lake fills behind the dam it will flood 1000 km² of land. The dam is being built for two reasons. Firstly, the dam will prevent flooding downstream. Secondly, it will provide **hydro-electric power**.

Q1 Describe the Three Gorges Dam project.

Q2 Why is Sandouping a good site to build a dam?

People

China's leaders see the Three Gorges Dam as a symbol of the importance of China. If it is successful, the dam will protect ten million people downstream from the threat of flooding. This is an important benefit, because over 300 000 people have died in floods in China this century. Nevertheless, the dam will cause huge problems for the people living upstream. Up to 1.9 million people will lose their homes under water. They have to move to new areas higher up. Higher up it is colder, the slopes are steeper and the soils are poor. It will be much harder to make a living from farming.

Some Chinese people have protested against the dam. Dai Qing spent ten months in prison for writing a book against the dam.

❛ The Three Gorges Dam is the most environmentally-destructive project in the world. ❜

Dai Qing

▲ **Fig 2** *One view on the dam.*

Q3 Why did the Chinese writer Dai Qing spend ten months in prison?

 Three Gorges Dam http://www.nextcity.com/ProbeInternational/ThreeGorges/index.html

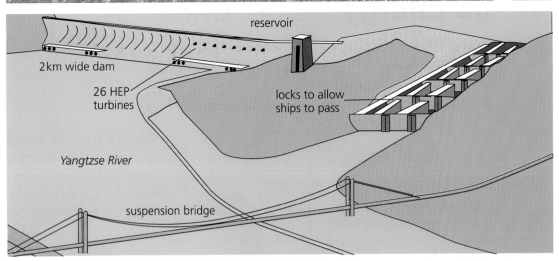

▲ **Fig 3** *An artists view of the dam when completed in 2009.*

Economy

China's economy is growing very fast in the east. Cities such as Shanghai need more and more energy to power its new buildings and industries. The Three Gorges Dam will contain 26 turbines which will generate over 18 000 megawatts of electricity. This will be enough to supply one-tenth of all China's electricity. At the moment, China relies on burning coal to produce most of its electricity. However, campaigners against the dam say this will only be a short-term benefit. Eventually, the **reservoir** will fill up with sediment. As this happens the dam will be able to produce less and less electricity.

Environment

The dam will benefit the environment if China burns less coal to produce electricity. Burning coal contributes to global warming. If global warming causes sea levels to rise, large areas of China's coast would be flooded. Up to 67 million people would have to leave their homes.

Despite this benefit, the dam will have a huge impact on the wildlife of the area. The Yangtze river dolphins, Chinese alligators and Siberian cranes could become extinct as their habitats are destroyed by the dam and reservoir.

Key words

dam – wall built to hold back water

gorge – a steep-sided river valley

hydro-electric power – electricity produced when water is released through turbines in a dam

reservoir – lake behind a dam

SUMMARY

- The Three Gorges Dam will be the largest dam in the world.
- The dam is being built to prevent flooding, and to provide electricity.
- The dam will have huge impacts on the Chinese people, economy and environment.

SUMMARY *activity*

Write two magazine articles about the Three Gorges Dam. One article should be by a Chinese official, who is in favour of the dam. The other should be by a Chinese environmentalist, who is against the dam.

 International Rivers Network – Rivers and Dams http://www.irn.org/basic/basic.shtml

82 Energy

In this section of the book you will investigate the following things:
- What is energy?
- What are the sources of energy?
- How do fossil fuels affect the environment?

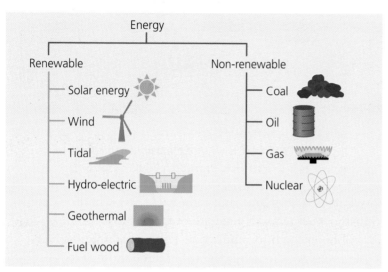

▲ **Fig 1** *Renewable and non-renewable energy sources.*

▼ **Fig 2** *World energy consumption, 1996.*

Oil	40%
Coal	27%
Gas	23%
Nuclear	8%
Hydro-electric	2%

Q1 Use Fig 2 to draw a pie chart to show the breakdown of world energy use.

Q2 What are fossil fuels?

Energy is power. People use energy in many different ways every day. Every time a person turns on a light or starts up a car, energy is being used. Sources of energy can be divided into non-renewable and renewable resources (Fig 1). The main non-renewable energy resources are coal, oil and gas. Coal, oil and gas are called '**fossil fuels**', because they take millions of years to form. Once they have been used up they cannot be replaced. Energy sources which last forever are called 'renewable resources'. **Renewable energy** resources include hydro-electric power, solar energy and wind power. At the moment, 90% of the world's energy comes from fossil fuels.

Coal

Coal is formed from the remains of trees and plants that grew in swamps 300 million years ago. After the trees and plants died, they were covered by layers of **sedimentary rock** (unit 11). Over millions of years, the weight of the rock above compressed the remains together. Eventually the remains turned into coal.

Large reserves of coal are found in areas such as the USA, Australia, South Africa and China. In the past coal was mined in tunnels underground. Today, it is cheaper and easier to dig it straight out of the ground. This method is called **opencast mining** (Fig 3). Most coal is burned in power stations to produce electricity. The known reserves of coal will last for another 300 years.

▲ **Fig 3** *Opencast coal mining.*

Q3 How long would it take for new coal to form?

Oil and gas

Oil and gas usually occur together. They are formed from the remains of tiny sea creatures that lived 200 million years ago. Their remains were buried under layers of sedimentary rock, and eventually turned into oil and gas. Oil and gas are brought to the surface by drilling deep holes through the rock (Fig 4). Huge platforms, called oil rigs, have been built to drill for oil and gas out at sea.

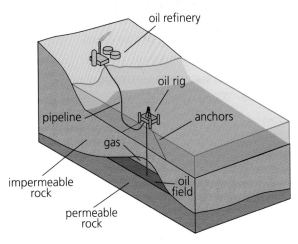

▲ **Fig 4** Drilling for oil.

The largest oil reserves are found in the Middle East, the USA, Russia and in the North Sea. Oil and gas are both burned in power stations to produce electricity. Oil is also refined to make petrol and plastic. The known reserves of oil will last for another 45 years, and gas for another 70 years.

Q4 Why is it important to conserve oil?

Environment

Using fossil fuels damages the environment in a number of ways:

- Opencast mining uses up large areas of countryside. It also causes noise and dust.
- Oil spills at sea kill fish, sea birds and mammals.
- Oil spills on land pollute water supplies and can affect people's heath.
- Burning fossil fuels releases chemicals which cause 'acid rain'. Acid rain kills trees and fish.
- Carbon dioxide is released when fossil fuels are burned. Carbon dioxide is causing 'global warming' (unit 63).

Q5 Draw two diagrams to show how fossil fuels harm the environment.

Key words

energy – the power needed to provide heat and light and to run machines

fossil fuel – an energy resource produced millions of years ago

opencast mine – mine where resources are dug straight out of the ground

renewable energy – energy which can be used forever

sedimentary rock – rock formed from particles of sediment

SUMMARY

- Coal, oil and gas are non-renewable energy resources.
- Non-renewable energy resources are called fossil fuels.
- Fossil fuels are damaging to the environment.

SUMMARY activity

Write a diary of the ways you have used energy over the past 24 hours. Are there any ways you could have saved energy?

 Energy Quest http://www.energy.ca.gov/education/

83 Nuclear power

In this section of the book you will investigate the following things:
- **What is nuclear power?**
- **What are the advantages and disadvantages of nuclear power?**
- **What were the causes and effects of the nuclear accident in Chernobyl?**

Nuclear power is produced using a radioactive mineral called **uranium**. Uranium **atoms** are split in a process called nuclear fission. Nuclear fission produces intense heat. The heat is used to boil water to produce steam. The steam drives turbines, which produce electricity (Fig 1).

Q1 How is nuclear power produced?

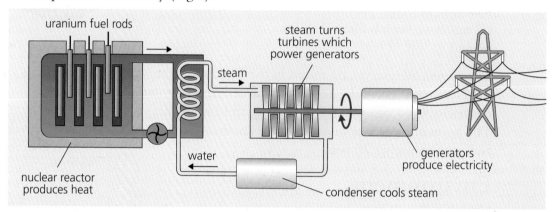

▲ **Fig 1** Nuclear energy.

The invention of nuclear power promised a supply of safe, cheap and clean energy. Richer countries spent huge amounts of money building nuclear power stations. Today there are 431 nuclear **reactors** spread across 44 countries. These nuclear reactors produce 8% of the world's electricity. This figure is unlikely to increase. There have been a series of leaks of **radioactive** material, and an explosion of a nuclear reactor in the Ukraine. These accidents have persuaded many people that nuclear power is just too risky.

Advantages of nuclear power	Disadvantages of nuclear power
Only small amounts of uranium are needed. One hundred grams of uranium produces as much energy as one tonne of coal.	There is a risk of radiation leaks from nuclear power stations. In the worst situation, a nuclear reactor can explode.
Reserves of uranium will last for at least 1000 years.	Radioactive substances can kill. A large dose is fatal immediately. Low doses cause cancer.
Nuclear power stations do not produce gases which pollute the atmosphere. They do not cause global warming or acid rain.	Nuclear power stations produce radioactive waste. High-level radioactive waste remains dangerous for hundreds of years.
Nuclear power can provide energy in countries which do not have reserves of fossil fuels.	There is no long-term solution for storing nuclear waste. Plans to bury it underground have been opposed. If the waste leaks, it could poison water supplies.
Nuclear power stations only produce a small amount of high-level radioactive waste.	Nuclear power stations have to be taken apart when they reach the end of their working life. This is a very expensive process.

 UKAEA http://www.ukaea.org.uk/

Chernobyl, Ukraine

On 26 April 1986, a leak of gas caused a reactor to explode at the nuclear power station in Chernobyl, Ukraine. The explosion released a cloud of radioactive dust which poisoned the surrounding area. After ten days, the radioactive cloud had spread across Europe, even reaching the UK, 2300 km away (Fig 2) .

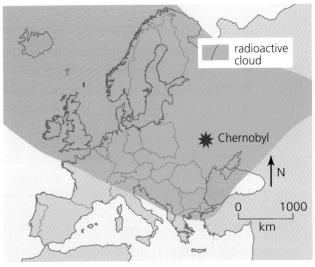

radioactive cloud

Chernobyl

N

0   1000
          km

▲ **Fig 2** *Nuclear fallout after the Chernobyl accident.*

The impacts of the disaster have been long-term. Around 135 000 people had to be evacuated from the Chernobyl area. An estimated 7000 of these people have since died from radiation poisoning. Many people who lived in Chernobyl have developed cancer, and children have been born with defects. A small number of people have moved back to the area illegally. Even today the food they eat and the water they drink is poisoned by radiation.

Q2 What caused the accident at Chernobyl?

▲ **Fig 3** *The Chernobyl nuclear reactor after the explosion.*

A concrete shelter was built over the reactor after the accident (Fig 3). But recently the shelter has begun to crumble in places, allowing radiation to escape. The USA and the European Union are helping Ukraine to re-seal the reactor, and to close down the two remaining reactors that are still running.

Q3 Describe the effects of the Chernobyl accident.

Q4 Why is it in the interests of the USA and Europe to help Ukraine make the Chernobyl reactor safe?

Key words

atom – the basic building block of all substances

radioactive – ability to release energy as radiation

reactor – machine which splits uranium atoms

uranium – a radioactive mineral

SUMMARY

■ Nuclear power produces energy from a radioactive mineral called uranium.

■ There are strong arguments both in favour of and against nuclear power.

■ The accident at Chernobyl has had terrible effects on people and the environment.

SUMMARY *activity*

Write an essay either in favour of or against nuclear power. Use facts to support your argument.

 BNFL http://www.bnfl.com/index1.html

84 Alternative energy

In this section of the book you will investigate the following things:
- Why is the demand for energy increasing?
- What is 'alternative energy'?
- What are the advantages and disadvantages of wind energy?
- How can energy consumption be reduced?

Globally, the demand for **energy** is increasing every year (Fig 1). This is happening because the world's population is increasing. The more people there are on the planet, the more energy is needed. At the same time, people are becoming richer. People have more money to buy things which use energy, such as cars, fridges and televisions.

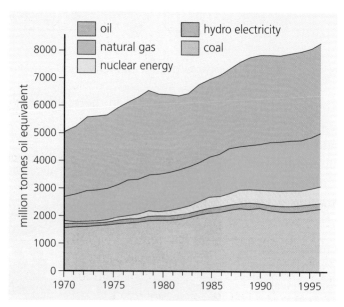

▲ **Fig 1** World growth in energy consumption.

Most of the world's energy is produced from **fossil fuels**, or nuclear power. Both of these sources of energy have problems. Fossils fuels cause pollution, and will run out in the future. Nuclear power is risky, and very expensive in the long run. Many people believe that the answer lies in '**alternative energy**'. Alternative energy means using renewable sources of energy such as the sun, wind, rivers, waves and tides to produce electricity.

Q1 Why is population growth increasing the demand for energy?

Q2 What is 'alternative energy'?

Wind power

Energy from the wind can be captured by large windmills, called 'wind turbines' (Fig 2). The rotor blades of wind turbines are turned automatically to face the wind. The wind turns the rotor blades at speeds of up to 400 km per hour. This drives a generator which makes electricity. There are over 300 wind turbines in the UK. The largest one, in the Orkney Islands, produces enough electricity for 2000 homes.

Wind power has several advantages. It is a 'clean' form of energy, which means it does not cause pollution. It is totally renewable – it will last as long as the wind blows! Wind energy is particularly useful in areas which have reliable, strong winds. It can provide power in places which are a long way from the main electricity grid.

▲ **Fig 2** Wind turbines.

 Crest – renewable energy http://solstice.crest.org/renewables/re-kiosk/index.shtml

The use of wind turbines is limited for a number of reasons. Wind energy is more expensive than energy from fossil fuels. It is also not very reliable. Power is only produced when winds are blowing. It would take thousands of wind turbines to produce enough electricity to power a city. The best places to locate wind turbines are in upland areas. These areas are often National Parks. Building thousands of turbines in National Parks would ruin the beautiful landscapes.

Q3 Which areas in Europe have the greatest potential for wind power?

Q4 Which areas in Europe have the least potential for wind power?

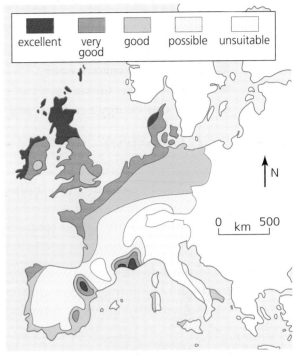

excellent | very good | good | possible | unsuitable

▲ **Fig 3** Possible wind turbine sites.

Reducing consumption

Rather than just producing more and more energy, we need to find ways of cutting down on the amount of energy we use. The governments of most countries have agreed to find ways of reducing energy consumption. The UK government is increasing the cost of petrol to try to persuade people to use their cars less. Road tax is also cheaper for smaller cars. Many electrical goods are now labelled to show how much electricity they use. At the same time, individuals can reduce the amount of energy they use (Fig 4).

- Turn down central heating and wear warmer clothes
- Walk or cycle rather than use a car
- Use low-energy lightbulbs
- Switch off the TV rather than leaving it on standby

▲ **Fig 4** Ways to conserve energy.

Q5 Give one way the UK government is trying to save energy.

Key words

alternative energy – energy produced from renewable sources
energy – power
fossil fuels – energy produced from coal, oil and gas

SUMMARY

- Globally, the demand for energy is increasing.
- Meeting the increased demand for energy with fossil fuels and nuclear power will harm the environment.
- Alternative energy sources could help provide the world with enough energy.

SUMMARY activity

Conduct an enquiry into energy use in your school. What could be done to make your school more energy efficient? You could present your report to your head teacher!

85 Land

In this section of the book you will investigate the following things:

- What is soil?
- What causes soil erosion?
- What are the consequences of soil erosion?
- What can be done to limit soil erosion?

Soil erosion

Soil is a very important renewable resource. It provides trees and plants with the **nutrients** they need to grow. Without soil, people are not able to grow food. Soil is formed from a mixture of weathered rock and dead plant matter. Although new soil is being formed all the time, it takes many years. It can take 1000 years to form 1cm of new soil. This means it is extremely important to look after soil.

Unfortunately, the United Nations estimate that one billion people live in areas at risk from soil erosion (Fig 1). Soil erosion is when soil is removed by wind or water. Soil erosion is increasing due to deforestation, intensive farming and overgrazing.

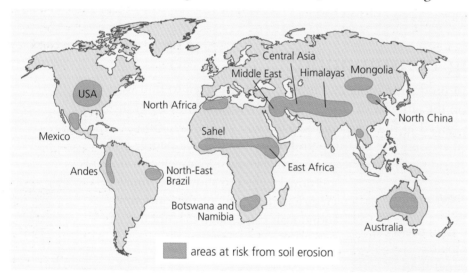

areas at risk from soil erosion

Q1 What is soil formed from?

Q2 Why is soil such an important resource?

Q3 What is soil erosion?

◀ **Fig 1** Areas at risk from soil erosion.

Nepal

Nepal is a country situated between China and India. The Himalayas make it one of the most mountainous countries in the world. Nepal is a poor country, where most people work as subsistence farmers. **Terraces** have been cut into the steep slopes to farm the land (Fig 2).

Q4 Draw a simple map of Nepal.

▲ **Fig 2** Terraces and soil erosion in Nepal.

 NASA – soil science http://ltpwww.gsfc.nasa.gov/globe/index.htm

Soil erosion

Soil erosion in Nepal has become a large problem in recent years. The population of Nepal has reached 24 million. This has created a need for more food and fuel. Farmers have increased the number of goats they farm to produce more food. As a result many of the steep slopes have been overgrazed. The vegetation has been removed leaving bare soil. At the same time, many trees have been cut down to provide fuel for heat and cooking. The trees used to protect the soil. Their leaves caught the rainfall, and their roots held the soil together. Today, heavy summer rains sweep the exposed soil down the slopes, causing massive soil erosion.

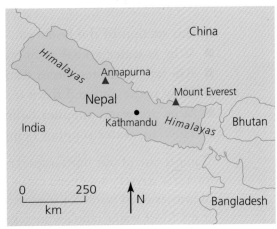

▲ **Fig 3** Nepal.

Consequences

It is estimated that 250 000 tonnes of soil are eroded in Nepal each year. This means that less food can be produced, at a time when more is needed. Farmers are forced to grow even more food in other areas. This again increases the risk of soil erosion. Much of the eroded soil is deposited in rivers. The soil can block rivers, making them more likely to flood.

Solutions

The Nepalese government have begun a number of schemes to reduce soil erosion. Local people have been involved in tree planting projects (re-forestation). By planting trees on the bare slopes, soil erosion is limited. The trees can also provide a sustainable supply of fuel wood and animal food.

Tourism has become increasingly popular in Nepal (Fig 4). Visitors enjoy walking holidays through the spectacular mountain landscapes. Tourists have to pay a fee to enter certain areas, such as the Annapurna district. This money is used to fund projects which benefit local people, including projects to protect the soil from erosion.

Year	Visits
1960	4 000
1970	4 500
1980	163 000
1990	255 000
1995	350 000
2000	500 000

▶ **Fig 4** Growth of tourism in Nepal.

Q5 How can tourism help to reduce soil erosion?

Key words

nutrients – chemicals needed for living things to grow

soil – mixture of weathered rock and decayed plant matter

terraces – steps cut into a hillside

SUMMARY

- Soil is a very important renewable resource.
- Soil erosion is a serious global problem.
- A combination of natural and human factors cause soil erosion in Nepal.
- Soil erosion in Nepal is being tackled by local re-forestation schemes.

SUMMARY activity

Draw a flow diagram to show the causes and consequences of soil erosion in Nepal.

NepalNet http://www.panasia.org.sg/nepalnet/Welcome.html

86 Water

In this section of the book you will investigate the following things:
- Why is water a vital resource?
- Are safe water resources distributed unequally?
- Why is the demand for water increasing?
- Why are water supplies falling?
- How are water supplies being polluted?

Water is one of our most important resources. Without water people can only survive for a few days. People need clean water in their homes for drinking and washing. Industries need water for manufacturing and processing. Farmers need water to irrigate crops. Most water supplies are taken from rivers, lakes and underground stores. Managing our water resources will be one of the biggest challenges of this century.

Q1 What are the three main uses of water?

Malaria – spread by mosquitoes breeding in stagnant water

Diarrhoea – spread by dirty water

Hookworm – parasite causing severe internal bleeding

Guinea worm – a worm which lives under people's skin

Bilharzia – parasite transmitted by water snails

▲ *Fig 1* Water-borne diseases.

Inequality

Although water is vital for life, 20% of the world's population do not have access to a safe water supply. Most of these people live in poorer countries; 90 million in South America, 375 million in Africa and 600 million in Asia. Most of these people have to collect dirty water from rivers, lakes and water holes. Collecting the water can take hours every day, and carrying the water can cause permanent injury. It is estimated that ten million people die each year from diseases caused by dirty water (Fig 1).

Q2 Use Fig 2 to name ten countries expected to have a severe water shortage by 2025.

▼ *Fig 2* Countries predicted to have a water shortage by 2025.

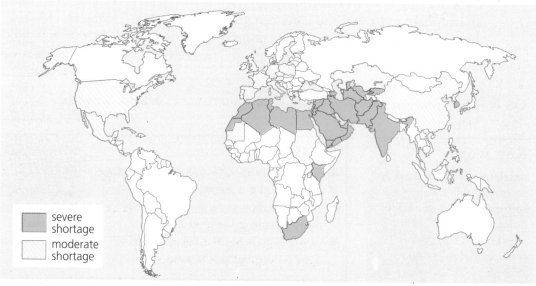

severe shortage

moderate shortage

Thames Water – water conservation http://www.thames-water.com/waterwise/index.html

Increasing demand

The global consumption of water has increased by six times since the beginning of the century. This is being caused mainly by population increase. The more people there are, the more water is needed. As a result, one-third of the world's population now live in areas at risk of water shortage. The United Nations estimate that by 2025, this figure will have increased to two-thirds of the world's population (Fig 2). Twenty-five of the worst hit countries will be in Africa. There are concerns that in the future, wars will be fought over access to precious water supplies.

Falling water tables

In some areas, rainfall seeps underground into **porous** rocks. Porous rocks hold water like a sponge.

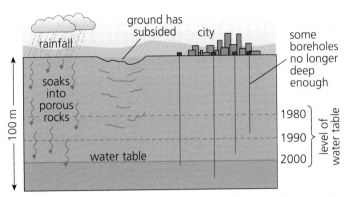

▲ **Fig 3** Water tables are falling.

These underground stores of water are called **aquifers**. Wells and boreholes are drilled into aquifers and water is taken out. Aquifers supply one-third of the world's water. In a number of areas, water is being removed faster than it is being replaced. In the USA, Russia, China and India the water level has fallen by tens of metres. As a result, some boreholes are now too shallow to reach the water (Fig 3). The land is also sinking, causing pipes to break and buildings to collapse.

Q3 Draw a labelled diagram to explain why underground water supplies are running out.

Pollution

The quality of the world's water is becoming worse. Millions of people in poorer countries have to use water contaminated with human **sewage**. Sewage is washed into rivers and aquifers because only 50% of the world's population have adequate sanitation (toilets).

Pesticides and fertilisers used in farming are increasingly poisoning water supplies. **Nitrates** from fertilisers cause brain damage and death. In parts of Africa nitrate levels in drinking water are eight times higher than 'safe' levels.

Q4 Explain how pollution of drinking water can affect people's health.

Key words

aquifer – underground water supply
nitrate – a nutrient used in fertiliser
porous – able to hold water like a sponge
sewage – human waste

SUMMARY

- Over one billion people do not have access to safe water.
- Two-thirds of the worlds population will run short of water by 2025.
- Underground water supplies are being used faster than they are replaced.
- Water supplies are being polluted by farming, industry and raw sewage.

SUMMARY activity

Draw a poster to persuade people to use water more carefully. Include ideas about how to save water.

 USGS satellite images of environmental change http://edcwww.cr.usgs.gov/earthshots/slow/tableofcontents

87 Air

In this section of the book you will investigate the following things:
- **What is the Greenhouse Effect?**
- **What is causing global warming?**
- **What will be the effects of global warming?**
- **What can be done to prevent global warming?**

The Greenhouse Effect

The Earth is surrounded by a layer of air called the **atmosphere**. The atmosphere is made up of different gases. Oxygen and nitrogen make up 99% of the atmosphere. The remaining 1% is made up of gases such as carbon dioxide (CO_2) and methane. Carbon dioxide and methane are very important gases because they absorb heat from the sun. These gases act like a blanket over the Earth, keeping it warm. This is known as the **Greenhouse Effect**. Without the Greenhouse Effect, the Earth would be permanently frozen.

Q1 What gases make up the Earth's atmosphere?

Q2 Draw a diagram to show how the Greenhouse Effect keeps the Earth warm.

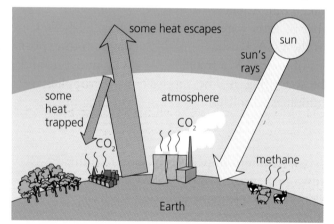

▲ **Fig 1** Global warming.

Global warming

In recent years scientists have discovered that the Earth's atmosphere is becoming warmer (**global warming**). This change is being caused by people. The amount of carbon dioxide and methane in the atmosphere is increasing. These gases are absorbing more of the sun's heat. As a result the Earth's temperature has increased by 0.5°C in the past 100 years.

Power stations and factories burn coal, oil and gas to produce energy. These fossil fuels release CO_2 when they are burned (Fig 2). Each year 5000 million tonnes of CO_2 are added to the atmosphere. This amount is expected to double by 2020.

Trees convert CO_2 into oxygen. Most of the world's temperate forests have already been cut down. Large areas of tropical rainforest are now being destroyed. Burning trees releases more CO_2 into the atmosphere.

Methane is being added to the atmosphere by bacteria living in rice fields, by rotting waste in rubbish dumps, and by cattle!

Q3 How are power stations causing global warming?

▼ **Fig 2** Carbon dioxide emissions in the UK, 1997.

Source	Emissions of CO_2 (million tonnes)
Power stations	40
Industry	37
Transport	37
Homes	23
Offices	12

 United Nations – Global Environment Outlook 2000 http://www.grida.no/geo2000/index.htm

174

Effects

Global temperatures are expected to rise by between 1°C and 4°C by 2040. This increase in temperature may have a number of impacts worldwide.

■ Sea water will expand as it becomes warmer. This could lead to a rise in sea levels of 1.5 metres.

■ Polar ice caps may begin to melt. If they melted completely, sea levels would rise by 5 metres.

■ Low-lying countries, such as Bangladesh, Egypt and the Netherlands, would be flooded. Millions of refugees would need new homes.

■ As the climates change, some areas will no longer be able to grow crops. Other areas may be able to grow more.

■ There will be an increase in extreme weather, such as hurricanes and droughts.

The possible effects of global warming on the UK are shown in Fig 3.

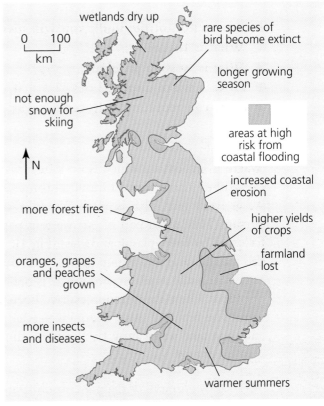

▲ *Fig 3* Possible impacts of global warming on the UK.

Q4 Why might global warming increase the number of refugees in the world?

Solutions

To prevent further global warming, the amount of greenhouse gases in the atmosphere must be reduced. Fewer fossil fuels should be burned and deforestation should be stopped. These are issues which need to be tackled at a worldwide level. At the Climate Change Summit in Japan in 1997, most of the world's richer countries agreed to cut emissions of greenhouse gases by 2012. Unfortunately, the USA refused because of worries about effects on American living standards. The world's poorer countries did not have to agree to reduce emissions.

Q5 Why is the Climate Change Summit of 1997 unlikely to prevent global warming?

Key words

atmosphere – layer of gases surrounding the Earth

global warming – increase in global temperature caused by people

Greenhouse Effect – absorption of Sun's heat by CO_2 and methane

SUMMARY

■ The Greenhouse Effect traps the sun's heat in the atmosphere.

■ Global warming is being caused by an increase in carbon dioxide and methane gas.

■ Sea levels will rise and climates will change if global warming continues.

■ Global warming can only be stopped by a worldwide effort.

SUMMARY *activity*

Draw a series of cartoons to show how global warming may affect life in the UK by 2100.

 Friends of the Earth http://www.foe.co.uk/

88 Waste and recycling

In this section of the book you will investigate the following things:
- What is waste?
- Why is waste a problem?
- How is waste disposed of?
- How can recycling help reduce waste?

Waste

Waste is something which is no longer useful to people. In the UK we throw away 25 million tonnes of household waste every year. That is nearly 350 kilos of waste per person! The largest part of our waste is paper and card, followed by food, plastic and glass (Fig 1). Throwing away this much waste is using up precious **resources**. Much of our waste, such as plastic and metal, is made from **finite** resources. Once these resources have been used up they cannot be replaced. Also, energy is needed to produce goods, and then take waste away. By throwing things away, we are wasting energy resources.

	Percentage of waste
Paper and card	33
Food waste	20
Plastic	11
Other	10
Glass	9
Dust	7
Steel cans	6
Textiles	2
Aluminium	2

Q1 Draw a graph, or diagram, to illustrate the contents of a typical dustbin in the UK.

▲ **Fig 1** What's in your bin?

Waste disposal

▲ **Fig 2** A landfill site.

Most of the waste that we throw away (83%) is put into large holes in the ground and buried. These holes are called **landfill sites** (Fig 2). Landfill sites take up a lot of space and create other problems. They look very unpleasant, smell bad and attract vermin. Landfill sites can contain poisonous substances. Dangerous chemicals can leak from batteries, or from discarded garden and household products. If landfill sites are not well sealed, these poisons can leak into water supplies.

A small amount of waste (9%) is **incinerated**. This is not a popular option because it releases pollution into the air. There is concern about dangerous chemicals being released when plastic is burned.

Q2 Describe the problems created by landfill sites.

 Waste Watch http://www.wastewatch.org.uk/

Recycling

Recycling is when things that have been used once, are used again. This includes turning waste into new products, or just re-using things rather than throwing them away. Currently we recycle just 8% of our waste. Studies show that it is possible to recycle 70% of our waste (Fig 3). Why should we bother?

■ Recycling saves resources.
■ Recycling saves energy.
■ Recycling reduces pollution.
■ Recycling contributes to sustainable development.

Q3 What are the benefits of recycling?

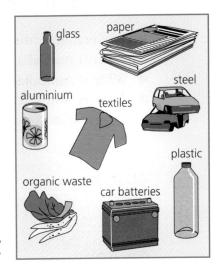

▶ **Fig 3** *What can be recycled in the UK?*

Glass

Glass recycling is helping to reduce waste, and save energy, in the UK. Recycled glass takes 20% less energy to produce, and causes 20% less pollution. People are encouraged to take their empty bottles and jars to recycling banks at waste centres and supermarkets. There are now 150 000 bottle banks nationwide. Of the six billion glass containers sold in the UK every year, 29% are recycled.

Q4 Where is your nearest recycling centre?

Aluminium

Aluminium is a metal used to make drinks cans and cooking foil. It is very costly to produce because it uses lots of energy. Recycled aluminium uses 95% less energy to make, and causes 99% less pollution. This makes aluminium one of the most valuable waste products. Of the 5 billion aluminium cans sold in the UK each year, 1.8 billion are recycled. This means that 3.2 billion cans, worth £24 million as scrap metal, are being buried in landfill sites. What a waste!

newspapers 30%
glass bottles 25%
aluminium cans 30%
clothing 25%

▲ **Fig 4** *How much is recycled in the UK?*

Q5 How could people be persuaded to recycle more aluminium cans?

Key words

finite – a limited supply
incinerate – to burn
landfill – burying waste underground
recycling – reusing waste
resource – natural product used by people
waste – items which no longer have a use

SUMMARY

■ Throwing away waste is using up the Earth's resources.
■ Disposing of waste damages the environment.
■ Recycling waste can save resources, energy and reduce pollution.
■ Only a small percentage of waste in the UK is recycled.

SUMMARY activity

☐ *Carry out an enquiry into litter and waste at your school. You could map the distribution of litter, or survey people about recycling.*

89 Australia – physical geography

In this section of the book you will investigate the following things:
- What is Australia's physical landscape like?
- What is Australia's climate like?
- What types of vegetation occur in Australia?

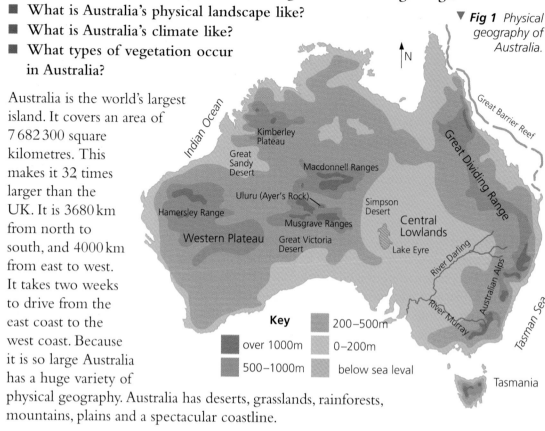

▼ *Fig 1* Physical geography of Australia.

Key
- over 1000m
- 500–1000m
- 200–500m
- 0–200m
- below sea leval

Australia is the world's largest island. It covers an area of 7 682 300 square kilometres. This makes it 32 times larger than the UK. It is 3680 km from north to south, and 4000 km from east to west. It takes two weeks to drive from the east coast to the west coast. Because it is so large Australia has a huge variety of physical geography. Australia has deserts, grasslands, rainforests, mountains, plains and a spectacular coastline.

Q1 Find Australia on a world map. Describe its location.

Physical landscape

▲ *Fig 2* Uluru (Ayer's Rock).

Q2 Name the three physical regions of Australia.

Australia is the world's flattest **continent**. Its landscape has been worn down by weathering and erosion over hundreds of millions of years. Australia's landscape can be divided into three areas (Fig 1). The Western Plateau is a vast, flat, area of ancient rocks. In the middle of Australia are the Central Lowlands. This area used to be a sea, and parts are still below sea level. The Central Lowlands contain mountain ranges such as the Macdonnells and Musgraves. This is where one of Australia's most spectacular landforms, Uluru (Ayer's Rock), is found (Fig 2). The Eastern Highlands are a chain of mountains running along Australia's east coast. These mountains include the Great Dividing Range and the Australian Alps.

 A guide to Australia http://www.csu.edu.au/australia/

Alice Springs	Jan	Feb	Mar	Apr	May	Jun	Jul	Aug	Sep	Oct	Nov	Dec
Average maximum temperature (°C)	36	35	32	27	23	20	20	23	27	31	33	35
Rainfall (mm)	42	41	33	16	16	14	13	10	9	20	25	36

Cairns	Jan	Feb	Mar	Apr	May	Jun	Jul	Aug	Sep	Oct	Nov	Dec
Average maximum temperature (°C)	32	31	31	29	28	26	26	27	28	29	31	31
Rainfall (mm)	405	434	424	197	99	49	30	27	35	38	89	175

▲ **Fig 3** *Climate statistics for Alice Springs and Cairns.*

Climate

After Antarctica, Australia is the world's driest continent. The centre of Australia is desert, with less than 250 mm of rainfall per year. Temperatures in the desert can reach 50°C in summer (Fig 3). To the north and east of the desert is a 'tropical grassland' climate. This has two seasons. It is hot and wet in summer and warm and dry in winter. The wettest areas in Australia are around the north and east coast. These areas have over 1000mm of rainfall per year. The north coast has a tropical **monsoon** climate. The monsoon winds bring heavy rain in the summer (Fig 3). Australia's northern coastline is at risk from violent tropical storms.

Q3 Use Fig 3 to draw climate graphs for Alice Springs and Cairns.

Q4 Describe the climates of the two places.

Vegetation

The huge variations in Australia's climate result in several different types of **ecosystem**.

■ Desert – the hot, dry deserts in the centre of Australia contain mainly scattered grasses. The grasses have adapted to the climate by growing very long roots (unit 34).

■ Tropical grassland – around the edges of the desert there is enough rainfall for grasses and Eucalyptus trees to grow. Australians call this area 'the bush'.

■ Tropical rainforest – the heavy rainfall, and high temperatures, of the northern coast support dense tropical rainforests (Fig 4).

▲ **Fig 4** *Tropical rainforest in Australia.*

Key words

continent – a large land mass

ecosystem – a community of plants and animals

monsoon – rain bearing winds

SUMMARY

■ Australia is a very large country.
■ Australia is mostly flat with low hills.
■ Australia has wide variations in climate.
■ Australia's ecosystems include desert, tropical grassland and tropical rainforest.

SUMMARY activity

Use Fig 1 to plan a car journey across Australia. Write a series of four postcards describing how the landscape, climate and vegetation change along the way.

 Australian Bureau of Meteorology http://www.bom.gov.au/

90 Australia – history

In this section of the book you will investigate the following things:
- What is the aboriginal history of Australia?
- What is the colonial history of Australia?
- How has Australia changed since independence?

To understand Australia today it is important to know about its past. The history of Australia can be divided into three periods.

Aboriginal history

▲ *Fig 1* An ancient Aboriginal ceremonial site.

Aboriginal people had lived in Australia for thousands of years before it was 'discovered' by Europeans (Fig 1). Aboriginal people are thought to have migrated from south–east Asia around 50 000 years ago. At that time sea levels were much lower. This would have made it possible to travel across small stretches of sea using rafts.

Aboriginal people have their own history known as the '**Dreamtime**'. They believe that during the Dreamtime, spirits were born from the Earth. The spirits travelled across Australia forming the landscape and creating all living things. There are many ancient aboriginal sites throughout Australia. A large number are sacred to **Aborigines**, for example Uluru (Ayer's Rock), the stunning rock formation near Alice Springs in the centre of Australia.

Q1 How did aboriginal people arrive in Australia?

Q2 What is meant by the 'Dreamtime'?

Aborigines lived off the land as hunters and gatherers. There were hundreds of groups of people who had their own territories. Each group developed their own language and customs.

Colonial history

Australia was not known about by Europeans until the early seventeenth century. The first European to land in Australia was the Englishman, Captain James Cook, who first landed at Botany Bay, on the east coast, in 1770. In 1788 he returned to Australia with a fleet of ships, carrying British convicts. Britain had decided to use Australia as a place to send criminals. This time Captain Cook landed at Port Jackson and founded a settlement called Sydney.

▶ *Fig 2* Captain Cook's chart of the Southern Hemisphere.

Any point Australia http://www.anypoint.net/default.htm

During the nineteenth century, as well as **convicts**, settlers from Britain began migrating to Australia. They went in search of adventure and possible wealth. Other **colonies** were established around Australia's coast. People began to move inland and set up large sheep farms. This caused conflict with aboriginal people. The settlers took the best land, forcing the Aborigines to move inland to drier areas. Aborigines who resisted were poisoned, or shot, by the settlers.

50 000 BP – Aboriginal people arrive

1606 – Australia discovered by William Jansz

1770 – Captain Cook lands in Botany Bay

1788 – Colony of Sydney established

1901 – Commonwealth of Australia becomes an independent country

1988 – Australia celebrates its Bicentenial – 200 years old

2000 – Australia hosts Olympic games

▲ *Fig 3* Key dates in Australia's history.

As each colony grew they established their own government. Australia became a number of separate colonies. In 1901, Australia gained independence from Britain. The colonies joined together to become the Commonwealth of Australia.

Q3 Why did people migrate to Australia from Britain?

Twentieth century

Since independence, Australia has developed its own identity and culture. It has developed closer links with countries in Asia. Its most important trading partners now include Japan, South Korea, Taiwan, Indonesia, New Zealand and the USA.

Although Australia is an independent country, the British Queen remains its head of state. During 1999 there was a referendum about whether Australia should become a Federal Republic. This would result in the Queen being replaced by an Australian President. The majority of Australians voted to keep the Queen.

In recent years, Australia has had to come to terms with the terrible ways the aboriginal people were treated in the past. Aboriginal culture and traditions are now valued and encouraged. Large areas of land in central and northern Australia have been returned to the Aboriginies.

Q4 Do you think land should be returned to aboriginal people?

Key words

Aborigine – original inhabitant of Australia
colony – an area, or country, ruled by another country
convict – a convicted criminal
Dreamtime – aboriginal creation story

SUMMARY

■ The original inhabitants of Australia were aboriginal people.
■ The British began sending convicts to Australia in the eighteenth century.
■ The colonisation of Australia resulted in conflicts with aboriginal people.
■ Australia became an independent country in 1901.
■ Australia has built up closer links with Asian countries.

SUMMARY activity

Use the data in Fig 3 and the text to draw a timeline to show key events in Australia's history.

 Australian government http://www.fed.gov.au/

91 Population and settlement

In this section of the book you will investigate the following things:
- Where do people live in Australia?
- Who are the Australian people?
- What is the population structure of Australia?

Population distribution

Australia has a population of 19 million people. The population is spread out very unevenly across the country (Fig 1). Few people live in the central part of Australia. The desert climate is harsh, with temperatures up to 50°C and very little rainfall. These conditions make it a difficult place to live and work. Most Australians live in towns and cities along the east and south-east coast. Coastal locations have a more pleasant climate. The most popular places to live are the cities of Sydney, Melbourne, Adelaide and Brisbane. These cities grew up around natural harbours, which are very important for trade with other countries. Perth, the main city on the west coast, developed because valuable minerals were discovered in the area. Canberra, the capital of Australia, is the only inland city.

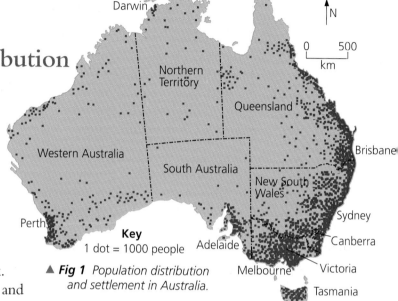

Key
1 dot = 1000 people

▲ **Fig 1** Population distribution and settlement in Australia.

Q1 Use Fig 1 to describe the population distribution of Australia.

Q2 Why do most people live on the coast?

Australian people

Almost all Australians are **immigrants**, or descended from immigrants (Fig 2). People began migrating to Australia after 1788, when Captain Cook founded the settlement of Sydney. At first Britain sent **convicts** to Australia. Later, many British people migrated to Australia in search of a better life. After World War II, many immigrants arrived in Australia from Europe. The largest groups were Italians and Greeks. Most recently, the largest group of migrants have come from Asian countries, such as Vietnam, the Philippines and Malaysia. Each group of immigrants have brought with them parts of their own culture and enriched the Australian way of life.

1	UK	1 107 119
2	New Zealand	264 094
3	Italy	253 332
4	Yugoslavia	160 479
5	Greece	136 028
6	Vietnam	121 813
7	Germany	111 975
8	Netherlands	94 692
9	China	77 799
10	Philippines	73 144

▲ **Fig 2** Origins of Australia's immigrants.

Q3 Which are the largest group of migrants to Australia?

 Australian Bureau of Statistics http://www.abs.gov.au/

Aboriginal people

Aboriginal people are the original inhabitants of Australia. They have been there for at least 50 000 years. When the British immigrants first arrived there were around 750 000 **Aborigines**. Their numbers quickly fell due to diseases introduced by the British, and because the British treated them very badly. Today there are around 400 000 Aborigines. Although most Aborigines now live in towns and cities, many still live in remote areas in the outback.

Q4 What percentage of the population are Aborigines?

Population structure

Fig 3 shows the population pyramid for Australia. The base of the pyramid is fairly narrow. This shows that Australia has a low birth rate, although the population is increasing slowly. The sides of the pyramid do not narrow significantly until people reach their sixties. This shows that Australia has a low death rate. The top part of the pyramid remains quite wide, showing that Australians have a long life expectancy. The average life expectancy is 80 years.

Aboriginal people have a very different population structure. Their birth rate is much higher, meaning 40% of the population are under 15. They also have a higher death rate resulting in a life expectancy of only 62 years.

Q5 Is the aboriginal population likely to increase or decrease?

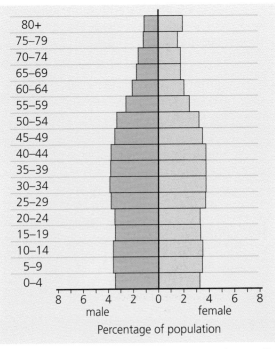

▲ *Fig 3* Population structure of Australia.

Key words

Aborigine – original people of Australia
convict – a criminal
immigrant – migrant moving into a country

SUMMARY

■ Most Australians live in coastal areas, especially the south and south east.
■ Almost all Australians are immigrants or descended from immigrants.
■ Aboriginal people were the first inhabitants of Australia.
■ The Australian population structure shows low birth and death rates and a long life expectancy.

SUMMARY activity

Draw a map to show where migrants to Australia have come from. Use arrows of different widths to show the numbers of migrants.

92 Australia – development

In this section of the book you will investigate the following things:

■ How developed is Australia?
■ How do standards of living vary?
■ Why do standards of living vary?

Standards of living

The United Nations ranks Australia as the seventh most developed country in the world (Fig 1). Most Australians have a good income and enjoy high standards of living. The average wage is £375 per week. In general the cost of living is cheaper in Australia, compared with Europe. This means money goes further. People are able to afford good-sized houses with large gardens (Fig 2). Almost everybody has access to a car. Food is plentiful, and cheap.

Population growth rate (%)		1.2
Birth rate (per 1000 population)		14
Death rate (per 1000 population)		7
Infant mortality rate (per 1000 population)		5.3
Life expectancy (years):	Men	77
	Women	83
Urban population (%)		86
People per doctor		400
Literacy (%)		99

▲ **Fig 1** How developed is Australia?

Australia has a high-quality health service. It is easy to visit a doctor, and there are plenty of modern hospitals. As a result, Australians have a long life expectancy. Education is compulsory for all children between the ages of 6 and 15. Many young people continue their education at university. Most people have a job in a **service industry**, although **primary industries** are still very important in Australia. Much of Australia's wealth has come from exporting agricultural products and minerals. Of course not everybody in Australia is

◄ **Fig 2** High quality housing.

wealthy and has a high standard of living. Out of the population of 19 million people, 4.4% live below the official **poverty line**. Unlike the UK, poverty is not concentrated in certain regions. Poverty is linked to particular groups of people, such as single parents and Aborigines.

Q1 Why does money go further in Australia compared with the UK?

Q2 How is poverty in Australia different to poverty in the UK?

 Australian Bureau of Statistics http://www.abs.gov.au/

Inequalities

The most disadvantaged group of Australians are aboriginal people. Aborigines are the group most likely to be unemployed. Those that do have a job receive a salary far below the Australian average. As a result Aborigines are three times as likely to be living in poverty. Fewer Aborigines are able to afford to buy their own home, or run a car. Aborigines receive less education and leave school or college with fewer qualifications. Aboriginal people are much more likely to be sent to prison, compared with white people who commit a similar crime. The average life expectancy for aboriginal people is 60 years. This is 20 years less than the average for Australia as a whole.

Aborigines are disadvantaged for a number of reasons. For many years after the arrival of European settlers they were mistreated and denied basic human rights. During the 1950s and 1960s it was government policy to end the traditional aboriginal lifestyle. Aboriginal children were taken from their parents to be raised in institutions, or adopted by white parents. Aboriginal culture was considered worthless. It was not until 1967 that Aborigines were recognised as Australian citizens. Although many aboriginal people now live comfortable lives, as a group they lag behind other Australians. Today there are many organisations working to improve standards of living for aboriginal people.

Q3 What reasons might explain why Aborigines have a shorter life expectancy than other Australians?

Q4 What do you think could be done to raise the living standards of aboriginal people?

	Total population	Aboriginal population
Life expectancy (years)	80	60
Average weekly income (£)	375	245
Home ownership (%)	70	30
Cars per household	1.5	1
Unemployment rate (%)	7	23
University education (%)	36	12

▲ **Fig 3** Inequalities in Australia.

Key words

poverty line – the minimum amount of money needed for a 'decent' standard of living

primary industry – farming, mining, fishing or forestry

service industry – work such as retail, administration, education, healthcare and tourism

SUMMARY

■ Most Australians enjoy high standards of living.

■ Standards of living have little regional variation.

■ Standards of living vary between different groups of people.

■ The most disadvantaged group are aboriginal people.

SUMMARY activity

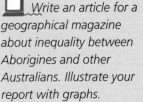

▢ Write an article for a geographical magazine about inequality between Aborigines and other Australians. Illustrate your report with graphs.

93 Australia – agriculture

In this section of the book you will investigate the following things:
- What types of farming are important in Australia?
- How has farming affected the environment?
- What is being done to restore the environment?

Farming has been a very important industry in Australia since the arrival of the first settlers. Today, **agricultural** goods, including wool, beef, wheat, fruit and wine, earn over one-third of Australia's **export** income.

▲ **Fig 2** Sheep farming.

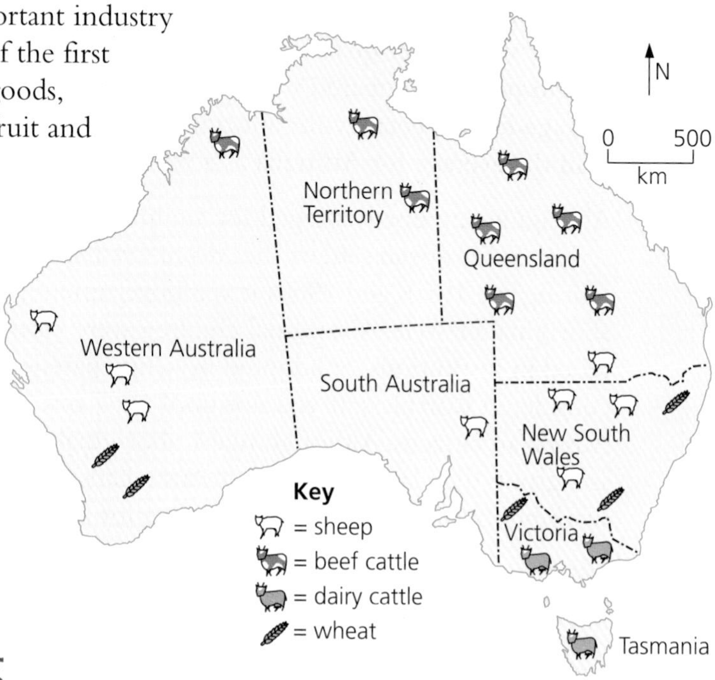

▲ **Fig 1** Farming in Australia.

Key
- = sheep
- = beef cattle
- = dairy cattle
- = wheat

Types of farming

Sheep – Merino sheep were brought to Australia from South Africa in the 1800s. Merino sheep produce high-quality wool. Money earned from exporting wool earned much of the country's early wealth, allowing it to develop. Australia remains the world's largest exporter of wool, producing 25% of the world's total. Sheep farms cover vast areas, especially the drier parts of New South Wales and Western Australia (Fig 2). The largest sheep farms are bigger than UK counties.

Cattle – Twenty six million cattle are farmed in Australia to produce beef and milk. The most important area for beef farming is the northern state of Queensland. Cattle are allowed to graze freely in the '**bush**' until it is time for them to go to market. Much of Australia's beef is exported to the USA and Japan. Dairy cattle are farmed in the southern states of Victoria and Tasmania, where the grass is of better quality. These farms are located closer to main cities where fresh milk is needed.

Wheat – Wheat is grown all over Australia, especially in the south east and south west. Technology has been used to increase the area that can be farmed. Poor soils have been improved with fertiliser, and crops are watered using irrigation systems. The main customers for Australia's wheat are China, Egypt and the USA.

Q1 Describe the distribution of farming in Australia.

 Australian agriculture http://agnet.com.au/

Soil degradation in Western Australia

In some areas of Australia, **soil degradation** is a problem. Soil degradation means the loss of soil. Soil can be blown away by wind, or washed away by water. Soil can also become too salty.

Q2 What is soil degradation?

Western Australia is an important wheat and sheep farming area. However, the amount of useful land is dwindling because the soil is becoming too salty for plants to grow. When farmers arrived in the area, over a hundred years ago (Fig 3), they cleared the land of trees to make more space for farming. The trees used to take excess water out of the soil, and release it back into the atmosphere. Now these trees have gone, the water table has risen and in low places the soil has become waterlogged. The sun evaporates the water to leave behind salty pools, or patches of hard salt (Fig 4). In some areas over one-third of farmland has been lost.

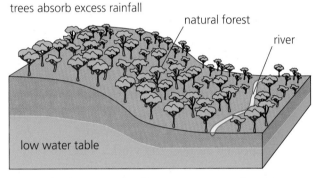

▲ **Fig 3** Farmland in Western Australia 150 years ago.

Farmers in Western Australia are trying to find solutions to the **salinity** problem. Some farmers are planting trees on surrounding slopes, in an attempt to lower the water table again. Others are adapting to the new conditions by farming animals such as fish, ostriches or goats. There is also a plan to build a network of canals to drain the salty water away. Although this plan may be the most effective, it would also be the most expensive.

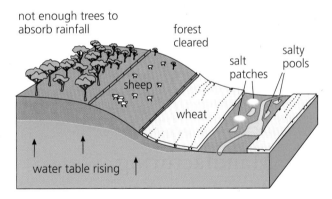

▲ **Fig 4** Farmland in Western Australia today.

Q3 What has caused the soil in parts of Western Australia to become salty?

Key words

agriculture – farming
bush – tropical grassland
export – goods sold abroad
saline – salty
soil degradation – loss of soil

SUMMARY

■ The most important types of farming in Australia are sheep, cattle and wheat.
■ In parts of Australia, soil has been damaged by farming practices.
■ Farmers are trying new methods of farming to solve the salinity problem.

SUMMARY activity

Draw a labelled diagram to show how farmers are providing solutions to the salinity problem in Western Australia.

94 Australia – industry

In this section of the book you will investigate the following things:
■ How important is mining to Australia's economy?
■ How important is manufacturing to Australia's economy?
■ How does mining create conflicts?

Mining

Australia is extremely rich in **mineral** resources (Fig 1). It has large reserves of metal **ores**, such as bauxite, iron ore, copper and nickel. It has energy resources of coal, oil, gas and uranium. It also has precious metals and gemstones, including gold and diamonds. Australia is self-sufficient in all of these resources. Surplus resources are exported all over the world. The money earned from exports has made Australia one of the world's wealthiest countries.

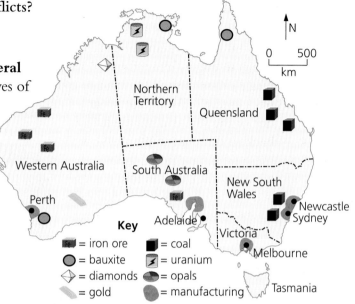

▲ **Fig 1** *Mining and manufacturing in Australia.*

Mining takes place all over the country, but is most important in Western Australia. Western Australia is home to iron ore mines in the Pilbarra region, bauxite (aluminium ore) mines around Perth, diamond mines in the Kimberley region and gold mines near Kalgoorlie. Coal mines and oil wells are found in Queensland. South Australia and Northern Territory are important uranium mining areas.

Q1 Describe the location of Australia's mineral resources.

Manufacturing

Manufacturing industry grew rapidly in Australia after 1945. The Second World War had made it difficult to import manufactured goods. As a result, some industries expanded while new ones were developed. Metal production has become the most important industry, followed by food processing and machinery. Manufacturing is concentrated around the cities of Sydney, Newcastle, Melbourne and Adelaide (Fig 1).

Q2 Why did manufacturing grow quickly after 1945?

Q3 Why do you think manufacturing is located close to main cities?

Conflicts

Mining Australia's resources creates conflicts between the mining companies, conservationists and aboriginal people. Many of the mining sites are located in sensitive environments, or on traditional aboriginal lands.

 Uranium Information Centre http://www.uic.com.au/

Kakadu National Park

Kakadu National Park is a wilderness area in Northern Territory (Fig 2). It is full of ancient rock landforms and rare wildlife. It is a world heritage site which attracts millions of visitors each year. The Kakadu National Park also has large reserves of uranium. Uranium is a valuable mineral used as a fuel in nuclear power stations. There are already two uranium mines in the National Park, and there are plans for a third. A mining company wants to open a new uranium mine at Jabiluka. There is disagreement over whether the Jabiluka mine should be allowed (Fig 3).

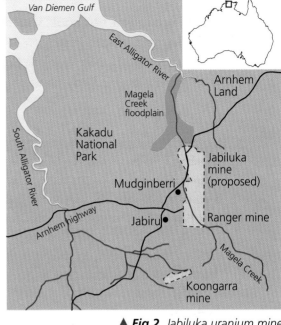

▲ **Fig 2** Jabiluka uranium mine in Kakadu National Park.

- Mining company – uranium has been mined in the area for over 20 years. The mining company say the land belongs to them. They argue that uranium mining provides jobs for local people, including Aborigines.

- Aboriginal people – land is sacred to Aborigines. They believe exploiting the land for profit is wrong. They argue that the land belongs to them, and they want the companies to stop mining (Fig 4).

- Environmentalists – uranium is processed on site and a leak of radioactive material is possible. Environmentalists are worried that a leak would harm wildlife. Experts say that so far there has been little impact on the area.

- Government – uranium exports earn the government money in taxes. They say the Aborigines can have their land back, but only if they allow mining to continue.

▲ **Fig 3** Protesting against Jabiluka mine.

❝ Let me make it plain. We say no to uranium mining now and for the future. Our right to say no comes from our ancestors, our heritage, our law and culture. ❞

Jacqui Catona of the Mirrar people

▲ **Fig 4** Aboriginal opposition to Jabiluka mine.

Q4 Why is Kakadu National Park a valuable area?

Key words

manufacturing – making things

mineral – a natural resource such as metal or rock

mining – extracting primary resources

ore – deposits of rock containing minerals

SUMMARY

- Australia is rich in mineral resources.
- Australia's mineral resources are exported all over the world.
- Manufacturing has become more important since 1945.
- Mining minerals creates conflicts between mining companies, Aborigines and environmentalists.

SUMMARY activity

Take the role of either a mining company, an Aborigine, an environmentalist or the government. Discuss in a group whether the Jabiluka mine should be allowed to go ahead in Kakadu National Park.

 Anti Uranium Coalition http://members.iinet.au/~fossil/index.html

95 Australia – the outback

In this section of the book you will investigate the following things:
- **Where is Coober Pedy?**
- **What is life like in Coober Pedy?**
- **How is Coober Pedy changing?**

Coober Pedy

Coober Pedy is an isolated town in the '**outback**' of Australia (Fig 1). The outback is the interior part of Australia, away from the coast. Coober Pedy is situated a long way from other towns and cities. The nearest large town is Alice Springs, which is 690 km to the north. The closest city is Adelaide. Adelaide is a long day's drive away, 850 km to the south.

Coober Pedy is an unusual town because most of its 2500 people live in underground homes called '**dugouts**'. Dugouts provide shelter from the harsh desert climate. Drilled ventilation holes keep the homes at a comfortable 26°C all year round. Coober Pedy gets its name from the aboriginal words, 'Kupa Piti'. This translates as 'white man's hole in the ground'.

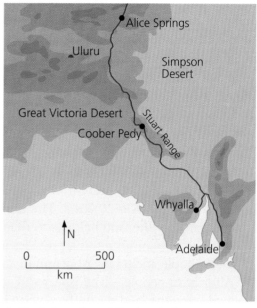

▲ **Fig 1** Location of Coober Pedy.

Q1 Where is Coober Pedy?

Q2 Why have people chosen to live underground in Coober Pedy?

Environment

Coober Pedy lies at the southern end of the Stuart Mountain Range. To the west is the Great Victorian Desert. Coober Pedy has one of the most extreme climates in Australia (Fig 2). It is very dry. The average yearly rainfall is only 157mm. During the day it can be extremely hot, even reaching 50°C. At night the temperature can drop to freezing. Dust storms can occur when it is windy. There is little vegetation apart from some patchy grassland.

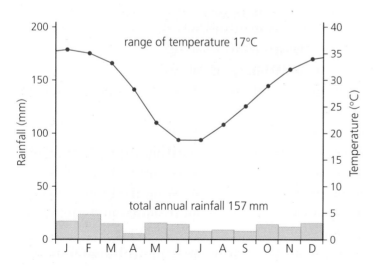

▲ **Fig 2** Climate of Coober Pedy.

Q3 Describe the climate in Coober Pedy.

 Coober Pedy http://www.opalcapitaloftheworld.com.au/

Opal mining

Coober Pedy has become the world's most important **opal** producing area. Opals are gemstones used to make jewellery. The sandstone rock around Coober Pedy contains layers of the valuable stones. In the 1960s European migrants came to Coober Pedy seeking their fortune. Today there are people from 53 different countries living in the town. The opal fields cover nearly 5000 square kilometres, and there are around 250 000 mine shafts. Opal mining has grown to become a multi-million dollar industry.

Tourism

Tourism is increasingly important to Coober Pedy. Around 100 000 tourists now visit the town each year. People come to see the unusual way of living, and are able to stay in underground hotels. Tourists have the chance to tour opal mines and to buy jewellery made in the town. A favourite activity is 'noodling'. Noodling is searching through discarded rock looking for pieces of opal missed by miners. Coober Pedy is also used as a setting for movies. 'Mad Max 3' was shot there because of its harsh and rugged appearance.

Q4 How do people make a living in Coober Pedy?

Change

Coober Pedy has changed a great deal since the 1960s. A tarmac road has been built through the centre of the town, and more shops have opened. Mains water was recently connected. Water is now supplied from an underground reservoir 24 km away. Although business in opals and tourism is doing well, there is little for the young people of Coober Pedy. There are no clubs, and the drive-in cinema has closed down. Many children attend boarding schools hundreds of miles away. Young people are leaving Coober Pedy to find work in the towns and cities on Australia's coast.

http:

❝ We had been driving along the highway for what seemed like days now. The surrounding countryside was vast and desolate. The occasional car passing was warmly greeted by smiling and waving. Some scrub-like vegetation appeared to have battled through and survived the harsh conditions of the South Australian outback.

Slowly in the distance the township began to emerge. Where on earth were we? Australia? It is difficult to describe how Coober Pedy looks as you are driving towards it but all I can say is that I honestly felt that I was no longer on earth. There is nothing. No trees, no grass, no buildings. All you can see are huge mounds of red dirt. Red dirt, red dirt and more red dirt. My first sighting of Coober Pedy will always stay in my mind. ❞

▲ **Fig 3** *A traveller's first impressions of Coober Pedy (posted on the Internet).*

Q5 Would you like to live in Coober Pedy?

Key words

dugout – an underground house

opal – a gemstone

outback – the dry interior of Australia

SUMMARY

■ Coober Pedy is an opal mining town in the Australian outback.

■ People live underground in Coober Pedy to shelter from the extreme weather.

■ Tourism is increasingly important to Coober Pedy's economy.

■ Although Coober Pedy is becoming more developed, young people are choosing to move away.

SUMMARY activity

☐ Write an extract about Coober Pedy to be included in a travel guide book about Australia.

96 Australia – Sydney

In this section of the book you will investigate the following things:

- ■ Where is Sydney?
- ■ What is life like in Sydney?
- ■ How is Sydney changing?

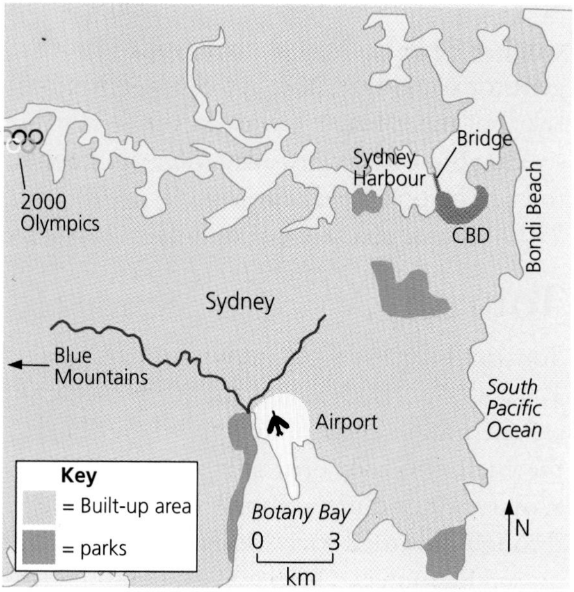

Sydney

Sydney is Australia's oldest, largest and most important city (Fig 1). It is located on the south-eastern coast. Sydney was the first place to be settled by the British in 1788. The site was chosen because of its excellent natural **harbour**.

Sydney's central business district (CBD), of shops and offices, is on the southern shore of Sydney Harbour. It is a densely packed mixture of old colonial buildings and modern skyscrapers. Large areas of housing stretch out from the CBD. The city has grown to cover a huge area of 12 400 square kilometres.

Sydney's population is around 3.7 million people. The city is a popular destination for **migrants**. There are a large number of people from the Lebanon, Vietnam, Turkey, China, Italy and Greece. The migrants give Sydney an international atmosphere.

▲ *Fig 1* *Sydney.*

Q1 Why was Sydney chosen as the site for Australia's first settlement?

Environment

Sydney has grown because of its excellent location and pleasant environment. It is bordered to the west by the Blue Mountains, to the north by the Hawkesbury River, and by the Southern Highlands in the south. The city has a pleasant climate (Fig 2). The average yearly rainfall is 1222 mm, which is spread fairly evenly throughout the year. During the summer, the average maximum temperature is 27°C. In the winter it remains mild with an average maximum temperature of 17°C.

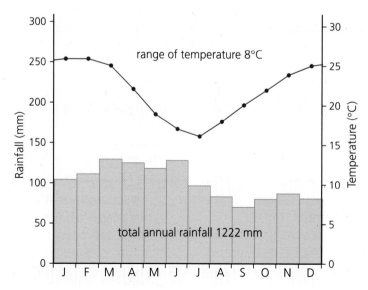

range of temperature 8°C

total annual rainfall 1222 mm

▲ *Fig 2* *Sydney's climate.*

 Sydney http://www.cityofsydney.nsw.gov.au/

Economy

Sydney is Australia's most important commercial centre. Over 60 large companies have their headquarters in the city, providing many office jobs. Manufacturing industries, such as oil refineries and textile mills, are also located around Sydney. Sydney Harbour and Botany Bay both have large shipping ports. Many of Australia's goods are exported through the city. Tourism is an important industry. Tourists come to see famous landmarks such as the Sydney Harbour Bridge and the Sydney Opera House (Fig 3).

▲ **Fig 3** *Sydney Opera House and Harbour.*

Q2 What kind of jobs are available in Sydney?

Change

Sydney is becoming an increasingly popular place to live. Unfortunately, it has no more room to expand, and almost every available space is already built on. This has caused house prices to rise. Some people have been forced to move further into the city **suburbs**, where houses are cheaper. Traditionally, Australian houses have been single-storey buildings with large gardens. In some places, these are being knocked down and replaced with blocks of flats.

▲ **Fig 4** *Sydney Olympic stadium.*

Sydney was chosen as the site for the 2000 Olympic Games (Fig 4). Although this brought several benefits, it has also increased pressure on the city. The site of the main Olympic stadium was a highly-polluted industrial wasteland. This area has been cleaned up and is now safe. The Olympics also created many jobs in construction, tourism and catering. At the same time, local facilities have been closed down to make space for Olympic buildings. Traffic congestion has also become worse as road layouts have been changed. This has angered many of Sydney's residents and business people.

Q3 What were the benefits of the Olympic Games?

Q4 What problems were caused by the Olympic Games?

Key words

harbour – sheltered area where ships can dock

migrants – people who have moved from one place to another

suburbs – housing at the edge of a city

SUMMARY

- Sydney's coastal location results in a pleasant climate.
- Sydney is Australia's most important commercial city.
- Pressure on Sydney is increasing as its population grows.

SUMMARY activity

Prepare a presentation for the International Olympic Committee to persuade them that Sydney is the best location to hold the Olympic Games.

97 Brazil – physical geography

In this section of the book you will investigate the following things:
- What is Brazil's physical landscape like?
- What is Brazil's climate like?
- What types of vegetation occur in Brazil?

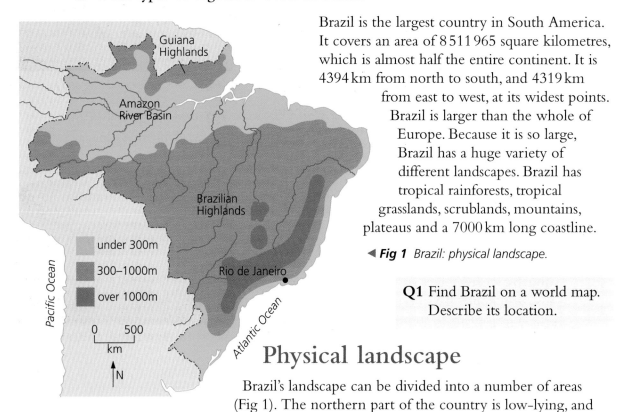

◀ **Fig 1** Brazil: physical landscape.

Brazil is the largest country in South America. It covers an area of 8 511 965 square kilometres, which is almost half the entire continent. It is 4394 km from north to south, and 4319 km from east to west, at its widest points. Brazil is larger than the whole of Europe. Because it is so large, Brazil has a huge variety of different landscapes. Brazil has tropical rainforests, tropical grasslands, scrublands, mountains, plateaus and a 7000 km long coastline.

Q1 Find Brazil on a world map. Describe its location.

Physical landscape

Brazil's landscape can be divided into a number of areas (Fig 1). The northern part of the country is low–lying, and contains the Amazon **river basin**. The Amazon is the largest river in the world. Its river basin covers four million square kilometres. To the south of the Amazon are the Brazilian Highlands. This area is a vast **plateau** which rises gently towards the south west. The plateau is crossed by several large rivers which are tributaries of the Amazon. The plateau rises steeply along the east coast to a height of over 1000 metres. It then drops steeply, as almost vertical cliffs. Running along the coast is a narrow strip of flat land. In some places it is up to 60 km wide, in others it disappears.

Q2 Name the two major physical regions of Brazil.

Rio de Janeiro	Jan	Feb	Mar	Apr	May	Jun	Jul	Aug	Sep	Oct	Nov	Dec
Temperature (°C)	29	30	29	27	25	25	24	25	24	25	26	28
Rainfall (mm)	125	122	130	107	79	53	41	43	66	79	104	137

Pôrto Nacional	Jan	Feb	Mar	Apr	May	Jun	Jul	Aug	Sep	Oct	Nov	Dec
Temperature (°C)	26	24	25	26	26	25	25	26	27	26	25	25
Rainfall (mm)	300	290	290	150	40	10	10	10	40	150	240	290

◀ **Fig 2** Climate statistics for Rio de Janeiro and Pôrto Nacional.

 Brazilian Embassy http://www.brazil.org.uk/welcome.html

Climate

Most of Brazil has a tropical climate, although there are variations throughout the country. The northern part of Brazil is on the Equator. The sun is overhead all year, meaning there is little seasonal variation. The average temperature is around 25°C. It rains every day, giving a yearly total of around 2200 mm. The Brazilian Highlands have a more seasonal climate. It is hot and wet in summer, and warm and dry in winter. The eastern corner of Brazil is usually hot and dry. It only rains for two or three months and often experiences **drought**. On average it receives less than 500 mm of rainfall a year. The most pleasant climate is along the south-eastern coast. Temperatures average 20°C in winter and 25°C in summer. There is reliable rainfall throughout the year.

Q3 Use Fig 2 to draw climate graphs for Rio de Janeiro and Pôrto Nacional.

Q4 Describe the climate of the two places.

Vegetation

The differences in Brazil's climate result in several different types of **ecosystem**.

- Tropical rainforest – in the north, the heavy rainfall and high temperatures support the world's largest area of tropical rainforest. This ecosystem contains a huge variety of trees, plants and animals. Less **dense** rainforest also grows along the eastern coast.

- Tropical grassland – the Brazilian Highlands contain a mixture of trees and open grassland. This area is known as the Cerrado.

- Scrubland – the eastern corner of Brazil only has enough rainfall to support small trees, thorn bushes and cacti. These plants have adapted to survive in a very dry climate. This area is called the Caatinga.

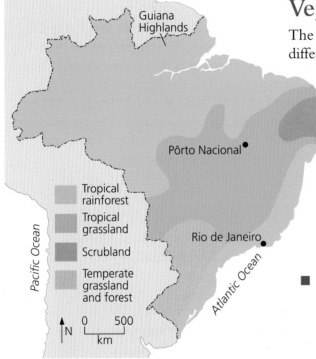

▲ **Fig 3** Brazil: vegetation types.

Key words

dense – crowded

drought – a long period of dry weather

ecosystem – a community of plants and animals

plateau – a large flat upland area

river basin – the area of land drained by a river

SUMMARY

- Brazil is the largest country in South America.
- The north of Brazil is a low-lying river basin.
- The south of Brazil is a gently sloping plateau.
- Brazil has a tropical climate, with regional variations.
- Brazil's ecosystems include tropical rainforest, tropical grassland and scrubland.

SUMMARY activity

Use the map in Fig 1 to draw a cross-section from Rio to the Guiana Highlands. Label your cross-section to show how the vegetation and climate change across the country.

 Instituto Nacional de Meteorolgia http://www.inmet.gov.br/index.html/

98 Brazil – history

In this section of the book you will investigate the following things:
- What is the pre-colonial history of Brazil?
- What is the colonial history of Brazil?
- How has Brazil changed since independence?

Pre-colonial history

▲ **Fig 1** Brazilian Amerindians.

Q1 Describe the route taken to South America by Amerindian people.

The original inhabitants of Brazil are known as **Amerindians**. Amerindians arrived in Brazil sometime between 5000 and 10 000 years ago. They are thought to have migrated from Asia via North America. At the time it would have been possible to cross the Bering Strait because sea levels were lower (Fig 2). Over many years the migrants made their way south, into the area that is now Brazil. They settled mainly in the Amazon Basin. They lived in small groups, which developed their own languages and cultures. The people lived off the land as hunters and gatherers, and through simple farming (Fig 1).

Colonial history

Brazil was discovered by the Portuguese in 1500. An explorer called Pedro Cabal was searching for a route to the Indian Ocean. He travelled too far west, and came across the continent of South America by mistake (Fig 3).

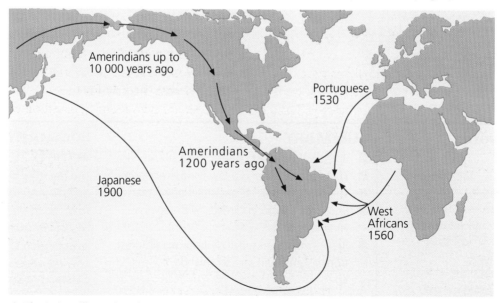

▲ **Fig 2** Brazilian migrations.

▲ *Fig 3* *Portuguese colonists arriving in Brazil.*

The first Portuguese **colonies** were settled on the north-east coast in 1530. The fertile soils in this area were suitable for growing sugar cane. The sugar cane was then exported back to Portugal. The Portuguese colonists tried to force the Amerindian people to work on sugar **plantations**. However, this was mainly unsuccessful. In 1560, thousands of Amerindians were killed by the smallpox virus, brought by Portuguese settlers. As a result, the Portuguese began importing slaves from West Africa to work on the plantations. Over the next 300 years over four million Africans were brought to Brazil.

Q2 How was Brazil discovered by mistake?

Q3 Why were slaves brought to Brazil by the Portuguese?

Independence

Brazil became independent in 1822, much earlier than other European colonies. The Prince of Portugal, who was living in Brazil, declared himself to be the Emperor of Brazil. He ruled the new country until 1831, when he gave the throne to his son, Pedro II. In 1850 the slave trade was abolished, due to pressure from Britain. Portugal could no longer import slaves. As a result, people from Italy, Spain and Germany migrated to Brazil to work on the plantations. Coffee became Brazil's most important export crop.

Q4 Why were migrants from other European countries encouraged after 1850?

Republic

In 1890 Brazil became a **republic**. This means it is a country without a king or queen. Army officers overthrew the Emperor and elected a government. Since this time, Brazil has twice been ruled by **dictators**. Brazil became a true democracy in 1989 when the public were able to vote directly for the President. In its short history, Brazil has developed its own identity, based on a blend of different cultures.

Key words

Amerindian – native people of South America
colony – an area, or country, ruled by another country
dictator – an unelected ruler
plantation – a large farm
republic – a country with a president as head of state

SUMMARY

- Amerindian people migrated to Brazil up to 10 000 years ago.
- Brazil was made a colony of Portugal in 1500.
- African slaves were forced to work on Brazilian sugar plantations.
- Brazil became independent in 1822.

SUMMARY *activity*

Draw a labelled timeline to show key events in Brazil's history.

99 Brazil – population and settlement

In this section of the book you will investigate the following things:

■ Where do people live in Brazil?

■ Who are the Brazilian people?

■ What is the population structure of Brazil?

Population distribution

Brazil has a population of 170 million. This makes it the fifth most populated country in the world. As in other countries, Brazil's population is spread out very unevenly (Fig 1).

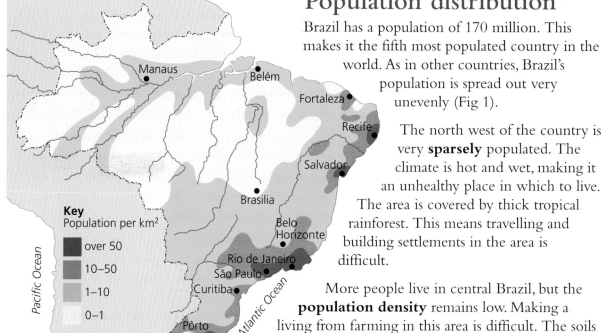

Key
Population per km²

- over 50
- 10–50
- 1–10
- 0–1

The north west of the country is very **sparsely** populated. The climate is hot and wet, making it an unhealthy place in which to live. The area is covered by thick tropical rainforest. This means travelling and building settlements in the area is difficult.

More people live in central Brazil, but the **population density** remains low. Making a living from farming in this area is difficult. The soils are quite poor and the rainfall is unreliable.

Most Brazilians live in towns and cities on the north–east and south–east coast. The climate here is cooler and more healthy. There is enough rain to ensure a reliable water supply. The area has fertile soils and is rich in natural resources.

▲ *Fig 1* *Population distribution and settlement in Brazil.*

The most popular places to live are cities such as Rio de Janeiro, São Paulo, Pôrto Alegre and Recife. Most of these cities grew up around natural harbours, which are important for trading with other countries. The most important inland city is Brasilia. Brasilia was a new settlement, built to become the nation's new capital in 1960.

Brazilian people

Brazil is a **multi-racial** society. Its people are descended from different groups of people who migrated to Brazil. Many people are 'mixed race' as a result of marriages between different **ethnic groups** (Fig 2).

Q1 Use Fig 1 to describe the population distribution of Brazil.

Q2 Why do most people live along the coast?

European	55%
Mixed race	39%
African	5%
Japanese	0.5%
Other	0.35%
Amerindian	0.15%

▶ *Fig 2* *Brazilian people.*

 US Census Bureau – International Data Base http://www.census.gov/ipc/www/idbnew.html

- Amerindians – the first inhabitants of Brazil arrived around 1000 years ago. They are thought to have migrated from Asia, via North America. Today there are only around 200 000 Amerindians left.

- Europeans – the first Europeans in Brazil were the Portuguese. They arrived and settled on the north-east coast in 1530. After 1850, people from Italy, Spain and Germany also migrated to Brazil.

- Africans – the Portuguese brought slaves from West Africa to work on plantations and in mines. This continued until 1850 when the slave trade was banned.

- Japanese – in the early 1900s a number of Japanese people settled on the east coast in São Paolo.

> **Q3** Why is Brazil described as a 'multi-racial' society?

Population structure

Brazil has had rapid population growth this century, although it has begun to slow down. In the 1960s women had an average of six children. Today the average number of children per woman is just over two. Nevertheless, Brazil still has a very young population. Two-thirds of its people are aged under 29 (Fig 3). This means the population will continue to increase as these people have children of their own. Brazil's death rate has declined, as health care has improved. As a result, life expectancy has increased to 67 years.

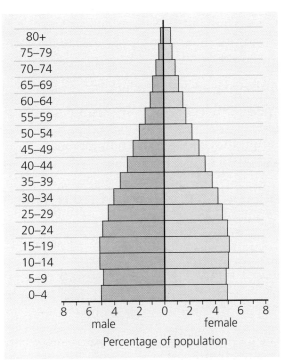

▲ **Fig 3** Population structure of Brazil.

> **Q4** What percentage of Brazil's population is over 60 years old?

Key words

ethnic group – people of the same racial group

multi-racial – people of several different races

population density – the number of people in a certain area

sparse – not crowded

SUMMARY

- The north west of Brazil is sparsely populated.
- Brazil's coast is densely populated.
- Brazil is a multi-racial society, descended from immigrants.
- Brazil has a young population.
- Brazil's population growth rate is slowing down.

SUMMARY activity

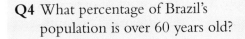
Use the data in Fig 2 to draw a pie chart to show the ethnic mix of Brazil's population.

100 Brazil – development

In this section of the book you will investigate the following things:
- How developed is Brazil?
- How do standards of living vary?
- Why do standards of living vary?

Standards of living

Brazil has **developed** rapidly since the 1970s. Growth in industry has made it the world's tenth largest economy. Brazil is now described as a **Newly Industrialised Country (NIC)** (unit 74). It is no longer a poor country, but is not yet as rich as Europe and the USA. The United Nations ranks Brazil as the 79th most developed country in the world.

As Brazil has become richer, the overall standard of living has risen (Fig 1). However, there are enormous inequalities between different regions and different groups of people.

Population growth rate (%)		0.8
Birth rate (per 1000 population)		20
Death rate (per 1000 population)		9
Infant mortality rate (per 1000 population)		53
Life expectancy (years):	Men	57
	Women	66
Urban population (%)		78
People per doctor		1000
Literacy (%)		81

▲ **Fig 1** How developed is Brazil?

Q1 Use the data in Fig 1 to compare standards of living in Brazil with the UK (see world statistics, pages 234–5).

Regional inequalities

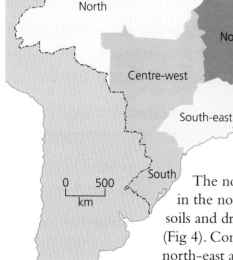

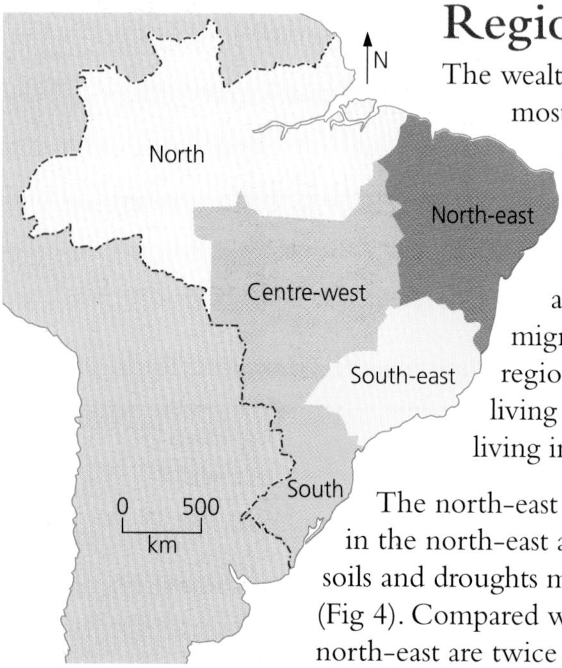

▲ **Fig 2** Brazil's regions.

The wealthiest area of Brazil is the south-east region. Brazil's most important cities, Rio de Janeiro and São Paulo, are located here. The region has developed since the 1950s as an important centre of industry. Money has been invested in the area to build factories and improve services such as electricity and water supply. Many thousands of people have migrated to the area in search of work. The south-east region is now home to 43% of the population. People living in the south-east have the highest standards of living in the country (Fig 3).

The north-east of Brazil is one of the poorest areas. Most people in the north-east are farmers who do not own their own land. Poor soils and droughts mean they struggle to make a living from farming (Fig 4). Compared with the people of the south-east, people in the north-east are twice as likely to be **illiterate**, earn half as much money and have a shorter life span (Fig 3).

Amnesty International – Brazil http://www.amnesty.org/ailib/countries/indx219.htm

Social inequalities

The richest 20% of the population own two-thirds of the wealth in Brazil. This means that although some people have a high standard of living, the majority of people are poor. Although there is little obvious **racism** in Brazil, the richest people tend to be white. The average income for white Brazilians is £150 a month. The poorest group tend to be black. The average wage for black Brazilians is only £60 a month. More white people live in the south-east, while more black people live in the north-east. The average wage for people of mixed race is £70 a month. Racial inequality began in the seventeenth century when white Europeans enslaved black Africans to work on their land.

Brazil	South-east	North-east
Birth rate (per 1000 population)	22	48
Infant mortality rate (per 1000 population)	49	109
Life expectancy (years)	66	56
People per doctor	875	2150
Adult literacy (%)	72	39
People employed in industry (%)	70	10
Brazil's energy consumption (%)	71	13
People with electricity (%)	82	15
People with clean water (%)	64	23
Car ownership (%)	66	10

▲ **Fig 3** *Differences between the south-east and north-east region.*

Q2 Describe how race can affect standards of living in Brazil.

Q3 How did racial inequality in Brazil begin?

Solutions

The government of Brazil has the difficult job of trying to reduce inequality. There are many schemes aimed at improving standards of living of the poor. In 1995, the government took 100 000 hectares of land from large landowners and shared it between 3 600 poor families. These poor families are now able to make a living from farming their own land. Of course, the landowners were very unhappy about this scheme.

Q4 Do you think land should be taken away from rich landowners and given to the poor?

▲ **Fig 4** *Poor living conditions in the north-east.*

Key words

developed – improvement in wealth and standards of living

illiterate – unable to read or write

Newly Industrialised Country (NIC) – country which has recently become industrialised

racism – belief that not all races are equal

SUMMARY

- Wealth in Brazil is shared out very unequally.
- The wealthiest region of Brazil is the south-east.
- White Brazilians have a higher standard of living than black Brazilians.
- The Brazilian government is attempting to reduce inequality.

SUMMARY *activity*

Write a report for the Brazilian government about inequality between the north-east and south-east regions. Illustrate your report with graphs.

101 Brazil – agriculture

In this section of the book you will investigate the following things:
- What types of farming are important in Brazil?
- How is farming changing?

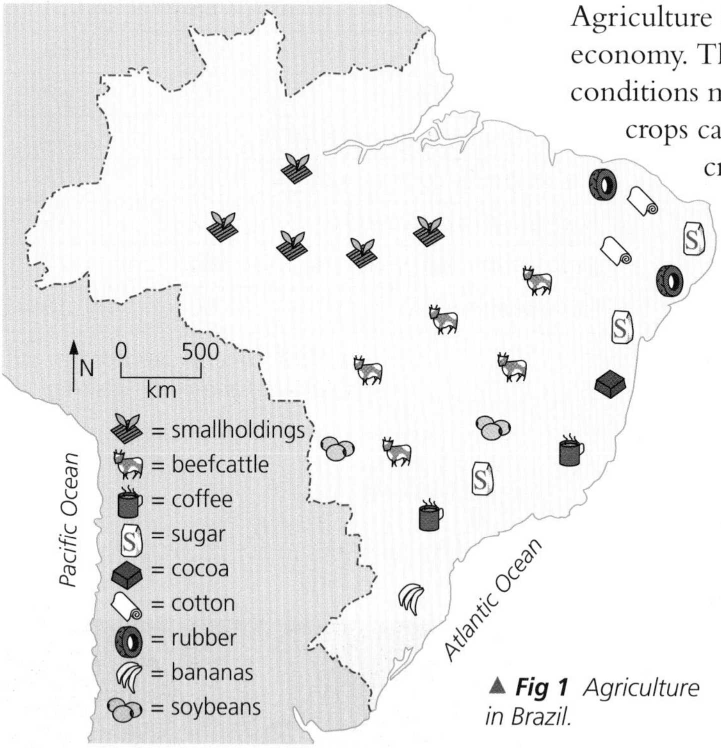

Agriculture is an important part of Brazil's economy. The range of soils and climatic conditions mean that many different types of crops can be grown (Fig 1). Brazil grows crops ranging from wheat to bananas. **Pastoral** farming is also important. Around 160 million cattle are reared for beef. Much of Brazil's farm produce is exported to other countries. These exports earn a third of Brazil's income.

Q1 What are Brazil's most important crops?

Fig 1 Agriculture in Brazil.

Pacific Ocean
Atlantic Ocean

N
0   500
km

= smallholdings
= beefcattle
= coffee
= sugar
= cocoa
= cotton
= rubber
= bananas
= soybeans

▲ **Fig 2** Plantation farming.

Plantations

The largest farms in Brazil are called 'plantations'. Many plantations were begun by Portuguese settlers in the sixteenth century. They tend to be located in the north-east and south of the country. Plantations often only grow one crop, usually for export. The most important crops are sugar cane, coffee and soybeans. Plantations can be extremely large. Farms of over 50 000 **hectares** are not unusual. This is 300 times larger than average UK farms (Fig 2).

Plantations are important employers in rural areas. Each plantation may provide work for hundreds of people. Workers may be paid by how much work they do. During harvest time, workers migrate from poorer areas, such as the north-east. Plantations often contain small towns built to house the workers. Housing, shops and healthcare are provided.

Plantations are having to change in order to compete with farms in other countries. They are increasing the range of crops they grow. Soybeans are a successful new export crop. Plantations are also becoming more mechanised.

 Brazil Agriculture http://www.planalto.gov.br/secom/co/ecao/agrain.htm

More profit can be made by using machines rather than human labour. As a result, many workers have lost their jobs. This has increased migration to the cities. Plantations are also processing more of their produce. For example, oranges are made into orange juice. Orange juice is more profitable than oranges.

Q2 What are plantations?

Q3 In what ways are plantations different to farms in the UK?

Small farms

The number of small farms is increasing in the Amazon region (Fig 3). Over 1200 km of roads have been built into the Amazon rainforest. This has opened up the area to settlers. The government gives free land grants, of up to 100 hectares, to settlers wanting their own farms. Before they can begin growing crops, settlers first have to clear the area of trees and undergrowth.

The government has allowed farming in the Amazon region to reduce pressure on cities in the south-east. Every year thousands of landless farmers migrate to cities, such as Rio and São Paulo, in search of work. The offer of free land has persuaded many people to migrate to the Amazon region instead.

Although some small farms are successful, a large number have failed. The forest appears to be fertile, but in fact the soil is quite poor. After the forest has been cleared, the soil is left exposed to the rain. The rain washes away **nutrients** in the soil, and even the soil itself. After a few years the farmer is no longer able to grow crops. Some farmers have given up and sold their plots to cattle ranchers.

▲ *Fig 3* A Brazilian smallholding.

Q4 Why is the number of small farms increasing in the Amazon region?

Q5 What problems are faced by farmers in the Amazon?

Key words

hectare – ten thousand square metres

nutrient – a chemical needed for living things to grow

pastoral – rearing animals

plantation – a large farm, usually in a poorer country

SUMMARY

- Brazil's climate allows a wide range of crops to be grown.
- Plantations are huge farms, often growing just one crop.
- Plantations are having to modernise to stay competitive.
- The number of small farms has increased in the Amazon region.

SUMMARY *activity*

Imagine you are the owner of a large sugar cane plantation. Explain the things you could do to make your plantation more profitable. Use the following subheadings: crops, machinery, processing.

102 Brazil – industry

In this section of the book you will investigate the following things:
- How important is mining to Brazil's economy?
- How important is manufacturing to Brazil's economy?
- How important is tourism to Brazil's economy?
- What are the destinations of Brazil's exports?

Brazil is extremely rich in **resources**. It has enormous reserves of timber, **minerals**, hydro-electric power and a young population. Since the 1940s, Brazil has used these resources to develop its industries. With government encouragement, there has been rapid growth in mining, manufacturing, finance and tourism. Brazil has become an industrialised country, **exporting** goods all over the world. Brazil's most important trading partners are the European Union, followed by the USA.

Primary	23%	
Secondary	24%	
Tertiary	53%	

◀ **Fig 1** Employment structure for Brazil.

Q1 💻 Use the data in Fig 1 to draw a pie chart to show the employment structure of Brazil.

Mining

Brazil has large reserves of iron ore, gold, copper, zinc, bauxite, manganese and tin (Fig 2). These minerals provide 10% of Brazil's export earnings. One of the world's largest deposits of iron ore is located at Carajas, in the Amazon rainforest. There are thought to be 18 billion tonnes of high grade iron ore, enough to last around 400 years. The Brazilian government set up a company called 'Companhia do Vale do Rio Doce' (CVRD) to mine the area. The mine is massive. It has already reached 200 metres deep, and has another 200 metres to go. The mine produces 8% of the world's iron ore, and has provided 7000 jobs on site. Most workers are housed in a specially-built town. The iron ore is transported 690 km to the coast by very long trains. Much of the ore is then exported to Japan, Korea and Germany.

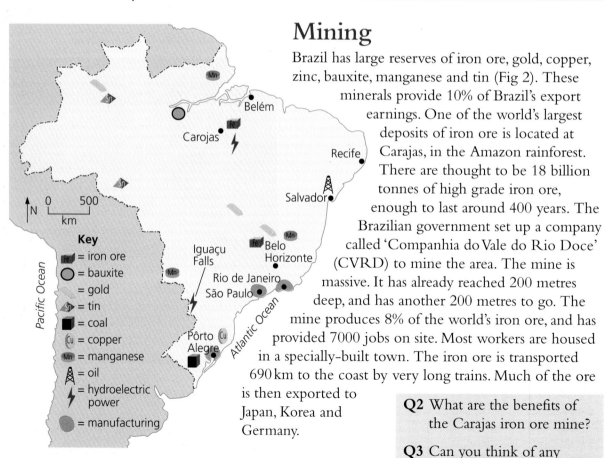

Key
- Fe = iron ore
- ○ = bauxite
- = gold
- Sn = tin
- ■ = coal
- Cu = copper
- Mn = manganese
- ⚡ = oil
- ⚡ = hydroelectric power
- ● = manufacturing

▲ **Fig 2** Mining and manufacturing in Brazil.

Q2 What are the benefits of the Carajas iron ore mine?

Q3 Can you think of any problems it might cause?

 Brazil Info http://www.brazilinfo.com/

Manufacturing

Manufacturing has been the key to Brazil's economic development. During the Second World War, shortages of imported goods forced Brazil to manufacture its own. The government encouraged the growth of many different types of industry. As a result, Brazil now exports a huge range of manufactured goods. Some of Brazil's most important exports include cars, aircraft, steel, machinery and chemicals. The government has allowed many foreign companies to invest in Brazil. Car manufacturers such as Fiat, General Motors and Volkswagen have set up large factories. Manufacturing industries are concentrated in the south-east of Brazil. Most factories are located around São Paulo, Rio de Janeiro, Pôrto Alegre and Belo Horizonte.

Q4 Why did manufacturing begin to expand in Brazil in the 1940s?

Tourism

Tourism is becoming more important to Brazil's economy. Around three million tourists visit Brazil each year. The most popular tourist destinations include the beaches of Rio de Janeiro, the historic cities of Bahia and Minas Gerais, and the Iguaçu waterfall (Fig 3). Recently the development of '**eco-tourism**' has made the Amazon rainforest a growing attraction. The government sees tourism as an important source of income. It has encouraged tourism by improving tourist facilities such as hotels and transport. After reports of violence against tourists in the 1990s, special tourist police squads have been established in popular destinations. The aim is for tourism to provide 10% of Brazil's earnings.

▶ *Fig 3* Iguaçu Falls – a popular tourist destination.

Q5 How has the Brazilian government encouraged tourism in Brazil?

▶ *Fig 4* Brazil's exports.

Export destination	$US billion	% total
European Union	12.6	27.0
United States	8.8	18.9
South America	6.6	13.3
Central America	3.3	7.2
Japan	3.1	6.6
Middle East	2.0	4.3
Other	10.6	22.7
Total	**47.0**	**100.0**

Key words

eco-tourism – holidays in natural areas with little impact on the environment
export – things which are sold to another country
manufacturing – making things
minerals – rocks which contain things useful to people
resources – natural things used by people

SUMMARY

■ *Brazil is rich in mineral resources such as iron ore.*
■ *Manufacturing industry now provides most of Brazil's export income.*
■ *The government is encouraging the growth of tourism.*
■ *Brazil's most important trading partners are the European Union and the USA.*

SUMMARY activity

Use the data in Fig 4 to show the destination of Brazil's exports. You could mark the information on to a map using arrows of different widths, or you could draw a pie chart.

CVRD mining company http://www.cvrd.com.br/

103 Brazil – deforestation

In this section of the book you will investigate the following things:
- Why is deforestation happening in Brazil?
- What are the effects of deforestation in Brazil?
- What can be done to protect Brazil's tropical rainforests?

Brazil is home to two-fifths of the world's remaining tropical rainforests. Tropical rainforests are the most diverse and complex **ecosystems** on Earth (unit 36). In Brazil, tropical rainforests are found in the Amazon basin, and in places along the Atlantic coast (Fig 1). Between the 1960s and late 1980s, **deforestation** in Brazil increased at an alarming rate. It is estimated that between 5% and 12% of the Amazon rainforest has been cleared.

◀ **Fig 1** *A satellite image showing deforestation in Brazil.*

Q1 Where are Brazil's tropical rainforests located?

Q2 Why is it difficult to calculate exactly how much of Brazil's rainforest has been cut down?

Causes of deforestation

Deforestation is happening in Brazil for the same reason it happened in Europe. Brazil needs land and resources to improve standards of living (Fig 2).

- Agriculture – forest is cleared to provide more farmland.
- Settlement – large-scale settlement programmes provide homes for Brazil's landless people.
- Ranching – the forest is burned then turned into pasture to graze beef cattle.

▲ **Fig 2** *Clearing the rainforest for farming.*

- Logging – valuable trees such as mahogany are harvested for export.
- Mining – the Amazon rainforest is rich in minerals such as gold, iron ore and bauxite.
- Dams – there are plans to build 73 dams to supply vital hydro-electric power. The reservoirs will flood, and kill, large areas of forest.
- Roads – 12 000 km of roads have opened up the Amazon rainforest to settlers.

Q3 How can deforestation improve standards of living for Brazilian people?

Effects

The loss of tropical rainforests is one of the world's greatest environmental problems. Tropical rainforests contain up to 90% of all known species of plants and animals. It is predicted that a minimum of 100 000 species will become extinct within the next 40 years. Unknown benefits to industry, agriculture and medicine will be lost forever.

Deforestation causes massive soil erosion (Fig 3). Without trees to intercept the heavy tropical rain, soil is easily washed away into rivers. This lowers the quality of the water and can cause flooding downstream. The deforested area quickly becomes infertile as nutrients are washed out of the remaining soil.

Deforestation may be contributing to **global warming** (unit 87). When trees are burned they release carbon dioxide, a greenhouse gas, into the atmosphere. Fewer trees mean that less carbon dioxide is converted to oxygen.

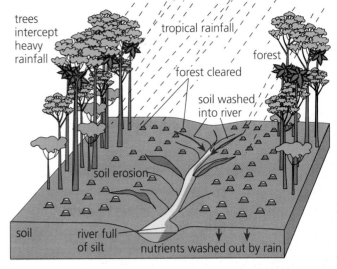

trees intercept heavy rainfall

tropical rainfall

forest

forest cleared

soil washed into river

soil erosion

soil

river full of silt

nutrients washed out by rain

▲ *Fig 3* *Deforestation causes soil erosion.*

Q4 Do people living in the UK have any right to tell Brazil not to cut down its forests?

Protection

The Brazilian government has taken a number of steps to protect the Amazon rainforest. In 1989 it abolished **tax incentives** for farming and ranching developments. In 1996 it stopped giving new licences for logging mahogany trees. A number of areas have been made into National Parks and given better protection. Satellite photos are used to monitor the rate of deforestation, and to spot illegal logging.

Sustainable ways of using the rainforest are being encouraged. Many rainforest products such as fruit and nuts can be harvested without damaging the forest. In places, selective felling is possible. Valuable trees are removed without damaging the surrounding areas.

Key words

deforestation – cutting down trees without replacing them

ecosystem – a community of plants and animals

global warming – a gradual warming of the Earth's atmosphere

tax incentives – lower tax rates for certain activities

SUMMARY

- Brazil has the world's largest remaining area of tropical rainforest.
- Deforestation is happening as Brazil becomes more developed.
- Deforestation can have disastrous effects, locally and globally.
- Rainforests need to be managed in a more sustainable way.

SUMMARY *activity*

💻 *Prepare a detailed presentation on one cause and one effect of deforestation in Brazil. Finish your presentation with a suggestion about how the rainforest could be used in a sustainable way.*

 Amazon Interactive http://www.eduweb.com/amazon.html

104 Brazil – Rio de Janeiro

In this section of the book you will investigate the following things:
- Where is Rio?
- What is life like in Rio?
- How is Rio changing?

Rio de Janeiro

Rio de Janeiro is located in south-eastern Brazil, on the Atlantic coast (Fig 1). The city has a spectacular setting (Fig 2). It is built on a narrow coastal plain, hemmed in by the sea on one side and by mountains covered in forest on the other. It is a city of enormous contrast. Stunning skyscrapers and sprawling shanty towns are found side by side.

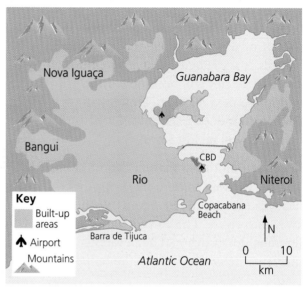

▲ **Fig 1** Rio de Janeiro.

▲ **Fig 2** Rio's spectacular setting.

Rio began to grow in the sixteenth century, when it was an important sugar milling centre. Rio became the capital of Brazil in 1763, after gold had been found inland. The natural harbour, Guanabara Bay, was an excellent site to develop a port. Rio soon became a very important trading centre. Although the capital of Brazil was moved to Brasilia in 1960, Rio remains a very important city for business and industry. It is the second largest city in Brazil, after São Paulo. It has a population of over ten million people and covers an area of 6500 square kilometres.

Q1 Why did Rio develop as an important city?

Favelas

A third of Rio's population live in **shanty towns**, called '**favelas**'. Favelas are areas of low-quality housing, built by migrants to the city (Fig 3). Favelas occupy the steep hillsides around the centre of the city. The risk of landslides make them dangerous places to live.

Forty years ago, favelas were nothing more than temporary wooden shacks. Today, some favelas have been transformed into permanent settlements. They have slowly been upgraded by the residents. Wood has been replaced by bricks, concrete and corrugated iron. The largest favela in Rio is Rocinha. Rocinha is home to around 700 000 people. Many parts of Rocinha now have services, including water and electricity. There are schools, shops and clinics.

Q2 What is a favela?

Q3 How has Rocinha favela changed?

▲ **Fig 3** A favela in Rio.

Barra

Barra is a new **suburb** of Rio, built to relieve overcrowding in the city. It is located in an area of flat land 20 km to the south. To provide good road links, tunnels have been bored through the mountains. In some places, where the mountains meet the sea, roads have been built on stilts. Barra is one of the wealthiest areas of Rio. It has high-quality apartments, with security on the gates. Standards of living are similar to those in Europe. Large American-style shopping malls have been built alongside the motorway.

Q4 Why was the new settlement of Barra built?

Change

The latest figures show that the centre of Rio has stopped growing. Middle-class people are in fact moving out of Rio, to live in Barra. At the same time, migrants from the countryside still arrive on the city outskirts with nothing. They build basic shelters from scrap materials. The newest favelas have no electricity, running water or sanitation. Standards of living are very low. The government is trying to improve life in the favelas by building new houses. In places, schools, clinics and childcare facilities are being provided.

Q5 How is the centre of Rio changing?

Key words

favela – a Brazilian shanty town

shanty town – area of low-quality, self-built, housing

suburb – housing at the edge of a city

SUMMARY

- Rio is Brazil's second largest city.
- A third of Rio's population live in shanty towns, called favelas.
- Barra is a suburb of high-quality housing, built to the south of Rio.
- Middle-class people are moving out of the centre of Rio.
- Migrants continue to arrive on the outskirts of the city.

SUMMARY activity

Write two diary extracts. One for a teenager living in Rocinha, and one for a teenager living in Barra.

 Encarta – Rio de Janeiro http://encarta.msn.com/find/Concise.asp?2=1&pg=2&ti=ooD2F000

105 Fieldwork

In this section of the book you will investigate the following things:
- What is fieldwork?
- How should a fieldwork enquiry be structured?
- How should questionnaires be used?

Fieldwork

Fieldwork is an important part of geography. It is an investigation which takes place outside the classroom (Fig 1). Fieldwork involves collecting **primary information**. This is information which is collected 'first-hand'. Primary information is gathered by counting things, measuring things, mapping, sketching, photographing and filling in questionnaires. When fieldwork is written up, it can also include **secondary information**. This is 'second-hand' information from books, magazines, CD ROMs and the internet.

◀ **Fig 1** *Fieldwork takes place outside the classroom.*

Q1 What is primary information?

Q2 What is secondary information?

Questions or hypotheses

A successful fieldwork investigation will be based on questions, or **hypotheses**. Questions are simply stated, investigated, and then answered in your write up. An example is 'Does the river become wider as it flows downstream?' Hypotheses are statements about the topic. For example, 'The river becomes wider as it flows downstream'. After the hypotheses have been investigated, they are either accepted, or rejected, in the write up.

Q3 Write three hypotheses that you could investigate.

Writing up fieldwork

Introduction – The introduction should say what the investigation is about. Include the questions, or hypotheses, that are being investigated. Say what information will be collected during the fieldwork. Locate the fieldwork area with a labelled map. Include background information on the chosen topic.

Data collection – The data collection section should describe exactly how the information was collected. This must include lots of detail, such as times and locations. Say why the method was

Questionnaires are a good way of finding out about people's background, actions and opinions.
Points to consider
- Always be polite and explain why you are carrying out the questionnaire.
- How many questionnaires will you carry out?
- Who will you ask?
- Only ask questions which are important to your investigation.
- Do not ask how old people are.
- Do not ask people what sex they are.
- Keep it short.

▲ **Fig 2** *Questionnaires.*

 Virtual Fieldtrips http://utexas.edu/depts/grg/virtdept/contents.html

chosen. It is a good idea to include labelled diagrams, or photos, of the methods. Remember to include an example of any data collection sheets, such as questionnaires.

Presentation and analysis – The
information collected must be presented using a range of different techniques. These could include graphs, tables, maps, sketches and photos. Make sure they all have titles and labels. The information then needs to be analysed. Describe each graph, table, map sketch or photo, including figures where possible. Try to explain what each of them shows.

Conclusion – This section should
summarise the main findings of the investigation. The original questions should be answered. If hypotheses were used, these should be accepted or rejected. Try to include figures.

Evaluation – This is a chance
to comment on how successful the fieldwork was. Describe any problems with the data collection. Say how the methods could be improved if the fieldwork was done again. Comment on the accuracy of the results. Say whether they were what was expected. Finally, comment on whether the conclusions might be different if the investigation took place in a different location, or at a different time.

▲ **Fig 3** *A sample questionnaire.*

Q4 Make a list of the sections that should be included in a fieldwork write up.

▶ **Fig 4** *Possible fieldwork topics.*

Topic	Unit
Weathering of rocks	12
River changes downstream	14
Longshore drift	19
School microclimate	30
Migration	43
Settlement hierarchy	53
Manufacture of sports shoes	73
Energy use	82
Recycling	88

Key words

fieldwork – an enquiry which takes place outside the classroom
hypothesis – a statement which is investigated to see if it is correct
primary information – original information
secondary information – second-hand information

SUMMARY

- Fieldwork is the collection of primary data for a geographical enquiry.
- Fieldwork must be based on questions, or hypotheses.
- Fieldwork should be written up in the following order: introduction, data collection, data presentation and analysis, conclusion and evaluation.

SUMMARY activity

☐ Carry out a fieldwork investigation based on one of the topics in this book (Fig 4).

 National Geographic http://www.nationalgeographic.com/

106 Atlas skills

In this section of the book you will investigate the following things:
- What information is contained in an atlas?
- How is an atlas used?
- What is latitude and longitude?

Atlases

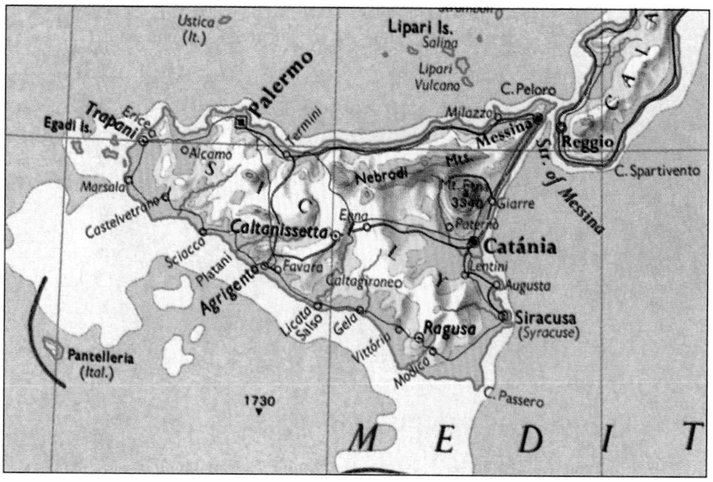

Geography often involves learning about places. It is important to know whereabouts in the world places are. One way of finding this out is to use an atlas. An atlas is a book which contains many different maps. The maps are at different scales, ranging from the whole world, to a region of a country. Maps may be physical or political (Fig 1). **Physical maps** show mountains, plains, rivers

▲ **Fig 1** Atlas map of Sicily, Italy.

Q1 What is the difference between a physical and a political map?

and seas. **Political maps** show towns and cities, roads, railways and borders between countries. Atlases also contain **thematic maps**. Thematic maps show information such as climate, vegetation, industry, agriculture and population.

Using an atlas

There are two ways of finding information in an atlas. The **contents** page at the front gives details about what is on each page. This is useful for finding

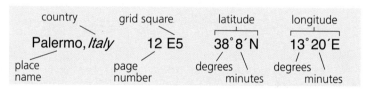

▲ **Fig 2** Atlas index.

thematic maps. The **index**, at the back of the atlas, is best for looking up countries, cities and towns. All the places are listed in alphabetical order. Each place name is followed by references, which tell you where to find it in the atlas (Fig 2). The first number is the page number. This is followed by a grid reference to locate the place on the page. The last references give the latitude and longitude of the place.

Q2 Where in an atlas is the index?

Q3 Find a map of Australia using the index in an atlas.

CIA world fact book http://www.odci.gov/cia/publications/factbook/

Latitude and longitude

Latitude and longitude are used to pinpoint a location anywhere in the world. Lines have been drawn onto the globe to make a grid (Fig 3). Each line is called a degree, and is written as the symbol °. To be even more accurate, each degree is divided into 60 minutes.

Lines of latitude run horizontally around the Earth. The Equator is the central point at 0°. This divides the world into a northern and southern hemisphere. Other lines of latitude run parallel to the Equator. In the northern hemisphere, the Tropic of Cancer is at $23\frac{1}{2}°$ north. The furthest point, at 90° north is the North Pole. In the southern hemisphere, the Tropic of Capricorn is at $23\frac{1}{2}°$ south. At 90° south is the South Pole. Therefore, latitude tells you how far north or south somewhere is from the Equator.

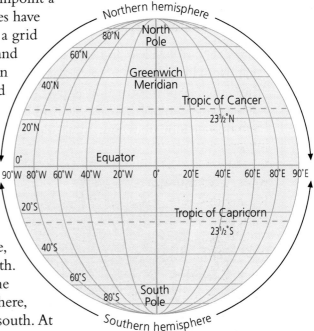

▲ **Fig 3** Latitude and longitude.

Lines of longitude run vertically, from the north pole to the south pole. They divide the world into segments, like an orange. The Greenwich Meridian is the central point at 0°. The Greenwich Meridian runs through Greenwich in London. Lines of longitude run 180° to the east, and 180° to the west. Therefore, longitude tells you how far east or west somewhere is from the Greenwich Meridian.

Q4 Which hemisphere is the UK in?

Q5 Think of a way to remember that latitude is horizontal and longitude is vertical.

Key words

contents – list of contents at the front of an atlas

index – alphabetical list of contents at the back of an atlas

physical map – map showing natural features

political map – map showing human features

thematic map – map showing information, such as climate or population

SUMMARY

- An atlas is a book containing maps and information about different countries.
- The contents and index can be used for finding things in an atlas.
- Lines of latitude run horizontally around the world.
- Lines of longitude run vertically around the world.
- Latitude and longitude can be used to give the exact location of a place.

SUMMARY activity

Use a world map in your atlas to work out the latitude and longitude of the following places: London, Athens, New York, Sydney, Rio de Janeiro, Tokyo, Delhi, Nairobi. Check your answers in the index of the atlas.

 Atlapedia Online Atlas http://www.atlapedia.com/

107 Ordnance Survey map symbols

In this section of the book you will investigate the following things:
- How are symbols used on Ordnance Survey maps?
- What different types of symbol are there?

Maps need to be clear and easy to read. If all the information was written as words, the map would become too crowded, and unreadable. For this reason, **symbols** are used to show important information (Fig 1). Symbols save space and make the map easier to understand. Symbols can also be read by anyone, no matter what language they speak. Symbols include drawings, lines, colours and letters. Some symbols are to scale, while others appear much bigger than they are in real life. All maps must include a **key** to explain what the symbols mean.

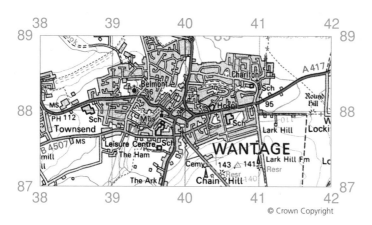

© Crown Copyright

▲ **Fig 1** Ordnance Survey map (scale 1:50 000).

Q1 What is a symbol?

Q2 Why are symbols used on Ordnance Survey maps?

Symbols

Small drawings – some symbols are drawings which look like the real thing. For example, a church with a tower, a glasshouse and a TV mast (Fig 2). Sometimes drawings are used which look nothing like the real thing. For example, a youth hostel, a bus station and a train station.

Lines – line symbols are used to show things such as roads, railways, rivers and footpaths (Fig 3). Line symbols also show boundaries between counties and areas such as National Parks. Contour lines are used to show how high the land is.

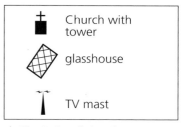

▲ **Fig 2** Small drawings as symbols.

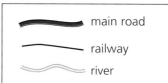

▲ **Fig 3** Line symbols.

Q3 How many different symbols are there in the OS map extract in Fig 1?

Q4 Draw the symbols, dividing them into drawings, lines, colours, letters, shortened words and tourist information.

Colours – coloured areas are used to show large areas of land use. Blue is used to show lakes and the sea. Green, sometimes with drawings, shows woodland and forests. Grey is used to show parks. Pink/orange is used to show buildings. The most common colour on Ordnance Survey maps is white. White areas are either farmland or open countryside (Fig 4).

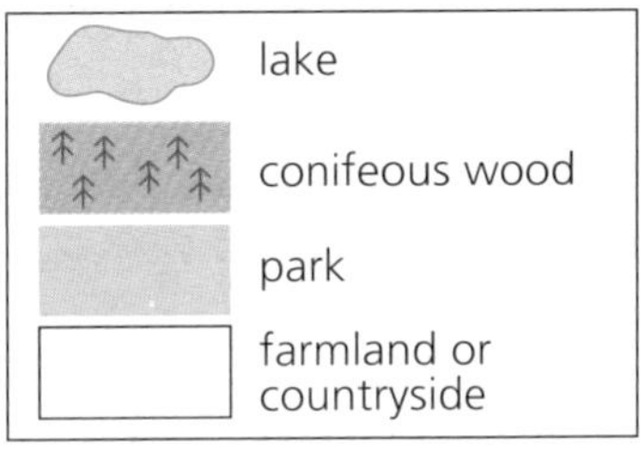

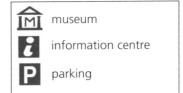

▲ **Fig 4** *Colours on maps.*

P	post office
PH	public house
MP	milepost

▲ **Fig 5** *Letters on maps.*

Letters – capital letters can be used, rather than writing the whole word. For example, P stands for post office, PH stands for public house and PC stands for public convenience (toilet) (Fig 5).

Sch	school
cemy	cemetery
Hospl	hospital
Fm	farm

▲ **Fig 6** *Shortened words on maps.*

Shortened words – words can be shortened to save space. Cemetery is shortened to 'cemy', hospital to 'hospl' and farm to Fm. These shortened words are not shown on the key (Fig 6).

Tourist information – tourist information symbols are always blue. They show areas which are interesting to visit or places of recreation. They include campsites, museums, preserved railways and theme parks (Fig 7).

museum
information centre
parking

▲ **Fig 7** *Tourist information on maps.*

The Ordnance Survey

Ordnance Survey (**OS**) is the organisation responsible for mapping Britain. They publish maps at a range of different scales for the whole country. Maps at a scale of 1:50 000 are called Landranger maps. Maps at a scale of 1:25 000 are called Outdoor Leisure maps, or Explorer maps. The symbols for these different scale maps are shown on pages 231 and 233. The 1:25 000 scale maps contain more detailed symbols. They also contain more tourist information symbols.

Key words

key – a list giving the meaning of symbols
OS – Ordnance Survey
symbol – something used to represent something else

SUMMARY

- Maps use symbols to save space and make them easy to read.
- Symbols may be drawings, lines, colours or letters.
- The Ordnance Survey are responsible for publishing maps of Britain.
- OS map symbols vary depending on the scale of the map.

SUMMARY *activity*

Make 16 cards with Ordnance Survey symbols drawn on the front and their meaning written on the back. Test yourself, and your friends, to see if you can remember what the symbols mean.

 Ordnance Survey Mapzone http://www.ordsvy.gov.uk/mapzone/main.html

108 Direction, scale and distance

In this section of the book you will investigate the following things:
- How is direction described?
- What is scale?
- How can distances be measured on a map?

Direction

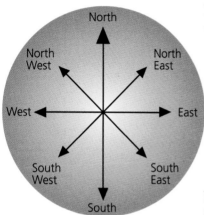

▲ **Fig 1** *Points of the compass.*

Direction is used to describe where one place is in relation to another. Direction is given using the points of a compass; north, south, east and west. One way of remembering the order of the points of a **compass** is with the saying 'Naughty Elephants Squirt Water'. The points of a compass can be divided into four further points: north-east, south-east, south-west and north-west (Fig 1). To give even more accurate directions, **bearings** can be used. The compass is divided into 360 degrees. This means up to 360 different directions can be described. For example, east is 90 degrees (Fig 2).

Q1 Draw the points of the compass.

Most maps have the points of the compass marked on them, although some maps only mark on the north point. If there are no compass points, then the top of the map should be north. On Ordnance Survey maps, light blue grid lines run from north to south, and from east to west.

Q2 Using the OS map on page 232, what direction is Thurston from Bury St Edmunds?

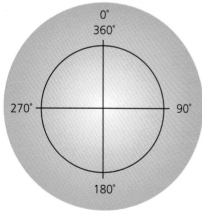

▲ **Fig 2** *Bearings.*

Scale

Scale shows how much smaller the distance on a map is, compared with the distance in real life. Ordnance Survey make maps at a variety of scales. The most common maps are 1:50 000 scale and 1:25 000 scale. Ordnance Survey always print a scale at the bottom of the map.

On a 1:50 000 scale map, the distance is 50 000 times smaller than real life. This means that 2 centimetres are equal to 1 kilometre. On a 1:25 000 scale map, the distance is 25 000 times smaller than real life. Therefore 4 centimetres are equal to 1 kilometre. As the scale increases, the level of detail on the map increases. It is worth remembering that whatever the scale of OS maps, the grid squares always equal 1 kilometre.

Q3 Which shows more detail, a 1:50 000 map, or a 1:25 000 map?

Distance

Maps can be used to measure the distance between places. The easiest way to do this is with a piece of paper (Fig 3). Place the piece of paper on the map, between the two places you want to measure. Mark the two places onto the piece of paper using arrows. Then, put the piece of paper along the scale at the bottom of the map. The distance between the two places can then be worked out (Fig 4).

To measure distances which are not in a straight line, the best option is to use a piece of string. If string is not available try marking off a piece of paper in small sections. It is always best to avoid using a ruler. It is easy to make mistakes converting centimetres into kilometres.

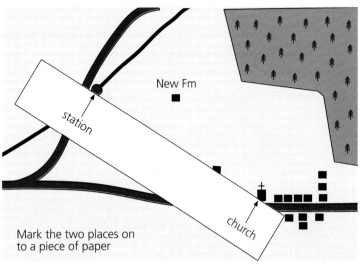

Mark the two places on to a piece of paper

▲ **Fig 3** *Measuring distance on a map.*

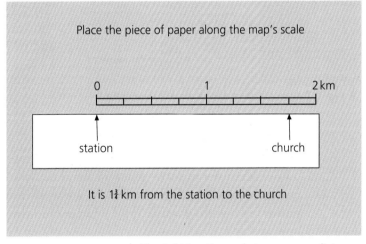

Place the piece of paper along the map's scale

It is 1¾ km from the station to the church

▲ **Fig 4** *Using the scale to measure distance.*

Q4 Using the OS map on page 232, what is the distance from Thurston railway station to Bury St Edmunds railway station?

Key words

bearing – compass direction in degrees

compass – instrument used to identify direction

direction – the location of one place in relation to another

scale – ratio between the distance on a map, and the distance in real life

SUMMARY

- Direction is described using the points of a compass.
- Scale shows how much smaller a map is compared with real life.
- The larger the scale of map, the greater the level of detail.
- Maps can be used to measure the distance between places.

SUMMARY *activity*

Draw a scale map of your classroom, or one of the rooms in your house.

109 Relief

In this section of the book you will investigate the following things:
- What is relief?
- How is relief shown on maps?

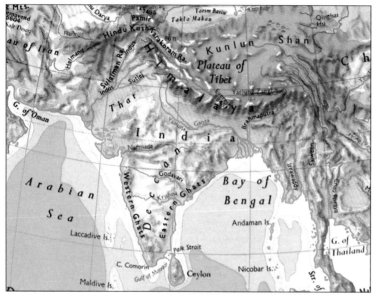

▲ **Fig 1** Layer colouring shows height in an atlas.

Relief

The surface of the Earth is rarely even or on one level. In mountainous areas the land is high with steep slopes. In other areas the land is low-lying, with gentle slopes. The shape and height of the land is called the '**relief**'. Since maps are drawn on flat paper, special symbols have been created to show relief. These symbols are layer colouring, contour lines, spot heights and triangulation pillars.

Q1 What does 'relief' mean?

Q2 Why is it difficult to show relief on a map?

Layer colouring

Layer colouring is used mainly on physical maps in atlases. Bands of different colours are used to show different heights. Low land is usually green and high land is brown. Very high mountains are shown in purple, while the very tallest points are coloured white (Fig1). Layer colouring always needs a key.

Contour lines

Contour lines are the main method used to show relief on Ordnance Survey maps. Contour lines are thin brown lines that join all places at the same height above sea level (Fig 2). Contour lines usually increase in 10 metre intervals, although this can vary depending on the relief. Contour lines have numbers written on them to show the height. It is sometimes necessary to follow the line along to find the number. Contour lines are very useful for

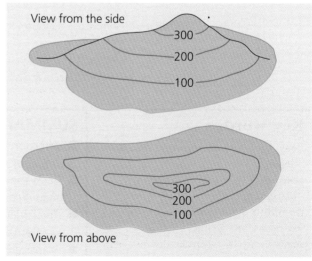

▲ **Fig 2** Contour lines.

working out the shape of the land. The simple rule is that the closer together the contour lines, the steeper the slope. The further apart the contour lines, the gentler the slope (Fig 3).

Q3 What are contour lines?

Q4 What is the height of the railway station in Thurston? (OS map on page 232)

Spot heights

Some points on an OS map are marked with an exact height in metres. These points are called '**spot heights**'. They are shown by a dot with a number written alongside (Fig 4). Spot heights have been measured very accurately by the Ordnance Survey.

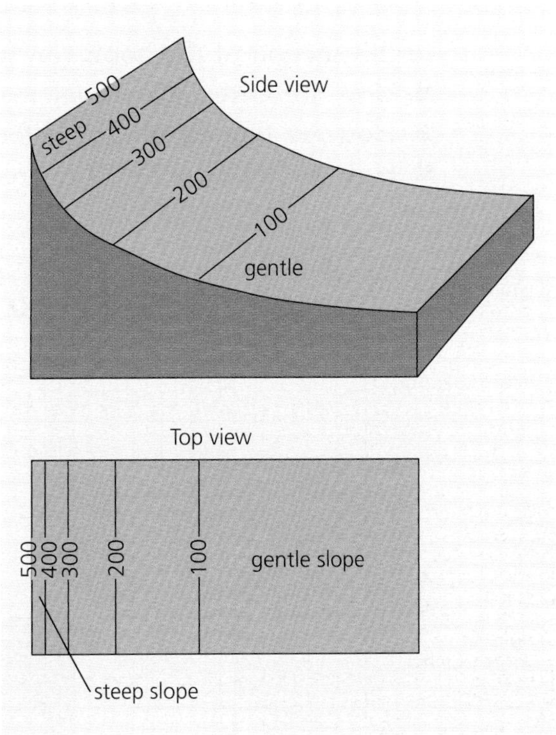

Triangulation pillars

Triangulation pillars are shown as a blue triangle with a dot inside. The height in metres is written alongside. Triangulation pillars show the highest point in the area. Triangulation pillars are the only height symbol that exist in real life. They are triangular shaped concrete pillars (Fig 5). They are used by the Ordnance Survey to make very accurate height measurements.

▲ **Fig 3** Contour lines show the gradient of the land.

• 364   364 metres above sea level

△ 678   678 metres above sea level

▲ **Fig 4** Spot heights.    ▲ **Fig 5** Triangulation pillars.

Q5 Describe the differences in relief between the OS maps on pages 230 and 232

Key words

contour line – line on an OS map joining all points of the same height
relief – the height and shape of the land
spot height – a very accurate height given on an OS map
triangulation pillar – a very accurate height, usually the highest in the area

SUMMARY

■ The surface of the Earth is uneven.
■ Maps use special symbols to show the relief of the land.
■ Layer shading is used in physical maps in atlases.
■ Contour lines, spot heights and triangulation pillars are used on OS maps.

SUMMARY activity

Make a model with layers of cardboard to show the relief of your local area. You will need to refer to your local Ordnance Survey map.

110 Grid references

In this section of the book you will investigate the following things:
- How are Ordnance Survey maps divided into grids?
- How are four-figure grid references used?
- How are six-figure grid references used?

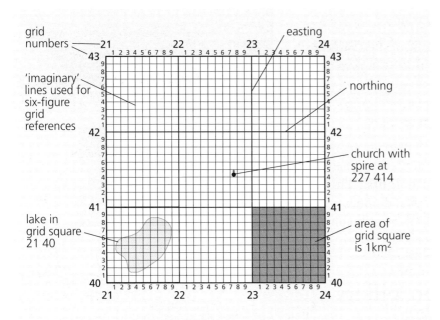

grid numbers

'imaginary' lines used for six-figure grid references

easting

northing

church with spire at 227 414

lake in grid square 21 40

area of grid square is 1km²

▲ **Fig 1** The grid.

▼ **Fig 2** Four-figure grid references.

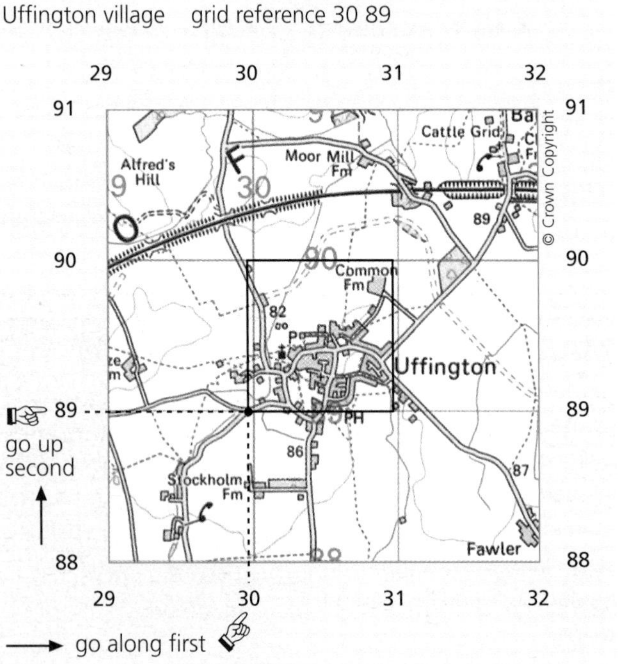

Uffington village   grid reference 30 89

© Crown Copyright

👉 89
go up second

→ go along first 👈

The grid

Ordnance Survey maps are criss-crossed by narrow blue lines. The lines running up and down the map are called '**eastings**'. The lines running across the map are called '**northings**'. Each line is numbered along the sides of the map, and also on the map itself. These lines divide the map into a grid of numbered squares. The grid is used to give each place on the map a four-figure, or six-figure **grid reference**. Grid references make it possible to find any location in Britain.

Q1 Why are grid references useful?

Four-figure grid references

Four-figure grid references locate one square on an Ordnance Survey map (Fig 2). This is an area of one square kilometre. Four-figure grid references are useful for finding larger features such as a lake, or a village.

1 Begin at the bottom left-hand corner of the map.

2 Move your finger along the bottom of the map until you come to the line with the first two numbers of the grid reference.

3 Move your finger up the map until you come to the line with the second two numbers of the grid reference.

4 This point forms the corner of four grid squares.

5 The correct grid square is always the one to the north east of this point.

Six-figure grid references

Six-figure grid references locate an area of 100 metres squared on an Ordnance Survey map (Fig 3). Six-figure grid references are useful for finding exact locations of features such as a car park or railway station.

1 Begin at the bottom left hand corner of the map.

2 Move your finger along the bottom of the map until you come to the line with the first two numbers of the grid reference.

3 To find the third number, imagine that the distance to the next gridline is divided into ten small parts. It helps to imagine number 5 being halfway. Move your finger along until you come to the right place.

4 Move your finger up the map, until you come to the line with the fourth and fifth numbers of the grid reference.

5 To find the sixth number, again imagine the distance to the next gridline is divided into ten small parts. Move your finger up until you come to the right place.

6 This point is the exact six-figure grid reference.

Q2 What is the main land use in grid square 2989 in Fig 2?

Q3 What is at grid reference 295 882 on Fig 3?

Q4 What is at grid reference 344 963 on Fig 3?

Stanford in the Vale church   grid reference 342 935

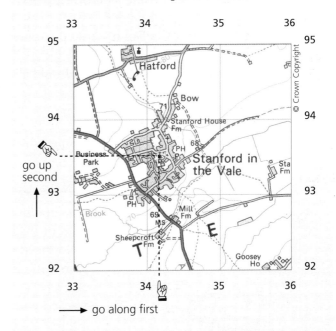

▶ **Fig 3** Six-figure grid references.

Key words

easting – grid line running up and down an OS map

grid reference – number which locates an area on a map

northing – grid line running across an OS map

SUMMARY

- Ordnance Survey maps are divided into numbered grid squares.
- Four-figure grid references locate an area of one square kilometre.
- Six-figure grid references locate an area of 100 square metres.
- Always give the number at the bottom of the map first, and the number at the side of the map second.

SUMMARY activity

Use the map on page 232 to give six-figure grid references for the following: a car park, a campsite, a tourist information centre, Thurston school and the train station in Bury St Edmunds.

111 Graphs 1

In this section of the book you will investigate the following things:
- How are bar graphs used?
- How are line graphs used?
- How are pictograms used?

Bar graphs

A bar graph is one of the simplest **graphs** to draw. Bar graphs are used to show amounts of things at a particular time. Bar graphs can be used to show one type of **data**, such as rainfall or pebble sizes. They can also be used to show different types of data, such as modes of transport or types of shop. The vertical **axis** has a **scale** to show the number of each item. The horizontal axis is labelled to show the types of data for each bar. If the bars all show the same type of data, such as rainfall, they should all be the same colour. If they show different types of data, they should be different colours.

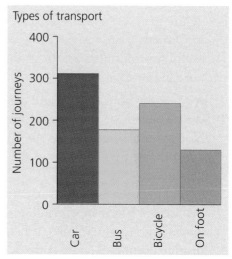

▲ **Fig 1** Bar graph.

Q1 Which is the most popular type of transport shown on Fig 1?

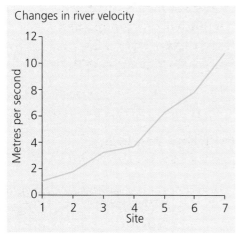

▲ **Fig 2** Line graph.

Line graphs

Line graphs are used to show how things change over time, or over distance. Line graphs can show changes in wind speed over a day, or changes in population over years. Line graphs can also show changes in the velocity of a river as it flows downstream. The vertical axis is labelled with a variable scale. The horizontal axis is labelled to show time or distance. Dots are plotted for each measurement and then joined up with straight lines. Line graphs can include more that one set of data, if different coloured lines are drawn.

Q2 Describe the change in river velocity shown in Fig 2.

Climate graphs

Climate graphs show the temperature and rainfall for a location over a year. They are a combination of a bar graph and a line graph. The left hand vertical axis should be labelled to show temperature in degrees Centigrade (°C). The right hand vertical axis should be labelled to show rainfall in millimetres (mm). Rainfall is shown as bars, which should be coloured blue. Temperature is drawn as a line, which should be coloured red. Climate graphs can also include the total rainfall for the year.

▶ *Fig 3* *Climate graph.*

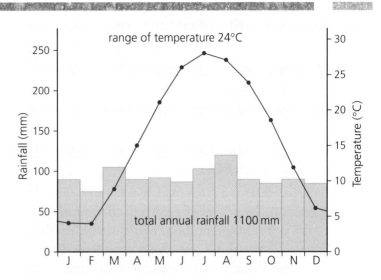

Q3 Describe the climate of New York shown in Fig 3.

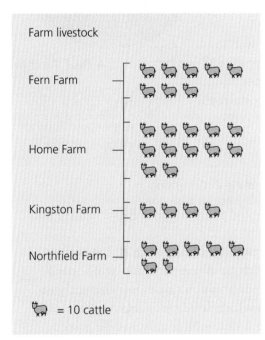

▲ *Fig 4* *Pictogram.*

Pictogram

Pictograms are used to show numbers of things. Small pictures or symbols are used to represent the things being measured. Pictograms can show one type of data or several different types of data. Pictograms could be used to show changes in village population, types of litter or farm produce. Each picture on the graph should be equal to a larger number in real life. It is important to label the horizontal axis to show what each picture represents. Pictograms should be used when visual impact is more important than accuracy.

Q4 Use Fig 4 to calculate how many cattle there are on Home Farm.

Key words

axes – the vertical and horizontal lines on a graph
data – a series of measurements
graph – a drawing to show data
scale – measurements on a vertical axis

SUMMARY

■ Bar graphs use solid blocks to show numbers of things.
■ Line graphs show changes over time or distance.
■ Climate graphs combine bar and line graphs.
■ Pictograms use small pictures or symbols to show numbers of things.

SUMMARY *activity*

What type of graph would you draw to show the following?
● *the climate of Nairobi*
● *changes in energy use over a decade*
● *average wages in a number of different countries*
● *types of litter*

112 Graphs 2

In this section of the book you will investigate the following things:
■ How are pie charts used?
■ How are scatter graphs used?
■ How are rose diagrams used?
■ How are triangular graphs used?

Pie charts

A pie chart is a circle which is divided into sections, like slices of a cake. Each section shows the **percentage** of **data**, which makes up the total. For example, pie charts can be used to show the percentages of people employed in different industries, or the percentage of ethnic groups in a population. Remember that pie charts can only be used to show percentages. Pie charts work very well to show between three and six groups of data. They should not be used for more or less than these amounts. One per cent is equal to 3.6 degrees on a pie chart (Fig 2). A protractor is used to divide the circle. Each section should be coloured or shaded. A key must be included.

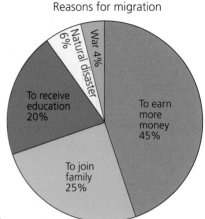
Reasons for migration

▲ *Fig 1* Pie chart.

Q1 What is the most important cause of migration (Fig 1)?

$$\text{Degrees} = \frac{\text{category}}{\text{total}} \times 360$$

◀ *Fig 2* Calculating degrees for a pie chart.

Scatter graphs

Scatter **graphs** are used to show links between two sets of data (Fig 2). Links can be shown between data such as income and health, or air pressure and wind speed. Scatter graphs have two **axes**. The **scale** for the data which causes the change, goes along the horizontal axis. The scale for the data which is being changed, goes along the vertical axis. Each pair of figures is plotted as a dot, which must not be joined up. The dots make a pattern which shows if there is a link between the data. There may be a positive relationship or a negative relationship. If the dots are random then there may be no relationship.

Q2 When should scatter graphs be used?

▼ *Fig 3* Scattergraphs.

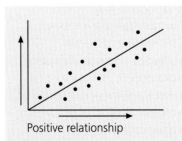
Positive relationship

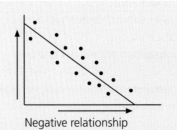
Negative relationship

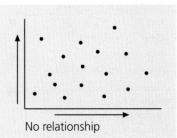
No relationship

Rose diagrams

Rose diagrams are used to show data in the form of compass directions, or bearings. They are especially useful for showing wind direction. Data must be placed into groups, such as the eight points of a compass. Bars are drawn outwards from a central point. The length of the bar shows the **frequency** of the measurement. A scale must be included to show the value of the bars. Rose diagrams should be in one colour.

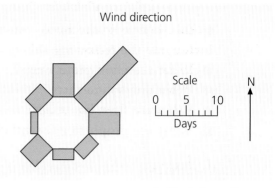

▲ *Fig 4* Rose diagram.

Q3 Use Fig 4 to work out the prevailing wind direction.

Triangular graphs

Triangular graphs allow three variables to be plotted onto a graph at the same time. They are used to show employment structures, which are divided into primary, secondary and tertiary industry. They can also be used to show types of mass movement and soil structure. The graph has three axes, each of which are divided into 100. This means triangular graphs can only be used to show percentages. Lines are drawn across the graph from each axis at an angle of 60°. A dot is plotted where the lines cross. Triangular graphs are useful for comparing several locations on one graph.

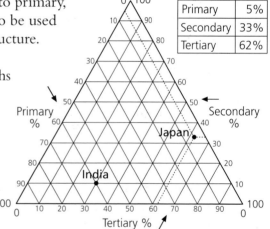

Employment structures
Japan

Primary	5%
Secondary	33%
Tertiary	62%

▲ *Fig 5* Triangular graph.

Q4 Use Fig 5 to work out the employment structure for India.

Key words

axes – the vertical and horizontal lines on a graph

data – a series of measurements

frequency – the number of times something occurs

graph – a drawing to show data

percentage – number out of 100

scale – measurements on a vertical axis

SUMMARY

■ Pie charts show the different percentages of data which make up the total.

■ Scatter graphs show relationships between two sets of data.

■ Rose diagrams show data with values for different directions.

■ Triangular graphs show data with three variables.

SUMMARY *activity*

What type of graph would you draw to show the following?

● *the relationship between population size and number of services*

● *wind direction over a month*

● *the population structure for Brazil*

● *the percentage of different types of housing*

 About.com – Geography http://geography.about.com/mbody.htm

113 Maps

In this section of the book you will investigate the following things:
- What are choropleth maps?
- What are isoline maps?
- What are flow line maps?
- What are proportional symbol maps?

Choropleth maps

Choropleth maps use shading to show differences between areas. They are useful for showing differences in many different things such as population density, standards of living and climate. **Data** must be divided into between three and nine groups. The divisions do not have to be equal, but no value must appear in more than one group. For example, 1 to 4.9, 5 to 9.9 etc. A base map is divided into different countries, regions or areas. The map is coloured or shaded to show different values. Darker colours should be used to show higher values. A **key** is used to show the value of each colour.

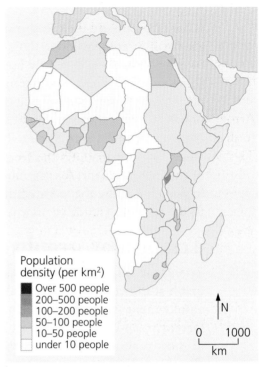

Population density (per km²)
- Over 500 people
- 200–500 people
- 100–200 people
- 50–100 people
- 10–50 people
- under 10 people

N

0   1000
km

▲ **Fig 1** Choropleth map of population density in Africa.

Q1 What are the most densely populated countries in Africa (Fig 1)?

Isoline maps

Isoline maps use lines to join up places of the same value. Isoline maps are used to show data such as height, air pressure, temperature and rainfall. Points are plotted onto a base map of an area. Measurements are then taken at each point. For some data, such as temperature, it is important that the measurements are made around the same time. Next, the points on the map with equal values are joined with a curved line. The isolines must never cross each other. The space between the isolines can be shaded. The higher the value, the darker the shading.

Q2 Name two areas at high risk from acid rain (Fig 2).

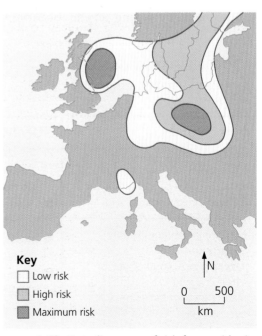

Key
- Low risk
- High risk
- Maximum risk

N

0   500
km

▲ **Fig 2** Isoline map of risk from acid rain.

Flow line maps

Flow line maps use lines of different widths to show the value of data. They are useful for showing data such as traffic and pedestrian flows, migrations and imports and exports of goods. Arrow lines are drawn onto a base map to show the direction of movement. The width of each line depends on the value of the data. A **scale** needs to be chosen that works for the highest and lowest value. The scale should be shown on a key. Two-directional flow can be shown if two arrows are used. Arrows are usually shaded black.

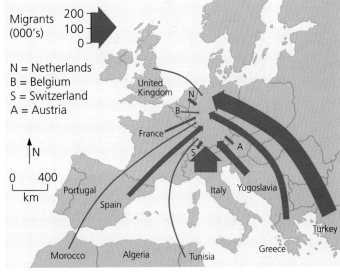

▲ *Fig 3* *Flow line map of migrants to Germany in the 1980s.*

Q3 Which were the largest group of immigrants to Germany in the 1980s (Fig 3).

Proportional symbol maps

Proportional symbols can be drawn on maps to compare data for different areas. Proportional symbols include bars, circles and squares. Whichever symbol is chosen its size should be in **proportion** to the value of the data. A key is used to show the value of each symbol. It is also possible to draw miniature bar graphs, pie charts or pictograms on a base map. The symbols, or graphs, should be drawn over the place the data was recorded.

Q4 Where are the most expensive house prices in the UK (Fig 4)?

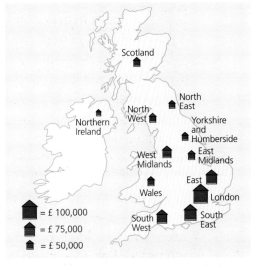

▲ *Fig 4* *Proportional symbols map of house prices in the UK.*

Key words

data – a series of measurements
key – a list giving the meaning of symbols
proportion – size relative to value
scale – proportional size

SUMMARY

- Choropleth maps use shading to highlight differences between areas.
- Isoline maps use lines to join places of equal value.
- Flow line maps show the value and direction of movements.
- Proportional symbol maps use symbols to show differences between areas.

SUMMARY *activity*

What type of graph would you draw to show the following?
- *the life expectancy for all countries in Africa*
- *the destination of Australia's exports*
- *air pressure*
- *the population of cities*

114 Maps, diagrams and sketches

In this section of the book you will investigate the following things:

■ How are sketch maps used?

■ How are diagrams used?

■ How are field sketches used?

Sketch maps

It is an important skill to be able to draw maps. Sketch maps are maps drawn freehand, rather than being traced. Rough sketch maps need only resemble the shape of the area being drawn. More accurate sketch maps can be drawn by using a grid. Just one square should be copied at a time. This helps to keep the map in the correct proportions. A sketch map is better than a photocopied map because it allows you to include only the detail you need. Maps should be drawn in pencil and **labelled** neatly in pen. Sketch maps must always include a **scale** and a **compass direction**. The map should be given a suitable title and surrounded with a border. Colour and a **key** can be added if appropriate (Fig 1).

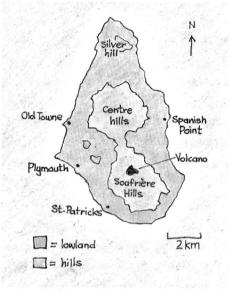

▲ *Fig 1* A sketch map of Montserrat.

Q1 Use an atlas to draw a sketch map of a country of your choice.

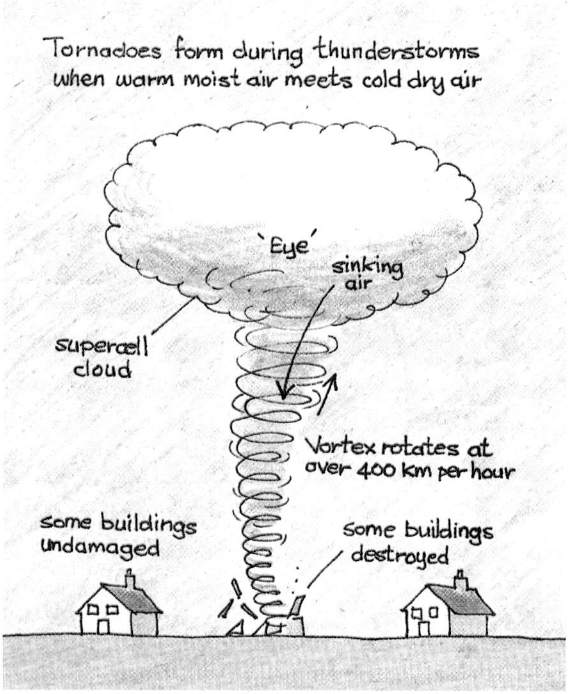

Diagrams

A diagram is a way of presenting information graphically. Diagrams can be used for both physical and human geography topics. Diagrams need not be artistic but should be neat. Always draw diagrams in pencil and label them in pen. Leave room around diagrams to add labels. Guidelines should be used to connect labels with the diagram. Some labels simply state what is there. Other labels describe or explain the diagram in more detail. Detailed labels are called **annotations**. When the diagram is finished, a border should be drawn around it. The diagram should be given a title which says what it is about (Fig 2).

Q2 What is an annotation?

Q3 Draw a diagram of an erupting volcano.

▲ *Fig 2* A diagram of a tornado.

Field sketches

A field sketch is an annotated drawing of geographical features made outside the classroom. Field sketches allow features to be described and explained in much more detail than just writing can. Field sketches are better than photographs because they can emphasise the important features. They can also be labelled during fieldwork, rather than waiting for photos to be developed. A field sketch should not contain everything that can be seen. Only things relevant to the topic should be included. Fig 4 is a field sketch of a river valley. Notice the information on it. Field sketches must include a title, a grid reference, a direction and a date. The sketch should be simple with clear annotations. It can be coloured later to make it clearer.

Q4 What are the advantages of field sketches?

▲ *Fig 3* A river valley.

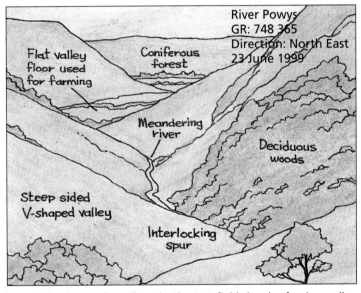

River Powys
GR: 748 365
Direction: North East
23 June 1999

Flat valley floor used for farming

Coniferous forest

Meandering river

Deciduous woods

Steep sided V-shaped valley

Interlocking spur

▲ *Fig 4* A field sketch of a river valley.

Key words

annotation – a detailed label which describes or explains
compass direction – arrow on a map to show north
key – a list giving the meaning of symbols
label – a note on a field sketch or diagram
scale – ratio between the distance on a map, and the distance in real life

SUMMARY

■ Sketch maps are maps drawn free-hand.
■ Diagrams present information in a creative and graphical way.
■ Field sketches are annotated drawings of geographical features.

SUMMARY *activity*

Draw a field sketch of the view from your classroom window. Alternatively, draw a field sketch based on one of the photographs in this book.

Yorkshire Dales 1:25 000

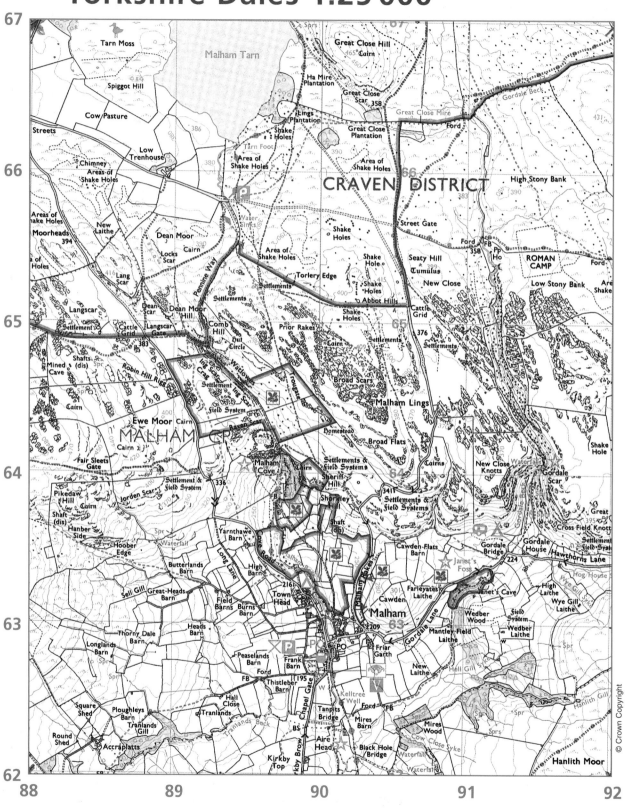

Outdoor Leisure™ and Explorer™ Series
1:25 000 Scale
MAP SYMBOLS

Communications

ROADS AND PATHS   Not necessarily rights of way

M1 or A 6(M)	Motorway
	Service Area
	Junction Number (7)
A 31(T) or A 35	Trunk or Main road
	Narrow roads with passing places are annotated
B 3074	Secondary road
A 35	Dual carriageway
	Road generally more than 4m wide
	Road generally less than 4m wide
	Other road, drive or track, fenced and unfenced
	Gradient: 20%(1 in 5) and steeper; 14%(1 in 7) to 20%(1 in 5)
Ferry	(V) Vehicle; (P) Passenger
	Path

RAILWAYS

	Multiple track / Single track — Standard gauge
	Narrow gauge Light Rapid Transit System
	Road over; road under; level crossing
	Station, open to passengers; siding
	Cutting; tunnel; embankment

PUBLIC RIGHTS OF WAY
(Rights of way are not shown on maps of Scotland)

	Footpath
	Bridleway
	Byway open to all traffic
	Road used as a public path

OTHER PUBLIC ACCESS

	Other routes with public access
	National trail or Recreational path
	Permitted Footpath
	Permitted Bridleway
	Permitted Bridleway coincident with right of way
	Selected cycle route, off and on road

General Information

GENERAL FEATURES

Place of worship	with tower; with spire, minaret or dome; without such additions
	Building; important building
	Glasshouse
	Youth hostel
	Bunkhouse/camping barn
	Bus or coach station
	Lighthouse; beacon
	Gravel pit
	Other pit or quarry
	Sand pit
	Refuse or slag heap
	Triangulation pillar; mast
	Windmill, with or without sails
	Wind pump; wind generator
pylon pole	Electricity transmission line
	Slopes

BP	Boundary Post		
BS	Boundary Stone		
CH	Club House		
FB	Foot Bridge		
MP ; MS	Mile Post ; Mile Stone		
Mon	Monument		
PO	Post Office	Rural areas only
Pol Sta	Police Station	
Sch	School	
TH	Town Hall	
NTL	Normal Tidal Limit	
W; Spr	Well; Spring	

BOUNDARIES

	County
	Unitary Authority, Metropolitan District, London Borough or District
	Civil Parish or Community
	Constituency (County, Borough, Burgh or European Assembly)
	National Park Boundary
	Forest Park Boundary

ARCHAEOLOGICAL AND HISTORICAL INFORMATION

	Site of antiquity	VILLA — Roman	Visible earthwork
1066	Site of battle (with date)	Castle — Non-Roman	

VEGETATION
Limits of vegetation are defined by positioning of symbols but may also be delineated by broken lines or dots

	Coniferous trees
	Non-coniferous trees
	Coppice
	Scrub
	Bracken, heath or rough grassland
	Marsh, reeds or saltings.
	Orchard

HEIGHTS AND NATURAL FEATURES

52 ·	Ground survey height
284 ·	Air survey height

Vertical face/cliff

Loose rock   Boulders   Outcrop   Scree

	Water
	Mud
	Sand; sand & shingle

ACCESS LAND

Land open to the public by permission of the owners. The agreement may be withdrawn.

	National Trust, always open; limited access - observe local signs
	National Trust for Scotland, always open; limited access - observe local signs
	Forestry Commission
AL	Other Access Land
	Access Information Point

Tourist and Leisure Information

V	Visitor centre	U Horse riding	Castle/Fort		Garden/Arboretum
	Information centre, all year/seasonal	Preserved railway	Building of historic interest		Nature reserve
PC	Public Convenience	P Parking	Public house/s	English Heritage	Water activities
C C C	Telephone, public/motoring organisation/ emergency	Picnic site	Theme/Pleasure park	Historic Scotland	Slipway
	Camp site	Walks/Trails	Cathedral/Abbey	Cadw: Welsh Historic Monuments	Fishing
	Golf course or links	Cycle trail	Museum	Country park	Other tourist feature
		Recreation/Leisure/Sports centre			
		Viewpoint			

© Crown Copyright

231

Bury St Edmunds 1:50 000

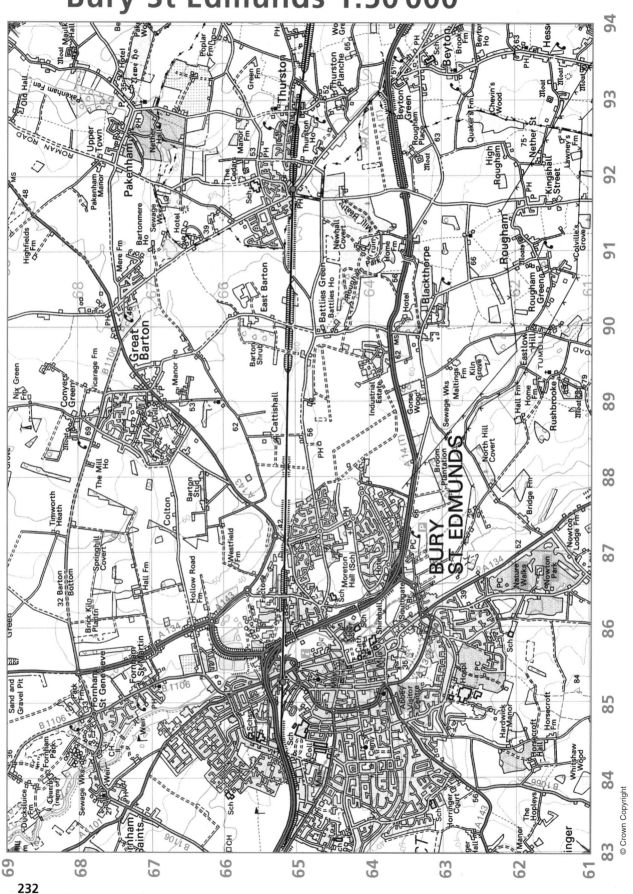

© Crown Copyright

232

Landranger® series (1:50 000 scale)
Map symbols

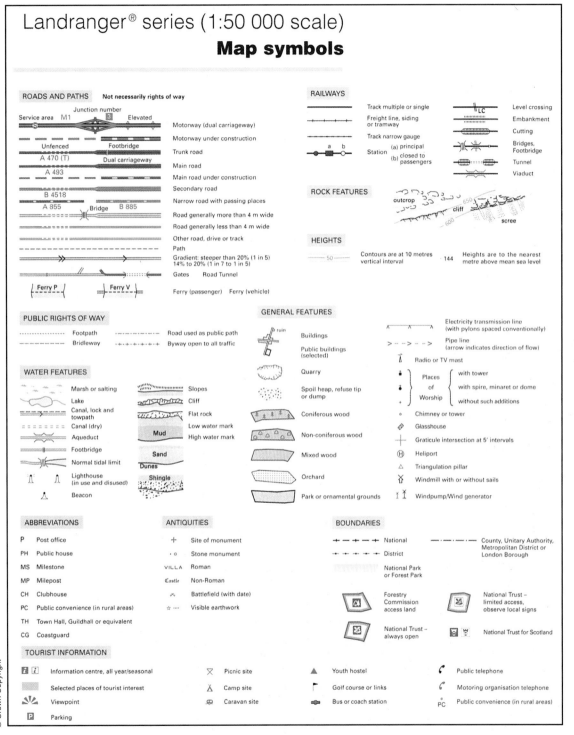

ROADS AND PATHS Not necessarily rights of way

Junction number

Service area M1   3   Elevated

Motorway (dual carriageway)
Motorway under construction

Unfenced Footbridge
A 470 (T) Dual carriageway

Trunk road
Main road

A 493

Main road under construction

B 4518

Secondary road
Narrow road with passing places

A 855 Bridge B 885

Road generally more than 4 m wide
Road generally less than 4 m wide
Other road, drive or track
Path
Gradient: steeper than 20% (1 in 5)
14% to 20% (1 in 7 to 1 in 5)
Gates Road Tunnel

Ferry P Ferry V

Ferry (passenger) Ferry (vehicle)

PUBLIC RIGHTS OF WAY

.... Footpath
– – – – – Bridleway
–·–·–·–·– Road used as public path
–+–+–+–+– Byway open to all traffic

WATER FEATURES

Marsh or salting
Lake
Canal, lock and towpath
Canal (dry)
Aqueduct
Footbridge
Normal tidal limit
Lighthouse (in use and disused)
Beacon

Slopes
Cliff
Flat rock
Low water mark
Mud
High water mark
Sand
Dunes
Shingle

RAILWAYS

Track multiple or single
Freight line, siding or tramway
Track narrow gauge
a b Station (a) principal
(b) closed to passengers

LC Level crossing
Embankment
Cutting
Bridges, Footbridge
Tunnel
Viaduct

ROCK FEATURES

outcrop cliff
600 650 scree

HEIGHTS

— 50 — Contours are at 10 metres vertical interval
144 Heights are to the nearest metre above mean sea level

GENERAL FEATURES

ruin Buildings
Public buildings (selected)
Quarry
Spoil heap, refuse tip or dump
Coniferous wood
Non-coniferous wood
Mixed wood
Orchard
Park or ornamental grounds

Electricity transmission line (with pylons spaced conventionally)
> – –> – –> Pipe line (arrow indicates direction of flow)
Radio or TV mast
Places of Worship { with tower
with spire, minaret or dome
without such additions }
Chimney or tower
Glasshouse
Graticule intersection at 5' intervals
Heliport
Triangulation pillar
Windmill with or without sails
Windpump/Wind generator

ABBREVIATIONS

P Post office
PH Public house
MS Milestone
MP Milepost
CH Clubhouse
PC Public convenience (in rural areas)
TH Town Hall, Guildhall or equivalent
CG Coastguard

ANTIQUITIES

+ Site of monument
· o Stone monument
VILLA Roman
Castle Non-Roman
Battlefield (with date)
Visible earthwork

BOUNDARIES

–+– –+– –+– National
–+– –+– –+– District
National Park or Forest Park
Forestry Commission access land
National Trust – always open

County, Unitary Authority, Metropolitan District or London Borough
National Trust – limited access, observe local signs
National Trust for Scotland

TOURIST INFORMATION

Information centre, all year/seasonal
Selected places of tourist interest
Viewpoint
P Parking

Picnic site
Camp site
Caravan site

Youth hostel
Golf course or links
Bus or coach station

Public telephone
Motoring organisation telephone
PC Public convenience (in rural areas)

© Crown Copyright

World statistics

	Capital city	Area (Km²)	Population (millions)	Birth rate (per 1000)	Death rate (per 1000)	Fertility rate (children per woman)	Infant mortality rate (per 1000)	Life expectancy (years)	Adult literacy (%)	GDP per person (US$)	Human Development Index
Albania	Tirana	28,750	3.6	22	8	3	47	72.8	85	2,120	0.699
Algeria	Algiers	2,381,740	29.3	28	6	4	47	68.9	57	4,460	0.665
Angola	Luanda	1,246,700	11.2	44	17	7	136	46.5	43	1,430	0.398
Argentina	Buenos Aires	2,766,890	35.4	20	8	3	19	72.9	96	10,300	0.827
Australia	Canberra	7,686,850	18.4	14	7	2	5	78.2	99	20,210	0.922
Austria	Vienna	83,850	8.2	11	10	2	6	77.0	99	22,070	0.904
Bangladesh	Dhaka	144,000	124.0	30	11	4	100	58.1	36	1,050	0.440
Barbados	Bridgetown	430	0.3	15	8	2	18	76.4	99	12,001	0.857
Belgium	Brussels	33,100	10.2	12	10	2	6	77.2	99	22,750	0.923
Benin	Porto-Novo	112,620	5.8	46	13	6	103	53.4	23	1,270	0.421
Bolivia	La Paz/Sucre	1,098,580	7.7	32	10	5	66	61.4	78	2,880	0.652
Botswana	Gaborone	581,730	1.5	33	18	5	55	47.4	74	7,690	0.609
Brazil	Brasilia	8,511,970	159.5	20	9	3	53	66.8	81	6,480	0.739
Bulgaria	Sofia	110,910	8.6	8	14	2	15	71.1	93	4,010	0.758
Burkina Faso	Ouagadougou	274,200	10.9	46	20	7	117	44.4	18	1,010	0.304
Burma	Rangoon	676,577	47.5	30	11	4	79	60.1	81	1,199	0.580
Burundi	Bujumbura	27,830	6.3	42	15	7	101	42.4	50	630	0.324
Cambodia	Phnom Penh	181,040	10.5	43	15	4	106	53.4	35	1,290	0.514
Cameroon	Yaoundé	475,440	13.8	42	14	6	78	54.7	54	1,890	0.536
Canada	Ottawa	9,976,140	30.2	13	7	2	6	79.0	99	22,480	0.932
Chad	Ndjamena	1,284,000	6.8	44	17	6	119	47.2	30	970	0.393
Chile	Santiago	756,950	14.7	18	6	3	13	74.9	93	12,730	0.844
China	Beijing	9,596,960	1,300.0	17	7	2	38	69.8	70	3,130	0.701
Colombia	Bogota	1,138,910	35.9	21	5	3	25	70.4	87	6,810	0.768
Congo	Brazzaville	342,000	2.7	39	17	7	106	48.6	57	1,620	0.533
Congo (Zaire)	Kinshasa	2,344,860	47.2	48	17	7	106	50.8	74	880	0.479
Costa Rica	San José	51,100	3.5	23	4	3	13	76.0	93	6,650	0.801
Cuba	Havana	110,860	11.3	13	7	2	9	75.7	75	3,100	0.765
Cyprus	Nicosia	9,250	0.8	15	8	2	8	77.8	94	14,201	0.870
Czech Rep.	Prague	78,864	10.5	11	11	2	8	73.9	99	10,510	0.833
Denmark	Copenhagen	43,070	5.4	12	10	2	5	75.7	99	23,690	0.905
Ecuador	Quito	283,560	11.8	25	5	4	33	69.5	88	4,940	0.747
Egypt	Cairo	1,001,450	63.0	28	9	4	71	66.3	49	3,050	0.616
El Salvador	San Salvador	21,040	6.0	27	6	4	30	69.1	70	2,880	0.674
Ethiopia	Addis Ababa	1,221,900	58.5	46	18	7	122	43.3	33	510	0.298
Finland	Helsinki	338,130	5.2	11	11	2	5	76.8	99	20,150	0.913
France	Paris	551,500	58.8	13	9	2	6	78.1	99	22,030	0.918
Gambia, The	Banjul	11,300	1.2	44	13	6	79	47.0	36	1,470	0.391
Germany	Berlin	356,950	82.3	9	11	1	6	77.2	99	21,260	0.906
Ghana	Accra	238,540	18.1	34	11	6	79	60.0	61	1,640	0.544
Greece	Athens	131,990	10.6	10	10	1	7	78.1	94	12,769	0.867
Guatemala	Guatemala City	108,890	11.3	33	7	5	49	64.0	54	4,100	0.624
Guyana	Georgetown	214,970	0.8	19	10	3	51	64.4	98	3,210	0.701
Honduras	Tegucigalpa	112,090	6.3	33	6	5	40	69.4	71	2,220	0.641
Hungary	Budapest	93,030	10.2	11	15	2	12	70.9	99	7,200	0.795
Iceland	Reykjavik	103,000	0.3	17	6	2	4	79.0	99	22.497	0.919
India	New Delhi	3,287,260	1,000.0	25	9	4	69	62.6	50	1,670	0.545
Indonesia	Jakarta	1,904,570	203.5	23	8	3	61	65.1	83	3,490	0.681
Iran	Tehran	1,648,000	69.5	33	6	5	51	69.2	65	5,817	0.715
Iraq	Baghdad	438,320	22.5	43	6	6	58	62.4	55	3,197	0.586
Ireland	Dublin	70,280	3.6	13	9	2	6	76.3	99	20,710	0.900
Israel	Jerusalem	21,060	5.9	20	6	3	8	77.8	95	18,150	0.883
Italy	Rome	301,270	57.8	10	10	1	7	78.2	97	20,290	0.900
Ivory Coast	Yamoussoukro	322,460	15.1	42	17	7	100	46.7	37	1,840	0.422
Jamaica	Kingston	10,990	2.6	22	6	2	15	74.8	84	3,440	0.734
Japan	Tokyo	377,800	125.9	10	8	2	4	80.0	99	24,070	0.924
Jordan	Amman	89,210	5.6	36	4	6	31	70.1	84	3,450	0.715
Kenya	Nairobi	580,370	31.9	32	11	6	55	52.0	75	1,190	0.519
Korea, North	Pyongyang	120,540	24.5	22	5	2	25	–	95	–	–
Korea, South	Seoul	99,030	46.1	16	6	2	8	72.4	97	13,590	0.852
Kuwait	Kuwait City	17,820	2.1	20	2	3	11	75.9	77	25,314	0.833
Laos	Vientiane	236,800	5.2	41	13	7	94	53.2	54	1,300	0.491
Lebanon	Beirut	10,400	3.2	28	6	3	35	69.9	91	5,940	0.749
Libya	Tripoli	1,759,540	5.5	44	7	6	58	70.0	72	6,697	0.756
Luxembourg	Luxembourg	2,590	0.4	13	8	2	5	76.7	99	30.863	0.902
Macedonia	Skopje	25,710	2.2	13	9	2	29	73.1	90	3,210	0.746
Malawi	Lilongwe	118,480	10.3	41	25	7	139	39.3	54	710	0.399
Malaysia	Kuala Lumpur	329,750	20.9	26	5	4	23	72.0	82	8,140	0.768
Mali	Bamako	1,240,190	11.0	51	19	7	101	53.3	27	740	0.375
Mauritania	Nouakchott	1,025,220	2.4	47	15	5	80	53.5	36	1,730	0.447
Mexico	Mexico City	1,958,200	97.4	26	5	3	24	72.2	87	8,370	0.786
Mongolia	Ulan Bator	1,566,500	2.5	25	8	4	68	65.8	81	1,310	0.618
Morocco	Rabat	446,550	28.1	27	6	4	41	66.6	41	3,310	0.582

	Capital city	Area (Km²)	Population (millions)	Birth rate (per 1000)	Death rate (per 1000)	Fertility rate (children per woman)	Infant mortality rate (per 1000)	Life expectancy (years)	Adult literacy (%)	GDP per person (US$)	Human Development Index
Mozambique	Maputo	801,590	19.1	44	18	7	123	45.2	37	740	0.341
Namibia	Windhoek	824,290	1.7	37	8	5	46	52.4	40	5,010	0.638
Nepal	Katmandu	140,800	22.1	37	12	5	77	57.3	26	1,090	0.463
Netherlands	Amsterdam	37,330	15.9	12	12	2	5	77.9	99	21,110	0.921
New Zealand	Wellington	270,990	3.7	15	8	2	7	76.9	99	17,410	0.901
Nicaragua	Managua	130,000	4.5	33	6	5	44	67.9	65	1,997	0.616
Niger	Niamey	1,267,000	9.2	54	24	7	116	48.5	12	850	0.298
Nigeria	Lagos	923,770	88.5	43	12	6	70	50.1	53	920	0.456
Norway	Oslo	323,900	4.4	11	11	2	5	78.1	99	24,450	0.927
Pakistan	Islamabad	796,100	143.6	35	11	6	95	64.0	36	1,560	0.508
Panama	Panama City	77,080	2.6	22	5	3	25	73.6	90	7,168	0.791
Paraguay	Asuncion	406,750	5.0	30	4	4	22	69.6	91	3,980	0.730
Peru	Lima	1,285,220	25.6	24	6	3	50	68.3	87	4,680	0.739
Philippines	Manila	300,000	67.2	29	7	4	35	68.3	94	3,520	0.740
Poland	Warsaw	312,680	38.6	12	10	2	12	72.5	99	6,520	0.802
Portugal	Lisbon	92,390	10.6	11	10	2	8	75.3	86	14,270	0.858
Romania	Bucharest	237,500	22.9	10	12	2	23	69.9	97	4,310	0.752
Russia	Moscow	17,075,400	148.4	11	16	2	24	66.6	99	4,370	0.747
Rwanda	Kigali	26,340	7.9	39	21	7	119	40.5	57	660	0.379
Saudi Arabia	Riyadh	2,149,690	18.4	38	5	6	44	71.4	61	10.120	0.740
Senegal	Dakar	196,720	8.3	45	11	6	63	52.3	31	1,730	0.426
Sierra Leone	Freetown	71,740	4.5	47	18	7	133	37.2	29	410	0.254
Singapore	Singapore	618	3.0	16	5	2	5	77.1	90	28,460	0.888
Slovak Rep.	Bratislava	49,000	5.4	13	9	2	11	73.0	99	7,910	0.813
Somalia	Mogadishu	637,660	9.2	44	13	7	119	56.0	27	–	–
South Africa	Pretoria	1,221,040	44.0	27	12	4	53	54.7	81	7,380	0.695
Spain	Madrid	504,780	39.7	10	9	1	6	78.0	98	15,930	0.894
Sri Lanka	Colombo	65,610	18.4	18	6	3	20	73.1	89	2,490	0.721
Sudan	Khartoum	2,505,810	29.9	41	11	6	74	55.0	43	1,560	0.475
Swaziland	Mbabane	17,360	0.8	43	10	5	86	60.2	74	3,350	0.644
Sweden	Stockholm	449,960	8.9	11	11	2	5	78.5	99	19,790	0.923
Switzerland	Bern	41,290	7.3	11	10	2	5	78.6	99	25,240	0.914
Syria	Damascus	185,180	14.6	39	6	6	39	68.9	68	3,250	0.663
Tanzania	Dodoma	945,090	29.7	50	13	6	105	47.9	64	580	0.421
Thailand	Bangkok	513,120	58.4	17	7	2	32	68.8	94	6,690	0.753
Tunisia	Tunis	163,610	8.9	24	5	3	34	69.5	63	5,300	0.695
Turkey	Ankara	779,450	61.3	22	5	3	41	69.0	81	6,350	0.728
Uganda	Kampala	235,880	21.4	45	21	7	98	39.6	59	1,160	0.404
Ukraine	Kiev	603,700	52.0	12	15	2	22	68.8	95	2,190	0.721
United Kingdom	London	244,880	58.3	13	11	2	6	77.2	99	20,730	0.918
United States	Washington, DC	9,809,431	263.6	15	9	2	7	76.7	99	29,010	0.927
Uruguay	Montevideo	177,410	3.2	17	9	2	15	73.7	96	9,200	0.826
Venezuela	Caracas	912,050	21.8	24	5	3	29	72.4	90	8,860	0.792
Vietnam	Hanoi	331,690	74.6	22	7	4	37	67.4	92	1,630	0.664
Zambia	Lusaka	752,610	9.5	44	24	6	97	40.1	75	960	0.431
Zimbabwe	Harare	390,760	11.5	32	19	5	73	44.1	83	2,350	0.560

Sources: *Philips Geographical Digest* and the
United Nations Human Development Report 1999

Internet activities

Current geographical news

Use the following news websites to investigate geographical stories that are in the news at the moment.

Electronic Telegraph

 http://www.telegraph.co.uk/

The Times

 http://www.the-times.co.uk/

The Guardian

 http://www.guardian.co.uk/

The Observer

 http://www.observer.co.uk/

The Independent

 http://www.independent.co.uk/www/

The Mirror

 http://www.mirror.co.uk/

BBC News

 http://news.bbc.co.uk/

CNN News

 http://www.cnn.com/

1 Choose one geographical story and investigate how it is reported by different organisations. What are the differences in the ways the story is reported?

2 Prepare a presentation on one geographical story. Copy and paste text and photos from the news websites into a software package such as Word or PowerPoint.

3 Make a list of all the geographical stories that are in the news. Label a world map to show where the events took place and what happened.

Farming

National Farmers Union

 http://www.nfu.org.uk/education/farmstud.shtml

■ Create a wall display about one of the farms featured on this website.
■ Include information on the following topics:
location, physical features, land use, labour, machinery, buildings, inputs, outputs, farming year, diversification and wildlife.
■ Copy and paste maps and photographs into your display.

Volcanic activity

Volcano World

 http://volcano.und.nodak.edu/vw.html

USGS Cascades Volcano Observatory

 http://vulcan.wr.usgs.gov/home.html

1   Find a photograph of the following volcanic features.
    a) A pyroclastic flow
    b) A strato-volcano
    c) A shield volcano
    d) A lava flow
    e) A lahar

    ■ Copy and paste the photos into a word processing package.

    ■ Write an explanation of each feature underneath the photos.

2   Search the sites for information on a volcano of your choice. Create a one-page 'Fact File' on the volcano, including text and photographs.

3   Find out the names of the most recent volcanic eruptions. Mark the volcanoes and the eruption dates onto a world map.

Rocks

The Essential Guide to Rocks

 http://www.bbc.co.uk/education/rocks/

1   Click on 'Britain's Rocky Past' and go to 'animation'. Watch the animation and answer these questions.
    a) When was the Universe formed?
    b) When were the Sun and planets formed?
    c) What was the Earth made from?
    d) When did dinosaurs appear?
    e) What geological period are we in now?

2   Click on 'Interactive timeline'.
    ■ Work your way through the interactive timeline.
    ■ Draw your own illustrated timeline to show the history of the Earth's rocks and fossils.

3   Click on 'Stones at Home' and then 'Graveyard Rockwalk'.
    ■ Note down the different types of rock you come across in the graveyard.
    ■ Decide whether each type of rock is igneous, sedimentary or metamorphic. If you are stuck, use the 'Rock Primer' to help you.

Traceable maps

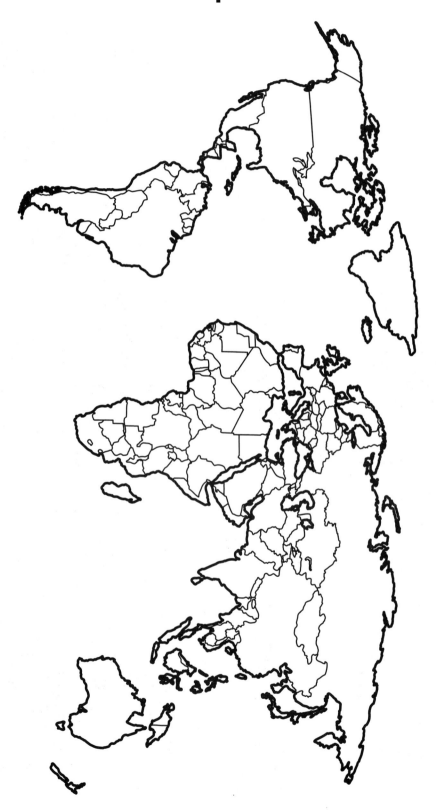

Europe

British Isles

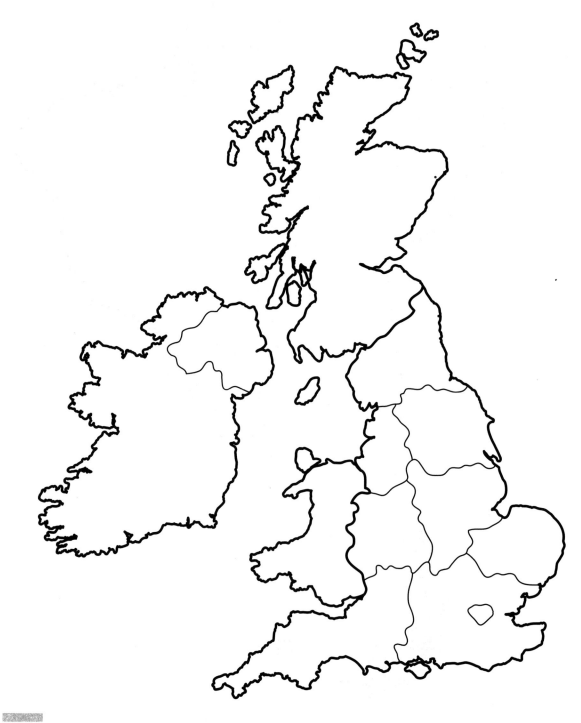

South America

Australia

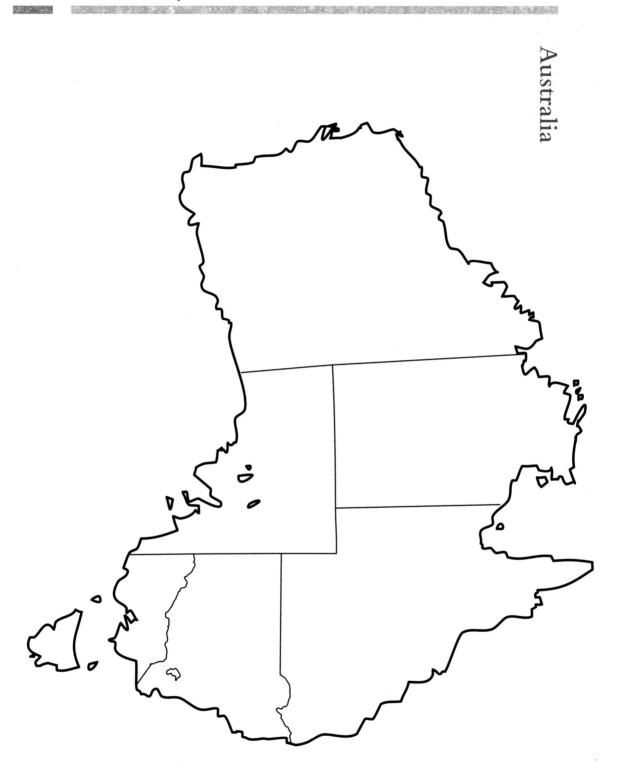

Glossary

A

Agenda 21 – sustainable development at local level

agriculture – farming

aid – transfer of resources from richer to poorer countries

air mass – a very large body of air

air pressure – the weight of the air

alternative energy – energy produced from renewable sources

anticyclone – area of high air pressure

appropriate technology – low technology aid based on local situation.

aquifer – underground water supply

arable – farming crops

atmosphere – a layer of air around the Earth

B

bedding plane – a horizontal crack between layers of rock

bilateral aid – aid given directly from one country to another

billion – one thousand million

biodiversity – the number and variety of all living things

birth rate – number of babies born per thousand people per year

brownfield site – land which has been built on before

business park – a development of offices and industrial units

bypass – a road built around a town

C

CAP – Common Agricultural Policy

carnivore – a meat-eating animal

census – a survey of the population

Central Business District – city centre containing shops and offices

cholera – a disease caused by dirty water

climate – the average weather over many years

clint – block of stone on a limestone pavement

collision boundary – where continental plates collide

colony – an area, or country, ruled by another country

compass – instrument used to identify direction

condense – gas becoming liquid

conservative boundary – where two plates slide past each other

constructive boundary – where two plates move apart from each other

continent – a large land mass

contour line – line on an OS map joining all points of the same height

contraception – family planning

convectional rainfall – rainfall caused by hot air rising, cooling and condensing

convict – a convicted criminal

core – the centre of the Earth

crust – the solid skin of rock around the Earth's surface

culture – way of life including language, dress, food etc.

D

dam – wall built to hold back water

death rate – number of people dying per thousand people per year

deciduous – trees that lose leaves in winter

decompose – broken down by bacteria and fungi

dense – crowded

depleted – run out

depression – area of low air pressure

desert – area receiving less than 250 mm of precipitation per year

desertification – the spread of desert-like conditions

destructive boundary – where an oceanic plate slides underneath a continental plate

dispersed – spread out

distributary – a small river which has split away from the main river

dormant – inactive

drought – a long period of dry weather

dyke – an embankment next to a river channel

E

easting – grid line running up and down an OS map

eco-tourism – holidays in natural areas with little impact on the environment

economic activity – a way people make a living

ecosystem – a community of plants and animals

emergents – the tallest rainforest trees

energy – the power needed to provide heat and light and to run machines

environment – the air, land, water, plants and wildlife

epicentre – the point on the Earth's surface directly above the focus of an earthquake

Equator – imaginary line running around the middle of the Earth

erosion – wearing away of the land

ethnic group – people of the same racial group

evaporate – liquid turning to gas

export – goods sold abroad

extinct – died out

F

fallow – land which is not farmed

family planning – contraception

fault – a line of weakness in rock

favela – a Brazilian shanty town

fertile – rich in nutrients

fetch – the distance travelled by a wave

fieldwork – an enquiry which takes place outside the classroom

finite – a limited supply

focus – the point underground where the energy of an earthquake is released

fog – cloud at ground level

foreshock – a small earthquake before a large one

fossil fuels – energy produced from coal, oil and gas

front – boundary between warm and cool air masses

function – the activities of a settlement

G

genetic modification – alteration of plants and animals to improve quality

geothermal energy – heat and electricity produced from hot underground water

global warming – a gradual warming of the Earth's atmosphere

GMO – Genetically Modified Organism

gorge – a deep steep-sided valley

graph – a drawing to show data

greenfield site – land which has not been built on before

Greenhouse Effect – absorption of Sun's heat by CO_2 and methane

grid reference – number which locates an area on a map

Gross Domestic Product (GDP) – the total amount of money earned by a country

gryke – weathered joint on a limestone pavement

H

habitat – area where plants and animals live

HDI – Human Development Index

hectare – ten thousand square metres

hemisphere – half of the globe

herbivore – a plant-eating animal

humid – moist air

hydro-electric power – electricity produced when water is released through turbines in a dam

I

igneous – rock formed from magma

immigrant – migrant moving into a country

imports – goods bought by one country from another

incinerate – to burn

Industrial Revolution - rapid growth of manufacturing industry

interception – raindrops landing on plants, trees and buildings

international migration – migration between countries

irrigation – artificial watering of crops

isotherm – line on a map joining places of the same temperature

J

joint – a crack in the rock

K

key – a list giving the meaning of symbols

L

land use – the use of the land

landfill – burying waste underground

lava – molten rock at the Earth's surface

LEDC – Less Economically Developed Country

linear – in a line

longshore drift – the movement of sand and pebbles along a beach

M

magma – molten rock beneath the Earth's surface

mantle – the semi-solid mass of rock beneath the crust

manufacturing industry – making products used by people

market – the place where goods are sold

MEDC – More Economically Developed Country

mega-city – city with over ten million people.

metamorphic – rock formed from other rocks under extreme heat and pressure

migration – movement from one place to another

mineral – a natural resource such as metal or rock

mining – extracting primary resources

monsoon – rain bearing winds

multilateral aid – aid distributed through international organisations.

N

National Park – an area of outstanding countryside which is protected from development

Newly Industrialised Country (NIC) – country which has recently become industrialised

nitrate – a nutrient which is important for plant growth

nomads – people who move from place to place.

Non-Government Organisation (NGO) – an independent organisation, often a charity

northing – grid line running across an OS map

nucleated – clustered together

nutrient – a chemical needed for living things to grow

O

omnivore – an animal that eats both plants and animals

ore – deposits of rock containing minerals

OS – Ordnance Survey

outback – the dry interior of Australia

P

pastoral – farming animals

percentage – number out of 100

permeable – allows water to flow through joints in the rock

physical map – map showing natural features

plantation – a large farm

plate boundary – the point where two tectonic plates meet

plate tectonics – theory explaining how the Earth's crust is able to move

plateau – a large, flat upland area

plunge pool – a deep pool which is eroded at the base of a waterfall

political map – map showing human features

pollution – damage to the environment

population density – the number of people in a certain area

population distribution – how people are spread out over an area

population explosion – rapid increase in world population after 1950

population pyramid – a graph showing the age and sex of a population

porous – able to hold water like a sponge

precipitation – rain, snow, hail or sleet

primary industry – farming, mining, fishing or forestry

primary information – original information

pull factor – something which makes a place attractive

push factor – something which makes a place unattractive

pyroclastic flow - a cloud of gas and ash ejected from a volcano

Q

quarry – an opencast mine for digging out stone

R

racism – belief that not all races are equal

raw material – natural products processed to make something else

recycling – reusing waste

refugee – a migrant forced to leave their home

relief – the height and shape of the land

renewable energy – energy which can be used forever

reservoir – lake behind a dam

resource – natural product used by people

retail – selling products to the public

river basin – an area of land drained by a river and its tributaries

river cliff – steep, undercut area on the outside of a river meander

rural – countryside

S

safari – a wildlife tracking holiday in the savanna

salinisation – the build up of salt on the surface of soil

salt marsh – a marshy wetland behind a spit

sanitation – safe toilet facilities

saturated – water-logged soil and rock

savanna – an area of tropical grassland.

science park – a development of high-tech industries close to a university

scree – piles of broken rock

secondary information – second-hand information

sedimentary rock – rock formed from particles of sediment

seismic wave – shock wave produced by earthquakes

seismometer – sensitive instrument used to measure earthquakes

service industry – work such as retail, administration, education, healthcare and tourism

settlement hierarchy – the order of importance of settlements

settlement pattern – shape of a settlement

settlement – a place where people live

shanty town – an area of self-built housing of very low quality

site – the exact location of a settlement

situation – the location of a settlement in relation to the surrounding area

slip-off slope – gently sloping area formed on the inside of a river meander

soil – mixture of weathered rock and decayed plant matter

source – the beginning of a river

sparse – not crowded

spur – a steep hill formed on the inside of a river bend

squatter settlement – an area of very low-quality housing

stewardship – looking after resources in a sustainable way for the future

suburb – housing at the edge of a city

sustainable – using resources in a way which means they will not run out

symbol – something used to represent something else.

T

tectonic plate – a large, rigid section of the Earth's crust

terraced houses – houses which are joined together

terraces – steps cut into a hillside

tertiary – a service industry

till – soft rock which is mainly clay

tourism – a holiday with at least one overnight stay

transnational company – companies with branches in more than one country

transportation – the movement of eroded material downstream

tributary – a river joining a larger river

tsunami – a sea wave caused by earthquakes and volcanic eruptions

U

uranium – a radioactive mineral

urban – town or city

urbanisation – increase in the percentage of people living in cities

V

vapour – a gas

vegetation – trees, shrubs and plants

volcanic bomb – lava exploded into the air which turns solid as it falls

WXYZ

waste – items which no longer have a use

wave-cut notch – undercut area at the base of a cliff

weather – the condition of the air

weathering – the breakdown of rocks by weather, plants and animals

Index

A

Aberfan disaster 42–3
aboriginal people 69, 180–1, 183, 185
acid rain 24, 26, 226
Africa 132–3, 138–9, 152–3
Agenda 21 agreement 157
agriculture see farming
aid 13, 19, 150–3
AIDS 139
air
  Greenhouse Effect 174–5
  masses 49, 51, 57
  pollution 24, 92, 126
  pressure 46, 50–1
alternative energy 168–9
altitude 55
Amazon 194
Amerindians 196–7
Antarctica 160–1
anticyclones 50, 58
appropriate aid 152–3
aquifers 173
arable farming 114–16
arches 37
Asia 102–3, 138, 147–9
atlas skills 212–13
atmosphere 174
attrition 36, 38
Australia 178–93
Ayer's Rock (Uluru) 178, 180

B

bar graphs 222
Barra suburb, Rio 209
bays 37
beaches 38–9
bearings 216, 225
Beaufort scale 47
Bhopal disaster 127
bilateral aid 150
biodiversity 74–5
biological weathering 25
birth rates 79, 82–3, 183
Bolivia 43
boundaries 7–9
Brazil 194–209
British Isles
  see also United Kingdom
  climate 58–9
  population 76–7, 80, 83
  weather 48–51
brownfield sites 108–9
BSE (mad cow disease) 117
buildings, earthquake-proof 20
business parks 124–5

C

Cane toads 65
carbon dioxide 174
carnivores 64
cattle farming 186
caves 26–7, 37, 158
censuses 82
central business districts 100, 104, 192
chalk 23, 37
chemical weathering 24
Chernobyl disaster 167
China 76–7, 84–5, 162–3
choropleth maps 76–7, 226
'circle of life' 64
cities 100–5
clay 23, 36–7
cliffs 36–7, 37, 41
climate 54–61
  Australia 179, 190, 192
  Brazil 194–5
  deciduous woodlands 66
  deserts 68
  Europe 56–7
  graphs 222–3
  Kenya 132
  tropical grasslands 70
  tropical rainforests 72
clouds 44–5, 47
coal 122–3, 163, 164
coasts 36–41
collision boundaries 9
colonial history 180–1, 196–7
Common Agricultural Policy (CAP) 117
compass directions 216, 225
composite volcanoes 10–11, 12
concentric land use models 104
condensation 44–5, 52
conflicts
  house building 108–9
  inequality 93
  Kakadu National Park 188–9
  road building 110–11
  Rwanda 91
coniferous forests 63
conservation 121
conservative boundaries 9
constructive boundaries 8
continental
  crust 6
  movement 5
contour lines 218–19
convection currents 7
convectional rainfall 49, 54
Convention on Biological Diversity 75
Coober Pedy 190–1
Cook, Captain 180

crust, Earth 4, 6
Cuba, Hurricane Lili 53
'cycle of poverty' 139, 154

D

dams 45, 162–3
data collection 210–11
death rates 79, 82–3, 183
debt 139, 154–5
deciduous woodlands 63, 66–7
defences, coastal 40–1
deforestation 63, 67, 73, 92, 206–7
deltas 33
deposition 29, 32–3, 38–9
depressions 51, 58
desertification 71
deserts 62–3, 68–9, 160, 179
destructive boundaries 8–9, 12
development 134–55
  Australia 184–5
  Brazil 200–1
diagrams 228
direction 216
disasters
  Aberfan 42–3
  aid 151
  Bhopal 127
  Chernobyl 167
  Kobe earthquake 18–19
  Montserrat 12–13
  River Rhine flood 34–5
diseases, water-borne 139, 172
dispersed settlements 96
distance 217
distribution, population 76–7, 182, 198
diversification 117
dykes 34–5

E

Earth, structure 4
Earth Summit 75, 126, 157
earthquakes 4, 6–7, 16–20
eastings 220
eco-tourism 205
economic
  activities 112–33
  indicators 134, 136–7
ecosystems 62–75
employment 112–13, 133, 146–7
energy 64, 93, 164–5, 168–9
enquiries 2–3
environment
  farming 120–1
  fossil fuels 165
  impact of development 142
  industrial effects 126–7
  resources 92–3, 156–7

Index